Tony Hulman

ALSO BY SIGUR E. WHITAKER

James Allison: A Biography of the Engine Manufacturer and Indianapolis 500 Cofounder (McFarland, 2011)

Tony Hulman
The Man Who Saved the Indianapolis Motor Speedway

Sigur E. Whitaker

McFarland & Company, Inc., Publishers
Jefferson, North Carolina

Library of Congress Cataloguing-in-Publication Data

Whitaker, Sigur E., 1948–
 Tony Hulman : the man who saved the Indianapolis Motor Speedway / Sigur E. Whitaker.
  p. cm.
 Includes bibliographical references and index.

 ISBN 978-0-7864-7882-8 (softcover : acid free paper) ∞
 ISBN 978-1-4766-1493-9 (ebook)

 1. Hulman, Tony. 2. Indianapolis Motor Speedway (Speedway, Ind.)—Biography. I. Title.
 GV1033.5.I55W45 2014
 796.7206'877252—dc23   2014012445

British Library cataloguing data are available

© 2014 Sigur E. Whitaker. All rights reserved

No part of this book may be reproduced or transmitted in any form or by any means, electronic or mechanical, including photocopying or recording, or by any information storage and retrieval system, without permission in writing from the publisher.

On the cover: Tony Hulman, 1951 (courtesy Indianapolis Motor Speedway)

Printed in the United States of America

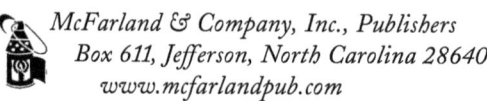

McFarland & Company, Inc., Publishers
Box 611, Jefferson, North Carolina 28640
www.mcfarlandpub.com

To my friend
and brother, Joel

Table of Contents

Preface — 1
Introduction — 2

1. Purchase of the Speedway — 9
2. The Hulmans Come to America — 18
3. Hulman & Company Early Years — 23
4. Hulman & Company Middle Years — 33
5. Clabber Girl — 43
6. Tony's Early Adventures — 51
7. Racing Resumes — 54
8. The Vukovich Era — 70
9. The Crisis in Auto Racing — 79
10. USAC's First Years — 95
11. The Golden Jubilee Race — 109
12. Breaking the 150 Mile-Per-Hour Barrier — 113
13. Celebrating the 50th Indy 500 — 121
14. Tough Times at the Speedway — 133
15. IMS Museum — 151
16. F. W. Cook Brewing — 156

17. Coca-Cola Bottler	162
18. Hulman, Orville Redenbacher and Popcorn	170
19. Diversification	174
20. Giving to Education	178
21. Giving Back	185
22. Dreams of Riding the Rails	188
23. Controversy	193
24. The End	199
Chapter Notes	203
Bibliography	220
Index	230

Preface

I grew up in Indianapolis, and my knowledge of Tony Hulman was limited to knowing that he had purchased the Indianapolis Motor Speedway and resumed the Indianapolis 500 after the track had been closed during World War II. He was also responsible for the resurrection of the Speedway's trademark event as the "greatest spectacle in racing." I was also aware that he was a Terre Haute, Indiana, businessman. This faint portrait left many questions, ranging from how did he have the financial wherewithal to buy the Speedway and to revive it, and how did he overcome the challenges he faced during his ownership of the Speedway? Researching Hulman further, I found a man who didn't seek publicity, who was one of Indiana's business leaders, a well-known sportsman and a prominent philanthropist.

Without the assistance of various librarians, this book would have been impossible. Laura Dodson of the Norfolk (VA) Public Library is responsible for much of the research by reaching out to other libraries for newspapers which had been preserved on microfilm. Jim Gilson of the Vigo County (IN) Public Library was my resource for the history of Hulman & Company throughout its 100-plus-year history. Also of great assistance were librarians at the Library of Congress, the Indianapolis-Marion County Public Library and the Indiana State Library.

Pictures were obtained through the efforts of Mary Ellen Loscar of the Indianapolis Motor Speedway, Richard Bernier of the Rose-Hulman Institute of Technology, and Jim Gilson of the Vigo County Public Library.

Introduction

On November 4, 1945, four men stood on the straightaway looking at the track of the venerable Indianapolis Motor Speedway.

The track was a shell of what it had been in its heyday. Weeds and some small trees were growing up through the cracks. More concerning were the grandstands, which looked like a strong gust of wind could topple them. With winter approaching, would this historic track survive? Or would it become, as many in Indianapolis speculated, another housing development? Given its condition on that November day, a vivid imagination was required to see the track's potential.

As Tony Hulman looked at the track, did his mind go back to 1914? The thirteen-year-old had accompanied his father to the fourth running of the Indianapolis 500. He wasn't impressed with the race: "It seems it took us an eternity to get into the track. When we finally did, we were

Portrait of Tony Hulman (courtesy Office of Communications & Marketing Rose-Hulman Institute of Technology, Terre Haute, Indiana).

both hot and dirty. I didn't enjoy that race and didn't think I ever would like to see another one."[1]

Hulman's hometown, Terre Haute, was on the National Road, a major east–west highway connecting St. Louis and points west to Indianapolis and points east. In a 1960 interview with Robert Shaplen of *Sports Illustrated*, Hulman recalled growing up in Terre Haute and race day: "Ever since I remember, I knew about Indy. Race day was always a big day for us kids in Terre Haute. Even if we weren't goin', we'd stand at the bridge on the side of town—it was the Old National Road then, dirt, before it got to be U.S. 40—and we'd watch the cars go by to Indianapolis, 70 miles away. Foreign makes and all. It was pretty darn impressive."[2]

In a subsequent interview with the *Indianapolis Star*, Hulman commented, "In the years when I couldn't go to Indianapolis as a kid, there used to be a lot of people come in from the West to go to the races. They'd drive through town in big automobiles, a lot better than we had in this town. There'd be some big fancy jobs from St. Louis ... so it's always been very much in my mind."[3]

Or while standing on the track that November day in 1945, did Hulman reminisce about going to the race with his Terre Haute buddies in the early 1920s? He recalled, "I saw the 1914 race first. Then I didn't see much until I got a little older—in the 20s. For about 20 years I was just part of the infield, hanging on the fence, on the inside, just enjoying the races."[4] He was there in the infield, hanging on the rail, when Peter DePaolo won the race in 1924.[5]

Hulman had been approached about buying the racetrack by Wilbur Shaw, a driving legend from the 1930s and a member of the elite group of men who had won the Indianapolis 500 three times—in 1937, 1939 and 1940. Shaw had an affinity for the Speedway and its traditions. In November 1944 with the permission of the federal government, he went to test tires at the Speedway for Firestone Tire & Rubber, leading to his mission to save the historic track. Shaw was the linchpin between Eddie Rickenbacker, the World War I flying ace, former race car driver and the owner of the Speedway, and Hulman.

"Rickenbacker wanted to get rid of the place," Hulman recalled. "Finally Wilbur Shaw looked me up and talked to us. He told me these stories about people, how they'd come there and spend a week—even longer. I just couldn't believe how anybody would go monkey around a race car and stay that long in that spot."[6]

When Shaw approached Hulman about buying the Speedway, Hulman's management team, led by Joe Cloutier, Hulman's chief financial officer, carefully reviewed the financial information Shaw had assembled about the operations of the Speedway prior to its being shuttered. Throughout World War

II, auto racing had been suspended not only in the United States but also in Europe.

There were no guarantees that if Hulman bought the track people would still be interested in auto racing. The due diligence of the purchase of the Speedway underscored Hulman's management style. "I've had a lot of disappointments in my life and I've learned from them that I can't always rely on my own judgment. I like to get the opinion of a lot of people before I do something. I don't like to go off hog wild on something because we might make it worse than it was."[7]

Hulman believed the Indianapolis Motor Speedway, the first superspeedway in the United States, was a jewel that should be preserved. He also knew that resurrecting the Speedway from years of neglect during the war with no maintenance and harsh Indiana winters would require deep pockets. As he made the decision about whether to buy the track, his overriding concern was that the Speedway be self-sustaining—that it would not be reliant upon the cash flow stream generated by Hulman & Company, the wholesale grocer which had been in Hulman's family for nearly a century.

Also at the track with Hulman that November day were Shaw, Cloutier, and Ted "Pop" Myers. Myers had a unique perspective on the track. He had been hired by Carl Fisher, one of the four original Speedway founders, to do odd jobs for another business, Prest-O-Lite. When Fisher and his business associates—James Allison, Arthur Newby and Frank Wheeler—built the two-and-a-half-mile oval, they needed someone to take charge of ticket sales. Fisher approached Myers about handling that part of the business. This would begin Myers' long association with the Speedway spanning some 44 years. By 1914, Myers, having earned the confidence of the Speedway's owners, was named general manager. When Rickenbacker purchased the track, Myers was named vice president.[8]

While at the track considering whether to buy the Speedway from Rickenbacker, Hulman asked Myers if he thought it was a good business proposition. Myers responded affirmatively. Ten days later, Myers watched as ownership of the Speedway was transferred from Rickenbacker to Hulman, assuring the track's continuation. Hulman's team faced the daunting task of getting the Speedway ready to begin racing in six short months. He chose his management team well, selecting Shaw who had a reputation in the auto racing world and management experience gained at Firestone Tire & Rubber, Myers who knew the track inside out and Cloutier. Some of Hulman's closest friends and family members, including his mother, thought the purchase of the track was a white elephant.

Hulman, a successful businessman in Terre Haute, thrived on making tough decisions and had a simple philosophy. "Whether in sports or business, play the game fair and you'll succeed. The success of anything depends on the amount of effort you put into it. When the going is tough, work harder."[9]

After graduating from Yale University, he had returned home to join the family business, Hulman & Company. The firm had been started by his great uncle and had been nurtured by the intervening generations. When Hulman joined the firm in 1924, his father had him start on the bottom rung. Over the next several years, Hulman was schooled in the operations of the firm. When he toured the Speedway in 1945, he was the president and majority owner of Hulman & Company, Indiana's largest wholesale grocer.

Although as a wholesale grocer Hulman & Company was a middleman between food manufacturers and grocers, it had some proprietary products including coffees, spices and baking powder. Hulman noticed that one of the products they manufactured had a pretty consistent market. With the rise of chain grocery stores in the late 1800s, the role of the wholesale grocery industry was under attack. By the 1930s, Hulman could see the threat posed by the rise in proprietary brands promoted by the grocery store chains. Could the baking powder manufactured by Hulman & Company become a national brand?

When his father gave him the opportunity to run the baking powder operation, Hulman developed a team to canvass the countryside painting signs on barns and fences and talking to housewives about the product. Under Hulman, the company's proprietary baking powder was transformed from a steady seller but a small portion of the total product line to a national brand. Clabber Girl Baking Powder became the new focus of the business. This action enabled the company to survive the consolidation in the wholesale grocery industry.

By 1945, Hulman was a seasoned businessman, having taken the helm of Hulman & Company in 1931. He had grown Clabber Girl Baking Powder into a national brand and had led the company through the turmoil of the Great Depression. His business interests extended beyond Hulman & Company into real estate and a family farm, the largest in Indiana, which also had a coal mining operation. Despite his success and being one of the richest men in Indiana, Hulman was virtually unknown to people outside of his hometown. He was quiet and shy and didn't seek publicity.

From his college days, Hulman's enjoyment in business came from fixing problems. He explained, "All I ever got to see about any of the business was the trouble. They brought the problems and I had to produce solutions. It was the same formula that I had studied at New Haven. This is the part of any job that appeals most to me. Certainly, I enjoy success, but I get more pure self-satisfaction from problem-solving. The every-day routine is not my dish."[10]

His business career was punctuated by opportunities to solve problems at Hulman & Company, the Indianapolis Motor Speedway, F. W. Cook Brewing and the Indianapolis Coca-Cola bottling franchise. Hulman did not see himself as a marketer, but in retrospect, this quiet, unassuming man had a good grasp of marketing.

The purchase of the Indianapolis Motor Speedway was obviously a turn-around project. Even after the race succeeded, there were challenges, including a potential drivers' strike in 1947, the pullout of the American Automobile Association Contest Board in 1955, and the uproar after a disastrous 1973 race in which there were multiple fatal wrecks.

In 1950, Hulman bought F. W. Cook Brewing, the oldest brewery in Evansville, Indiana, with a signature product, Goldblume beer. Like the wholesale grocery trade, the beer industry was in a consolidation mode. Based upon his success in taking Clabber Girl Baking Powder national, Hulman planned a campaign to make F. W. Cook a large regional or national company. F. W. Cook provided new challenges for Hulman. Unbeknown to him when he purchased the brewery, the beer foamed too much. Ultimately, when the union struck for additional wages and benefits, Hulman recognized that time had run out for turning around the business and decided to cut his losses.

The purchase of the Coca-Cola bottling franchise in Indianapolis in 1965 undoubtedly had some challenges as the franchise had been owned by one individual for fifty years. As with the Indianapolis Motor Speedway, Hulman set into motion the building of a new facility with higher capacity. The Coca-Cola franchise was also representative of other Hulman purchases in that it focused upon the cash flow of the business. With ready demand for the product, Coca-Cola franchises were very valuable properties, if properly run.

Hulman also invested in commercial real estate. The first purchase was an office building in Evansville, Indiana, during the height of the Great Depression. It had been occupied by a bank which failed, so a goodly portion of the building was vacant at the time of purchase. His second purchase was the tallest office building in Dayton, Ohio, and he later added the largest office building in Louisville, Kentucky, to his holdings.

Subsequent investments in companies which generated steady cash flow included the Terre Haute newspaper, several television stations, and natural gas companies.

Following in the footsteps of his grandfather and father, Hulman was also a philanthropist. He gave much of his fortune to colleges based in Terre Haute, including Indiana State University, where a multipurpose arena bears his name. But his largest contribution was to Rose Polytechnic Institute, where he served on the board. His multimillion-dollar donation nearly tripled the school's endowment. In recognition of this gift, the school changed its name to the Rose-Hulman Institute of Technology, recognizing the two individuals with the largest impacts upon it, Chauncey Rose, the school's visionary and founder, and Tony and Mary Hulman. Hulman also gave of his time to various civic enterprises; he was the World War II war bond chairman for Vigo County and served on several Indiana boards.

Underscoring his success was a positive outlook. Hulman commented, "I'm an optimist. I sometimes like to think things are going to go better than they can around here. I make plans on that basis and sometimes we find out I was wrong. Then we have to cut back and change things."[11] Despite his optimistic outlook, Hulman was also a realist who wasn't afraid to set a course and then make midcourse corrections if things don't go as planned.

Fortune magazine accurately described Hulman as "a man who would like to avoid being recognized as the manager and effective owner of an eminently substantial company and an even more substantial family fortune."[12] Hulman preferred to not be in the limelight, but he became a beloved person in the Indianapolis community as well as in Terre Haute.

1

Purchase of the Speedway

It took Hulman several months to decide to buy the Indianapolis Motor Speedway. As a savvy businessman, he knew if action wasn't taken, the track would become a memory to those involved in racing prior to World War II.

The track was the brainchild of four Indianapolis businessmen, Carl Fisher, James Allison, Arthur Newby and Frank Wheeler, who were passionate about improving the American automobile. Built in 1909, it was unique among auto tracks, which were dominated by dusty one-mile dirt tracks normally used for horse racing, owned by municipalities, counties or states, or road courses utilizing public roads. This track was the first paved oval dedicated to auto racing.

The seller of the track was Eddie Rickenbacker, the World War I flying ace and famed driver from earlier times. Growing up in Dayton, Ohio, Rickenbacker became obsessed with speed at an early age—first bicycles during their heyday in the 1880s and then on to automobiles and airplanes. Rickenbacker's association with the track went back to the first Indianapolis 500 as a relief driver for Lee Frayer of the Columbus Buggy Company team.

By 1915, Rickenbacker was a member of the Maxwell racing team. When the decision was announced that Maxwell would dissolve the racing team, Rickenbacker approached Indianapolis Motor Speedway principals Carl Fisher and James Allison. Allison and Fisher had recently established the Speedway Team Company with five racing machines. Would they be interested in starting a second racing team?

Allison and Fisher were highly successful Indianapolis businessmen, having founded the Prest-O-Lite Company, a manufacturer of the power source for automobile headlights, in 1904.[1] In order to have racing cars for speedway racing, Allison and Fisher organized the Speedway Team Company in September 1915. Allison and Fisher organized the Prest-O-Lite Team on September 14, 1915, purchasing two Maxwell racing cars and hiring Rickenbacker as the head of the team. Given a choice of two compensation packages, Rickenbacker chose to assume all expenses of the team in return for 75 percent of the team's earnings. The Prest-O-Lite team won the first race it entered at the Narragansett Speedway in Providence, Rhode Island.[2] By the end of 1916, the Prest-O-Lite Team had been dissolved.

By 1927, Allison was the majority owner of the Indianapolis Motor Speedway. He also owned Allison Engineering which started as a high-end machine shop to maintain the racing cars for the Speedway Team Company.[3] During World War I, Allison Engineering had designed jigs and models for the Liberty engine.[4] With the Armistice ending World War I, Allison Engineering returned to racing cars. After Allison's Peugeot won the 1919 Indianapolis 500, he sold the racing cars. Allison Engineering returned to aircraft engines.

One of the problems with the Liberty engine was it didn't run long before there was a bearing failure. The engineers at Allison Engineering discovered a way to extend the engine life to hundreds of hours, resulting in the company gaining a contract from the U.S. government to retrofit hundreds of Liberty engines in storage with reduction gears.[5] The company over the years earned a reputation of strong engineering and did a lot of work for both the U.S. government as well as aircraft manufacturers, particularly with aircraft reduction gears.[6]

In 1921, Rickenbacker purchased a Sheridan automobile dealership, beginning a long association with General Motors. The pace car for 1927 was a LaSalle produced by General Motors and driven by Rickenbacker.[7] Through his association with General Motors, Rickenbacker knew the company was interested in getting into the aircraft business. Also knowing that Allison Engineering had lucrative government contracts, Rickenbacker approached Allison about buying Allison Engineering. Allison declined but wondered if Rickenbacker would be interested in buying the Speedway.

In 1927, the Speedway was sold for $750,000 to a consortium of investors led by Rickenbacker. Rickenbacker assumed the presidency of the Speedway, but the operations continued to be headed by "Pop" Myers. Rickenbacker made improvements to the Speedway including a golf course and guided the Speedway through the Great Depression.

Auto racing was very popular, and although dirt tracks continued to dominate the landscape, multiple board tracks sprung up during the 1920s throughout the United States. The consortium was able to weather the Great Depression when the board tracks failed and most dirt tracks returned to their historic roots—horse racing. Throughout the Great Depression, the Indianapolis Motor Speedway continued with its signature event, the Indianapolis 500.

When World War II was declared, Rickenbacker instinctively knew that there would be rationing, not only of gasoline but also of rubber and metals, essential for the building of race cars. After the U.S. military declined his offer to use the facility, he had the Speedway shuttered. For four long years, the track stood empty, subjected to the Indiana winters, with the exception of the golf course which remained open.[8]

It would take significant funds to bring the physical facility back to life. Without an interest to reviving the Speedway, Rickenbacker, who was by then the president of Eastern Airlines, let it be known that he was interested in selling. Rickenbacker's motivation was that the demands of running an airline made it impossible to devote the necessary time to the track's future.

Most people in Indianapolis thought the track would be torn down for residential development. The town of Speedway had grown. The town was anchored by two Allison and Fisher companies, Prest-O-Lite, then owned by Union Carbide, and Allison Engineering, then a part of General Motors. Both had significant manufacturing facilities in the area, leading to the need for housing. Also with operations in Speedway, Indiana, was Esterline-Angus, Electric Steel Casings Company and American Art Clay Company.

Like Rickenbacker, Wilbur Shaw had been an Indianapolis 500 driver, winning the 1937, 1939 and 1940 races. During World War II, he was an employee of Firestone Tire & Rubber Company. His association with Firestone Tire & Rubber began as a representative of the firm traveling around the United States promoting the company's products during the late 1930s. On a visit to Akron, Ohio, in 1939, Shaw visited with Leonard Firestone who was interested in Shaw heading the aircraft subsidiary of Firestone Tire & Rubber.[9] Shaw agreed to work for Firestone Tire & Rubber subject to having time off in May to participate in the Indianapolis 500.

During World War II, Firestone developed a new technology they believed could be applied to automobile tires. Anxious to capitalize on the new technology with the end of hostilities, Firestone executives wanted them tested. After getting the permission of the U.S. government to hold a special test at the Indianapolis Motor Speedway, Firestone management asked their employee and former race car driver, Wilbur Shaw, to conduct the test.

In his book *Gentlemen, Start Your Engines*, Shaw described the test during bitter cold weather on November 29 as "the longest, coldest 500-mile high-speed run I ever made in my life. The temperature was about five degrees above zero and the absence of competition made it seem like 5,000 miles instead of 500."[10]

In a visit with Rickenbacker, Shaw learned that an Indianapolis realtor wanted to buy the Speedway property and turn it into a real estate subdivision. This conversation spurred Shaw to action, as he badly wanted to save the track from demolition. He got financial information from the Speedway for the years of ownership by the Rickenbacker consortium. Shaw then sent out prospectuses to multiple individuals and businesses hoping to form a group to purchase the Speedway. Although there was interest, most was from groups wanting to promote their products rather than buy the track for the betterment of automobiles. Shaw backed away from developing a group to buy the Speedway.

An Indianapolis native, Shaw learned that Homer Cochran, an Indianapolis investment banker, had connections which could be helpful in finding a purchaser for the track. As it turns out, Cochran was an essential linchpin in the sale of the track as he made the connection with Hulman. According to Dave Cassidy, an Indianapolis Motor Speedway employee since 1960 and a friend of Hulman, Cochran was a trusted adviser to Hulman. Cochran brought Hulman several business opportunities during World War II. Cassidy said regarding Cochran's pitching of the transaction to Hulman, "It was from someone he knew and recognized. It was not like some flake coming in off the street."[11]

Through his business transactions with Hulman, Cochran knew that Hulman had the financial strength and business savvy to pull off the purchase of the Speedway. And Shaw, with knowledge of racing and whose name was synonymous with the sport, had the necessary industry knowledge and contacts.[12]

Cochran approached the Hulman organization about the purchase of the Speedway in the summer of 1945. Leonard Marshall, Hulman's attorney, and Cloutier broached Hulman about the subject during a golf game in Terre Haute. Marshall related, "We got Tony steamed up during a golf game one afternoon but nothing was done right then. Tony always moves deliberately until he makes up his mind, and after that you can't keep up with him."[13]

Without the prior relationship with the Hulman organization, it is unlikely that this transaction would have occurred. Joe Cloutier, Hulman's right-hand man, recalled in an interview with Ron Dorson, "The man who came to see us about the Speedway had at times brought a variety of things to our attention. When he brought the Speedway to us, I said, 'You brought a lot of things to us over here but this is the most ridiculous yet.' I told him, 'We're just conservative wholesale grocers over here. This is a very promotional type of thing and were not good promoters.'"[14]

Given the prior interactions with Cochran, the Hulman organization listened to the proposal, and after several meetings, review of the financial information and an inspection of the track, the decision was made to purchase the track. Hulman financed a portion of the transaction with money borrowed from two banks.[15]

Of the purchase, Cassidy said, "It was a flat out business decision. It was an opportunity enhanced by the fact that he was a race fan, but it was a business decision. Granted, it turned out far in excess of anything in their wildest dreams." Cassidy continued, "I don't think he perceived the Speedway being show business, but he thought he knew something about what people wanted."[16]

When the Indianapolis Motor Speedway was purchased on November 15, 1945, Hulman, Rickenbacker, Cloutier, and Myers were at the Indianapolis Athletic Club where the announcement was made. Rickenbacker was paid $750,000,[17] equaling the amount paid for the track in 1927. Through the intervening years, Rickenbacker had made improvements to the track from the profits derived from the racing, including the building of a golf course in 1929.

Hulman expressed his vision for the Speedway: "Our first aim will be to look to spectator comfort and convenience and provide a track and competition that should be an invitation and challenge to the greatest drivers in the world. We think the fans in Indiana will be glad to know that the Speedway is home-owned now."[18]

Rickenbacker paid homage to the founders of the Speedway and Hulman for the purchase of the facility. "It is fitting that Hoosier management and Hoosier capital should continue the most famous venture in the mechanical competition. Wilbur Shaw is of the track, as I was, and brings to it not only sound ability to carry on the top traditions of racing in America but the sincere affection for automobile racing that is so necessary for the proper conduct of this international event. Carl Fisher and Jim Allison, both Hoosiers, built the Speedway in 1909 and in 1911 bricked it and inaugurated the 500 mile race."

Rickenbacker continued, "I have always felt that the people of Indiana should have had more than an observation interest in this great state institution. Mr. Hulman and Shaw will bring to the track 'home-state' ownership which it deserves along with Shaw's knowledge of racing which he learned the hard way—on the track itself. I have no doubt that the new ownership will continue its successful operation."[19]

Pop Myers, a fixture at the Speedway since the ownership by Allison and Fisher, was also positive about the change in ownership. "It is a great thing that the track comes back to Indiana under Hoosier ownership. It was built by public-spirited sportsmen and will be operated in the future by men of the same type, who will carry on the ideals of the past."[20]

With significant investments including Hulman & Company, a gas company and real estate ventures, Hulman did not need the Speedway to provide for his livelihood. He gave an indication of his philosophy on the Speedway: "I don't care whether or not I make any money out of it. The Speedway has always been a part of Indiana, just as the Derby is a part of Kentucky. The 500-mile race should be continued. But I don't want to get into something that will require additional capital each year to keep it going. I'd like to make sufficient income each year so that we can make a few improvements each year and build the Speedway into something everyone can really be proud of."[21]

Hulman's normal strategy when acquiring a company was to leave existing management in place, if they were competent and wanted to stay. It was different with the Speedway acquisition. Cloutier explained, "At the Speedway they didn't have too much of an organization, because when we purchased them they'd been down for four years."[22] Hulman skillfully knit together a management team including people with the breadth and depth knowledge of racing, the track and people with whom he had worked for many years at Hulman & Company. Management of the Speedway included Shaw as president, Myers as vice president, Leonard Marshall as secretary and Cloutier as treasurer. Cloutier was vice president and treasurer of Clabber Girl while Marshall was a Terre Haute banker. Hulman was the chairman of the board.[23]

The *Indianapolis News* heralded the change of ownership and predicted the rebirth of the track in a November 15, 1945, editorial:

> Mr. Hulman and Mr. Shaw and their associates are men of vision and of a high caliber of sportsmanship. They can be expected to put into good condition the property which has been permitted to run down. The public has long been aware of the hazardous condition of some of the stands and of the necessity for additional repairs to the track itself. Mr. Hulman's reputation and record indicate that he will not hesitate to take that opportunity to rebuild this giant property with dispatch.
>
> Under his and Mr. Shaw's guidance, the 500-mile race undoubtedly will again become one of the country's greatest sporting events and will make a real contribution to automotive progress.[24]

The *Indianapolis Star* in a November 16, 1945, editorial was also enthusiastic about Hulman's purchase of the Speedway:

> Sports thrills in anticipation of the 1946 renewal of the 500-mile Speedway race have been intensified by the return of the famous oval to Hoosier ownership. Anton Hulman, Jr., Terre Haute sportsman and financier, acquires the property which has made the name of Indianapolis familiar to the entire world.
>
> Both the daring dash for gold and glory and the byproduct of automobile development will benefit from the sale. The new management presents a fine balance of sports enthusiasm, executive and race experience. Mr. Hulman adds personal zest for various sports to extensive business and financial interest.[25]

1. Purchase of the Speedway

Not everybody was positive about the purchase of the Speedway. When Hulman asked his mother, Grace Smith Hulman, what she thought of the purchase, her response was, "Tear it down and start over."[26] According to James Laycock, others, including some of his close friends, thought that "it was a white elephant and that he was going to lose his shirt."[27]

There were reasons to be concerned about the viability of the track. Beyond the concern about the condition of the physical plant, would there be demand for racing after World War II? Auto racing had experienced difficulty during the Depression, and most tracks from the 1920s had folded. There was also the lack of new race cars. Would spectators want to see cars which were six, seven or eight years old?[28]

The management team faced a huge challenge to get the track ready for the 1946 Indianapolis 500. Rickenbacker had managed to keep the track going throughout the Depression, but during World War II, it had been shuttered. The place was falling down. Laycock, in charge of the Indianapolis Motor

The Speedway in 1943; the deterioration of the track is evident. This picture is taken from turn 1 looking back down the main straightaway (Indianapolis Motor Speedway).

Speedway Media Center from 1953 through 1995, described the poor condition of the track:

> They just let it go during the war, except for when they ran the Firestone test. There were weeds everywhere. Down by the bridge over the creek between Turns 1 and 2, you couldn't even see the track because trees had sprouted up. I saw how bad it was. In fact, I thought it was going to be impossible to get the place ready in time for the '46 race, but, of course they did.[29]

Within a day or two of purchasing the Speedway, Hulman had Clarence Cagle, an employee of Hulman & Company, tour the facility with Shaw and Myers. Cagle described his initial impression of the Speedway: "We unlocked the gate and it fell down. Everything was rotten, there were weeds everywhere. It was a terrible mess."[30]

Despite the condition of the Speedway, Cagle knew Hulman would be successful in his efforts to restore the racetrack. "I knew [the track] was salvageable, because Tony Hulman bought so many broken-down things and made them work. We knew it was going to take time. Pop and Wilbur knew a lot about racing but nothing about construction."[31]

Cagle, working alongside Jack Fortner, the grounds superintendent for Rickenbacker, developed a strategy for bringing the track back to life. Complicating the task was the Indianapolis winter, which would delay improvements to the track, as well as continued shortages of many crucial supplies used in commercial construction.

Hulman wanted the track to be self-sustaining. With the track in need of substantial improvements over the next several months, Hulman pondered how to finance the improvements without depending upon Hulman & Company. His solution was to sell the concessions business to Sportservice for a ten-year period for $1,000,000—generating $250,000 in excess cash flow which could be used for the most crucial improvements. At the end of the ten years, the concession business would revert to the Speedway.[32]

With a mere five months until the Speedway opened for practice, a plan to refurbish the track began to take shape. The most critical need was to restore the track to racing condition and to ensure that the grandstands were safe. Rather than replacing the grandstands with wooden stands, Hulman wanted the new seating to be constructed out of steel. Like many other materials, steel wasn't readily available. Harry Tousley, an Indianapolis contractor, brought an idea to Hulman to construct the new grandstands out of the steel they could get rather than the steel they wanted. With this, Tousley's construction company got the contract for building the new grandstands.

Renovations of the Speedway were helped by a strike at the Allison Transmission Division of General Motors. Allison, located in close proximity to the Speedway, provided a skilled labor force. Track superintendent Jack Fortner hired Allison employees to tear down the grandstands which couldn't be rehabilitated and to make repairs to those which could. Cassidy, then a high school junior, assisted in the work and described the work by the carpenters: "They had these big hatches. One by one they would tap the boards. If it was rotten, they'd chop it out. My job was to keep them supplied with new boards. So I'd hand one to them, they would put a couple of nails in it, and would go on to the next one."[33]

As the opening day approached, the Speedway continued to hum with improvements. Shaw called this time "Duesenberg Days," as the long hours reminded him of when he worked with Augie Duesenberg. "We did report for duty early each morning, take time off for hamburgers and coffee late in the afternoon, and then rush back to the shop to start the night shift. About 2 or 3 a.m. Augie would put his tools aside and say, 'well, boys, let's knock off and get a good night's sleep. Be back about 7:30.'"[34]

On the day of the race, Fortner, the track superintendent, was so exhausted, Shaw found him with his head on his desk crying.[35] But despite the long hours, the track was ready to open ... and Hulman would find out if there was an interest in the race.

2

The Hulmans Come to America

Tony Hulman was a descendant of German immigrants who brought to America a sense of family, hard work, community and philanthropy. Without the grounding provided by previous generations, Hulman might not have had the financial security to invest in the Indianapolis Motor Speedway.

Although his family firm, Hulman & Company, was started by a great uncle, his grandfather, Herman Hulman, put the business on a stable footing. Herman Hulman loved Terre Haute. He was generous to his adopted hometown, and this trait was passed on to succeeding generations.

The Hulmans trace their ancestors to Lingen, a small town in northwestern Germany. Located on the Ems River, the medieval town was a crossroads between Holland to the west, the Rhine River to the east and the Baltic Sea to the north.[1] As with most medieval cities, the town was surrounded by a wall. Three roads converged outside of the town, with the only access being through a gate.

The story behind the Hulman name originates from the clansmen who guarded the gate to the city. Originally, they were called Huilerman, which roughly translates to "hole men." Over time, the spelling was abbreviated, first to Huileman and later to Hulmann. When the family immigrated to the United States, they dropped the extra "n" resulting in Hulman.[2]

Located in the central part of Lingen near the watchtower and the gates to the city, the Hulman ancestral home dates back 450 years.[3] The last Hulman to occupy the house was Hulman's great grandmother, Anna Maria Catherine Pullman Hulmann, the second wife of Johann Heinrich Hulmann.[4]

2. The Hulmans Come to America

In hope of finding a better life, Johann Diedrich, the eldest son of Johann Heinrich Hulmann and his first wife, decided to immigrate to the United States. He was probably influenced not only by information sent back to Lingen by other immigrants but also by promotional literature sponsored by various states to encourage immigration.[5]

Johann Diedrich, who was called Diedrich, traveled to New York City in 1842. Unable to find employment, he traveled to Cincinnati, Ohio, which had a thriving German community. Diedrich encouraged his brother, Francis, the second son of Hulmann Sr. and his first wife, to join him in the United States. Francis, who had been working in Paris, France, as a bookkeeper decided to join Diedrich in Cincinnati.

The Hulmans immigrating to the United States were among the large influx of Germans who ultimately settled in Indiana. The immigrants to America had political ideas closely aligned with those in the United States rather than with their home country which still operated as a feudal society. They believed in individual rights, a democracy based upon equality before the law, free enterprise and the separation of church and state. They also brought with them an ethic of hard work and community involvement.[6]

When Francis Hulman arrived in Cincinnati, he formed a partnership with Charles B. Mayer for the sale of "fancy goods" such as toys, jewelry and other personal items. While in Cincinnati, Francis Hulman met John B. Wudowici who owned a grocery store.

On November 14, 1849, Francis wrote his younger brother, Herman, an impassioned letter encouraging him to immigrate to America for a better life. Even though Francis was planning to relocate to Terre Haute from Cincinnati and was going to start a business with Wudowici, he was confident that the outlook was better than it would have been in Germany.

> I have concluded to give up this business next spring in February or March. I have already found another partner, a very good and sober man about forty years old, and married. He has about two or three thousand dollars capital and I have known him ever since I came here. We intend to go farther into the country and establish a wholesale grocery store.
> This is a very profitable business, especially in the country, with the prospects to make money in time. My future partner has at present, a business of this kind here and therefore knows it through and through, and I will quickly work myself in.
> We have chosen a place called TERRA HAUTE, three hundred miles west of here in the State of Indiana. This is a place of about 6,000 inhabitants, very well laid out, flourishing and growing rapidly, in a clean and healthy location. Besides this, the territory is rich with wealthy farmers (peasants) in the surrounding country and beautiful prairies (flat land, or widely spreading meadows). This place is, as I have said, one of the best in this vicinity and if we have any luck we are sure to make money.[7]

Francis Hulman continued urging Herman Hulman to be firm with his mother about his desire to immigrate to America.

> Then, too, try to persuade her to let you come over here. Speak up courageously as I did. Tell her you have no desire to labor away in that poor Germany and then become stunted, toiling our life through where not even one with capital can make anything, much less one without it. Tell her you are positively sure that there you never could succeed.[8]

The land Francis Hulman would adopt as his home was established as the Indiana Territory in 1800. The territory included most of Indiana, all of Illinois and Wisconsin, some of Michigan and a little bit of Minnesota. Roads were nonexistent. The majority of travel was by river, although there were Indian trails which could also be used. The territorial capital was established in southwest Indiana at Vincennes, located on the banks of the Wabash River.

President Thomas Jefferson appointed General William Henry Harrison as the first territorial governor who arrived in Vincennes in 1801.[9] In 1806, the government appropriated funding for roads; however, it would be several years before construction began.

Despite the majority of the lands in the Indiana Territory being held by the Indians and a very small population, one of Harrison's goals for Indiana was statehood. In order to accomplish that, he negotiated treaties with various of the native Indian chiefs for land. Harrison also built a series of forts to provide a sense of security for the settlers, one of which was Fort Harrison, located about three miles north of where Terre Haute would be located.

With the sense of safety being secured by the presence of Fort Harrison and the granting of statehood to Indiana in 1816, settlement of the former territory escalated. One of the first settlers to come to the Terre Haute area was Abraham Markle in 1816. He found a prairie with high grasses and wildflowers and an abundance of trees, including sycamore, dogwood, maple, oak and crab apple.[10]

More important was the river that flowed by the town. In an era of travel dominated by flatboat or Indian trails, the navigable Wabash River was sufficient for riverboat travel. For eight or nine months a year, the Wabash River is navigable about seventy miles north of Terre Haute.[11] This was significant in that although there were other towns in Indiana located on rivers, most were not on an inland waterway.

When Francis Hulman arrived in Terre Haute in 1850, he found a small community with 4,051 residents. The town consisted of forty blocks. The central business area surrounded the town square. Animals roamed wild through the streets which were unpaved.

Buntin's House was the gathering point of the community for both conducting business transactions and gossiping. Mail arrived twice a week when the stagecoach stopped at Buntin's House.[12] Early resident Chauncey Rose described the early transportation to Terre Haute:

> There were no direct roads. The trip East was made by way of Louisville, Baltimore, and Philadelphia. It was a source of great rejoicing when the first steamboat landed at Terre Haute, in 1822.[13]

Goods were shipped by Conestoga wagons from Baltimore or Philadelphia. Loaded with up to five tons of cargo, the trip from the east would take up to six weeks from Baltimore to Terre Haute. The cargo would travel either to Wheeling, West Virginia, where it would be shipped by boat down the Ohio River then up the Wabash River, or as far as Louisville where the cargo would be taken off the steamboat and carried overland to Terre Haute.[14]

The rise of railroads would change the world of transportation, making the inland waterways less important to the towns. Rose, with significant landholdings in the Terre Haute area, recognized the importance of railroads to Terre Haute's development. He is credited with being the driving force behind the Richmond & Terre Haute Railroad, the first railroad to reach Terre Haute, chartered in 1847.[15] The railroad opened in February 1852, providing a direct connection between Indianapolis and Terre Haute.[16]

By April 1851, Hulman and Wudowici had established a mercantile business in Terre Haute. Total capitalization was $2,100, with Hulman contributing $700 and Wudowici contributing $1,400. Wudowici, who had controlling interest in the firm, managed the books while Hulman was responsible for developing business.[17]

Two years later in March 1853, the partnership was dissolved. Hulman found Wudowici too conservative. There was also a dispute about the sale of liquor, with Wudowici being opposed to it.[18] At that time in Terre Haute, liquor consumption was significant, partly because it was considered to be a medicine.[19]

With the proceeds from the dissolution of the business, Francis Hulman had the capital to start another mercantile store, F. T. Hulman Wholesale Store, in April 1853.[20] Hulman's store carried a large variety of goods including tobacco, castor oil, flour, sugar, salt, beans, beef, whiskey, and peach brandy. Although it was a small operation, it was successful and relocated to a larger storefront directly across from his former partner, Wudowici.[21]

With the arrival of railroads to Terre Haute in 1852, the receipt of goods became easier and more frequent. The population of Terre Haute was growing, and there was plenty of business for all of the stores in the area. Hulman's business continued to expand and thrive and he sold goods to people from surrounding communities.[22]

After many years of encouragement, Herman, who had established a mercantile store in Onasbruck, Germany, in 1849, joined Francis Hulman in Terre Haute in 1854.[23] Hulman was also urging his younger brother, Theodore, to join him in Terre Haute. Theodore became part of the Terre Haute Hulman clan in 1857.[24] After nearly a decade in the United States, Francis began planning a trip to Germany to visit his mother.

Since traveling was very dangerous in those days, Francis Hulman also thought about making provisions in case something happened on the trip. On April 15, 1858, he drafted a will distributing his assets. He also transferred the ownership of three pieces of property including the family homestead to his brother, Herman Hulman.[25]

Francis Hulman and his family enjoyed an extended vacation in Germany. The return passage was booked on the *Austria* which sailed from Hamburg, Germany, on September 2, 1858. The *Austria* had 558 on the sailing from Hamburg and picked up additional passengers at Southampton, England. While en route to the United States with an estimated 600 on board, the ship's crew disinfected the steerage passage area to prevent the spread of disease while at sea. The methodology used was to dip a hot iron into tar. Unfortunately, the tar ignited, and very quickly the *Austria* burned. Only 99 passengers were rescued by two nearby ships, the *Catarina* and the *Maurice*.[26] Among the passengers lost at sea were Francis Hulman and his family.

3

Hulman & Company Early Years

As part of the settlement of Francis Hulman's estate in 1858, Herman Hulman bought the business.[1] By 1860, Terre Haute was a thriving town of 8,495 people. The growth was driven by a variety of forces including the expansion of rail service to Terre Haute and the growth of banking interests. This in turn fed the growth of commerce and industry. Terre Haute's major industries included pork packing, rope production, milling of lumber and flour, canning and ironworks.[2]

Herman Hulman took over the company just as the clouds of war were darkening. Like many Germanic immigrants, Hulman supported the federal efforts in maintaining the unification of the United States.[3] Believing war was inevitable, Hulman increased his offerings to include writing paper and ink for the troops to write their loved ones and fresh fruit, such as lemons, limes, oranges and pineapples, when they were available.[4] With the beginning of hostilities between the Union and Confederate forces, commerce to the South was cut off. Despite the loss of the southern market during the conflict, the company prospered.

In 1861, seven years after his engagement, Hulman wrote to his fiancée, Antonia Risfinstahl, in Germany and asked her to join him. She arrived by steamer in New York City in October 1862 where she was met at the dock by Hulman. They were married in New York City on October 9, 1862, before establishing their home in Terre Haute.[5] Mary, their first child, was born on July 20, 1863, but she died within a year. A son, Anton, was born on October 4, 1864, and the family expanded with the birth of a second son, Herman Jr. on July 15, 1867.[6]

One of the anchors of immigrant families was participation in a homogeneous community. This was true of the Germans, the Italians, the Polish, the Irish and others who came to America. Many immigrant communities were built around the church, which provided not only salvation but also a social connection. In the 1800s and the first half of the 1900s, active participation in a church community could also help bring social status.

The Hulmans were Roman Catholic. In the early days of Terre Haute, the Hulman family attended services at St. Joseph's Catholic Church, established in 1837 by Simon Brute, the first bishop of the diocese of Vincennes.[7] The fervent hope of the German Catholics in Terre Haute was to establish their own parish in order to have German spoken for sermons and devotions and their traditions to be continued. This was not an unusual desire. There was a significant population of German Catholics in America, but most of the priests had an Irish heritage. German Catholics wanted priests who spoke their native language and had the same background.[8]

On January 17, 1864, thirteen men met with the Reverend Father Martin Marty to discuss the establishment of a German Catholic church. Less than a month later on February 7, 1864, the Reverend Father Fintan Mundwiler and the committee agreed to purchase a large property located on Ohio Street at 9th Avenue. At this meeting, they decided also to build a school and a rectory.[9] The cornerstone was laid on October 2, 1864, of the parish to be known as St. Benedict's Church. Shortly after the church opened, the parish added a rectory and, not surprisingly, a school.[10]

As a community, Germans held education in high regard. Unfortunately, although Indiana had included a mandate for public education as part of its state charter, the state of Indiana lagged in its efforts. Of the ten Midwestern states, Indiana ranked seventh in per-pupil spending on primary education and ninth in literacy. Germans in Indiana also favored having schools which taught the German language.[11] Within fourteen years, the school had outgrown its building, and a committee headed by Herman Hulman, Sr., was formed for the construction of a larger St. Benedict's School.[12] The cornerstone for the two-story school was laid on June 12, 1887. The school had an enrollment of 200 with lessons taught in both German and English.[13]

In 1863, Hulman met John Dymond, a traveling salesman for Stanton, Sheldon & Company of New York. This was a fortuitous meeting. After Dymond became a principal in the firm of Dymond & Lally, a broker of coffee and sugar, the company extended the Hulman firm a line of credit between $50,000 and $75,000 to support the purchase of merchandise, which allowed the business to expand.[14]

Among Hulman's competitors in Terre Haute was R. S. Cox & Son. The

3. Hulman & Company Early Years

two firms were about the same size and carried similar product lines. Herman and Theodore Hulman started discussions with R. S. Cox and David B. Dick about combining the two companies. In July 1869, the resulting firm was trading as Hulman & Cox Wholesale House.[15] The expansion of the operations resulted in the business using the top two floors of its building, which was described as "the largest of its kind in the State of Indiana."[16]

Hulman's firm had carried coffee for many years. In 1869, Hulman decided to construct a spice mill to grind spices as well as coffees. The 63-by-90-foot spice mill was added to the backside of the Hulman company building.[17] The spice mill allowed the company to buy green coffee, roast, ground blend it and sell it under a trade name rather than carrying coffees produced by others.[18] This was a significant step for the firm, as it was the first venture into manufacturing a product rather than wholesaling. With a ninety-horsepower engine, the company could roast up to 100 sacks of coffee a day plus other spices.

The countryside surrounding Terre Haute was dominated by farming. The primary crop was corn, used not only as a food source including corn meal but also as seed corn. The by-products of the agriculture industry were used to make distilled spirits. Terre Haute had a thriving liquor industry, with much of the product being transported by steamer and sold downstream.

The largest distillery in Terre Haute was the Alexander McGregor Distillery[19] founded by Ezra Smith and Horace Button in 1840. After the original distillery burned in 1847, it was rebuilt by Smith. Alexander McGregor acquired the distillery in 1850.[20] Like Hulman, McGregor astutely navigated the trials and tribulations of the Civil War.

With a need to support the war effort, the federal government increased taxes. The tax on the manufacture of whiskey resulted in the profit on whiskey for many being nominal.[21] Prior to the implementation of the packaging tax in 1863,[22] McGregor had a large amount of whiskey in storage. During the war years, when his competitors raised the prices of their whiskey to cover the cost of the manufacturing tax, McGregor would follow the market and raise the price of his whiskey. Since McGregor's whiskey was distilled prior to the passage and implementation of the packaging tax, his whiskey was not taxed. This resulted in a tidy profit reported to be $1 million during the Civil War.[23]

Seeking to diversify his business interests, Hulman purchased the McGregor Distillery in August 1869.[24] After buying the distillery, Hulman began expanding its operations and improving profitability. By June 1871, the distillery was producing 2,400 gallons per day. To improve profitability Hulman used mash, one of the by-products of the distillery operation, to fatten hogs and cattle. During 1871, 220,000 bushels of grain were used to produce 609,679 gallons of distilled spirits, and 1,400 hogs were fattened.[25]

During 1872, demand dropped for liquor, and the plant experienced the blowout of a still, causing a work stoppage of several days. One of the strategies used by Hulman to increase the distillery's profitability was to lower the transportation costs for importing raw materials and exporting the finished product. In 1872 Hulman received approval to lay a railroad spur of the Crawfordsville & Terre Haute Railroad to the distillery.

By 1873, demand for whiskey improved, and the distillery was running at full capacity of 4,800 gallons per day. With additional mash being produced, Hulman actively advertised the feeding activities. To support the growing feeding operations, Hulman bought four additional properties behind the distillery. Under Hulman's guidance, the distillery became the third largest in the United States and the largest in Indiana. Between May 5, 1869, and May 19, 1873, the distillery contributed $1,175,965.98 of the $1,875,592.48 taxes paid to the state of Indiana.[26]

The 1875 Revenue Bill enacted into law on March 3, 1875, increased the tax on whiskey to $0.90 per gallon. March was also the most profitable month for the distillery since it had been purchased by Hulman. Due to the size of the operation, he was able to undercut his competitors' price yet recorded a 15 percent profit margin.[27]

The 1870s were a time of significant growth as Hulman & Cox became a general-line wholesaler, selling a broader line of merchandise in addition to staples. The company also added a produce department for fresh fruits and vegetables.[28]

The firm also sold tobacco and spirits. In the early 1870s, the firm started carrying its first patented item, Dr. Gottlieb Flak's Bitters. This item was promoted by its manufacturer as the cure to all human ills. With the growth of tobacco use in the 1870s, Hulman & Cox increased the volume of tobacco products sold. They began buying cigars by the carload, with one order having 30,000 boxes of cigars.[29]

The 1870s had been a period of growth for Hulman & Cox. By 1879, the company was among the largest wholesalers in the nation.

The two sons of Herman and Antonia Hulman, Anton and Herman Jr. grew up in Terre Haute and were educated at St. Benedict's Catholic School as well as being tutored by two German priests. Most of their summers were spent at the family home outside of Terre Haute, Strawberry Hill, where they enjoyed playing in the fountain. During the heat of the summer, the family would spend time on the shores of Lake Michigan in Petoskey, Michigan, and at Lake Maxinkuckee, Indiana's second-largest natural lake.[30]

In the summer of 1875, Hulman took his family on an extended vacation to Europe. He sold the MacGregor Distillery to Crawford Fairbanks, the son of a prosperous Vigo County farmer. Upon his return from Europe in October 1875, Hulman bought back stock in the distillery, forming a partnership with Fairbanks. The distillery was renamed "The Phoenix."[31]

Prior to selling the operation to Fairbanks, Hulman had given up the fattening of hogs to concentrate solely on cattle. In 1878, a fire destroyed a significant portion of the cattle pens and the livestock within. As an efficient use of the by-product from the distillery operations, the cattle feeding operation was subsequently reestablished.

On January 1, 1879, a disastrous explosion occurred at the distillery. Shipments did not resume until April 1879. On April 16, 1879, Hulman traded his interest in the distillery for Cox's interest in Hulman & Cox. He remained the sole owner of the wholesale house until 1885.[32]

On April 19, 1879, representatives for the distillery were summoned to appear on May 8 before the grand jury in Indianapolis. The grand jury was investigating three charges against Hulman and Fairbanks:

(1) illegally operating on Sunday,
(2) untaxed whiskey was found underneath one of the stockpiles of corn, and
(3) a $57,000 deficit in the account with the state of Indiana.

At the grand jury meeting, Hulman and Fairbanks admitted the distillery was running on Sundays but maintained that they had an exception to the law to do so. On this charge, the court ruled that since the state had benefited from the extra taxes paid on the whiskey produced, the charge was a technical one. Hulman and Fairbanks indicated they would pay the amount due to the state of Indiana. On the charge of the untaxed whiskey being found, Hulman and Fairbanks maintained that they had no knowledge of this, and given the size of the operation, employee smuggling was always an issue. The witness testimony against Fairbanks and Hulman was questionable. On May 20, 1879, the grand jury dismissed the charges against Hulman and Fairbanks, stating that the evidence brought forth did not prove fraud.[33]

But Hulman was not only about business. One of his first philanthropic gestures addressed one of Terre Haute's needs—a hospital. Until the establishment of a hospital, the ill would be taken to the jail or county poorhouse for treatment. The driving force for a hospital in Terre Haute was Dr. L. L. Willen, an abdominal surgeon in the Wabash Valley area, who was expressing a need for both a facility as well as nurses to care for his patients, After Dr. Willen negotiated with a convent in Lafayette, Indiana, to supply two nuns, a hospital with room for eighteen patients was established. Within a year, the hospital couldn't meet the demand for beds. One of the volunteers helping the sisters tend to the ill was Antonia Hulman, Herman's wife. During her last illness, she was cared for by the sisters and expressed a desire to repay them through an expansion of the hospital.[34]

After Antonia Hulman died on April 17, 1883, Hulman purchased the site of the Terre Haute Female College. The college, built in 1856 by John Covoert, had closed in 1867. Hulman donated the property bordered by College, Farrington, 4th and 6th streets to the Sisters of Saint Francis on June 12, 1883, as a tribute to his wife. In the donation, Hulman specified the property was "to be used as a hospital and only as a hospital." He also provided $10,000 for renovations to the property. This new hospital, named St. Anthony's in honor of Antonia Hulman, provided much-needed new facilities with twenty-four private rooms and twenty-seven ward beds.[35] It opened on January 1, 1884.[36]

As Anton and Herman Jr. were coming of age, they, like many of their compatriots, became bicycle enthusiasts. Anton and Herman Jr., along with their friend Fred Baur, were the first in Terre Haute to have bicycles. They spent many hours bicycling throughout the countryside.[37] Along with Benjamin McKeen, John G. Mack, Alexander Crawford, Fred Probst, Harry P. Townley, Edwin Elder and Gus Ayers, they founded the Terre Haute Cycling Club in June 1884. The club's focus was both social as well as cycling.[38]

Herman Hulman Jr. was the more outgoing of the two boys. Although Anton was the more serious and enjoyed mechanics, architecture and invention, he also enjoyed the challenges of long-distance cycling. In 1895, he took a multiple-day bicycle ride leaving Terre Haute and traveling first to Logansport, Indiana, in two days, then on to Lake Maxinkuckee where he stayed for four days. He then ventured to Dayton, Ohio, before turning westward to Indianapolis. About four miles west of Indianapolis, his bicycle broke and couldn't be repaired, resulting in him riding the train for the final leg of the trip.[39] He also won the silver cup for winning the state's cycling championship three years in a row.[40]

After finishing high school in Terre Haute, Anton Hulman continued his education at a boarding school in St. Louis for two years before journeying east to Worchester Polytechnic Institute where he studied engineering. His brother, Herman Jr., also studied engineering, but at Rose Polytechnic in Terre Haute. Neither of the sons of Herman and Antonia Hulman would finish their college studies. Anton dropped out of college shortly before his mother's death in 1883, and Herman Jr. decided to elope shortly before completing his collegiate studies.[41]

After the death of his wife, Hulman and his two sons, Herman Jr. and Anton, sailed to Europe for an extended vacation, touring England, France and Germany, on June 22, 1883. They returned to Terre Haute on September 15, 1883.[42]

3. Hulman & Company Early Years

Upon returning from Europe, Anton Hulman did not join the family firm. Rather, for the first two years he worked for the Vandalia Railroad as a shop mechanic.[43]

After operating the firm for the previous six years, in 1885 Hulman formed a partnership with his son, Anton, and B. C. Cox, the son of his former business partner. The firm was incorporated as H. Hulman & Company.

There had been a close relationship between the Hulman and Cox families throughout the years. When Robert Cox had joined forces with Hulman in 1869, he was the first of several family members to join the Hulman operation. In 1870, a brother, George Cox, joined the Hulman operation, and in 1871, Benjamin and James Cox joined the company. In 1885, when H. Hulman & Company was formed, Benjamin Cox was the personnel manager. Anton Hulman was being schooled in the various operations of the firm. When Benjamin Cox died, Anton Hulman became the active head of the firm.[44]

Herman Hulman, Sr., continued to be a community leader. When the business community wanted to promote the benefits of Terre Haute, it formed the Citizens Manufacturing Association in 1887. At the initial meeting, Hulman bought five of the twenty-two shares sold. Within two weeks, the association had met its goal of 100 subscriptions each at $30 per year.[45]

Through the 1880s, the most profitable product line carried by H. Hulman & Company was tobacco. The firm carried products manufactured by Liggett & Myers of St. Louis, Missouri; P. Lorillard & Company of New Jersey; and Blackwell & Company of Durham, North Carolina. In 1890, H. Hulman & Company sold 312,796 pounds of Star Tobacco, a product of Liggett & Myers, more than any other wholesaler in the country.[46]

One of the issues facing H. Hulman & Company salesmen was the large variety of goods available. When the salesmen visited their clients, they needed to be able to communicate the prices on the products carried. By 1876, Herman Hulman, Sr., started exploring the possibility of issuing a catalog by writing to various manufacturers who utilized catalogs. The company's first catalog was published in 1882. Although it solved the issue with the large number of goods available for sale, the company had difficulty finding a printer to regularly publish it. By 1894, the company established a printing division.[47]

By 1888, H. Hulman & Company was in need of additional space to support the continued growth of the firm. The company's market area stretched to Indianapolis in the east, St. Louis in the west, Louisville in the south and Chicago in the north.[48] Property was purchased at the corner of 9th Street and Wabash Avenue.[49] Hulman hired Cincinnati architect Samuel Hannaford to design the building in the Romanesque style. Hannaford was well known to Hulman as he had also designed the Vigo County courthouse in 1888.[50]

The cornerstone for the new Hulman building was laid on April 12, 1892.[51] With 1,500 men working on the seven-story building twelve hours a day, it was completed in September 1892. In order to make for the efficient loading and off-loading of merchandise, the ground floor of the building was level with railroad cars on tracks adjacent to the building. The railroad tracks were three feet lower than the building. The three private tracks which led to the H. Hulman & Company property were connected to the Vandalia Railroad Yards.[52] The new building was the largest wholesale trade building west of the Alleghany Mountains when it was built.[53]

An adjacent five-story building was built on the north side of the property for the spice and coffee operations.[54] The spice operation was connected to the main facility by an elevated walkway connecting the fourth floor of the Hulman building to the fifth floor of the spice building. In order to maintain quality control, all materials used in the spice building would be received in the bottom floor of the main building and then transported to the spice building when needed.[55] The spice building also contained the engine room providing the entire property with electricity.[56] Also constructed as part of the property was a new facility for the distillery.[57]

One of the unique features of the structures was an alarm system tied directly into the Terre Haute Fire Department. It was designed by Adolph Meyer, H. Hulman & Company's cashier. If there was a fire, the person spotting the fire would break the glass of one of the strategically located alarm boxes and pull the cord. This would cause a break in the circuit, causing an alarm to sound at the fire department.[58]

The buildings were opened to the public on September 28, 1892. Approximately 5,000 people accepted invitations for the grand opening.[59] In the afternoon of the grand opening, many people went to the Vigo County fairgrounds to see the horse races where Nancy Hanks, a trotter, set a new world record. At 7:00 p.m. a large sign reading "GRAND OPENING—H HULMAN & COMPANY" was lit. Additionally, from the flagpole atop the building, fifty-foot streamers in red, white and blue lit the sky, visible for several miles. The celebration continued with fireworks lasting nearly an hour.[60]

That evening, a large banquet was held on the grounds of the Terre Haute House. A large tent had been erected on the grounds of the hotel. The 2,000 guests at the first seating and 1,500 guests at the second seating enjoyed the evening entertainment provided by Peter J. Breinig's Ringgold Orchestra as they ate dinner served on china with silver eating utensils.[61]

One of the speakers at the opening ceremonies for the new building was Eugene Debs, a Terre Haute native, who at an earlier age had worked for the firm. After having worked for the railroad, he found his calling as a union organizer and ran for president several times on the Socialist ticket. In his prepared remarks, Debs said, "The completion of this magnificent building, which accounts for this enjoyable occasion, is a monument of faith in the future."[62]

Beginning in the early 1880s, wholesale grocers in New York and New England started forming associations followed closely by wholesalers in Ohio and Michigan. Soon, associations were forming in Indiana, Illinois and Missouri. The original focus of the associations was the sale of sugar. Although many wholesale firms joined the associations, wholesalers in St. Louis, Chicago, and Indianapolis, along with H. Hulman & Company, did not join. By 1895, the firms which had originally opposed the associations in Illinois, Indiana and Missouri joined. Shortly thereafter, the state associations began issuing rules governing the sale of all goods. The main rules included the prohibition of salesmen collecting for the sale, a limit on the terms of sale of sugar to net thirty days or a 1 percent discount on sales which were paid within ten days, a mandate that the interest charge on the sale of sugar between ten and thirty days would be 6 percent, elimination of delivery and cartage charges being absorbed by the wholesaler, and implementation of a minimum delivery charge of two cents per $100. Additionally the only goods which could be sold on a price including delivery were cigars when it was outside of another shipment. These rules were not acceptable to the larger firms, who used items such as the terms of sale as a way to increase their sales volume. Shortly after the establishment of the rules, the associations collapsed when the larger firms withdrew.[63]

Over the years, St. Benedict's Church had prospered to the point that the facility was inadequate. Parishioners wanted a new building, and in late 1895, fund-raising began. Herman Hulman, one of the members of St. Benedict's, wanted the church to have a grander appearance, one that would hearken back to the cathedrals in his native Germany.[64] At a meeting in early 1896, Hulman was elected president of the building committee which included Frank Prox, John Brinkman, Joseph Frisz, Sr., Ernest Bloomel, John Dommerschausen, Anton Haring and August Fuchs.[65] The building committee decided on a Romanesque-style church to be built at the corner of 9th Street and Ohio Street.[66]

Representing the church, Hulman, Frisz and Haring traveled to Chicago and Quincy, Illinois. After looking at several churches, they decided that they liked the architectural style of St. George's Church in Chicago. St. George's Church was built in the Romanesque style, a departure from the Gothic style favored by German immigrants. After returning to Terre Haute, Adolphus Druing, the Chicago architect who had designed St. George's, was hired.[67]

The old church was demolished in April 1896, with the altars, pipe organ and church furniture being stored in the school.[68] Construction of the new building began in July 1896 with Herman Hulman and the Reverend Peter W. Scharoun laying the first brick of the foundation. F. H. McCormack & Company of Columbus, Indiana, was selected as the contractor.[69] The interior of the church was crafted by tradesmen from the United States as well as Germany. The windows were painted by Victor Vonderforst of Westphalia, Indiana, in his home before being transported to the church.[70] The new St. Benedict's Church was opened on June 8, 1898, with a two-hour organ recital played by Hulman's niece, Anna Hulman. The dedication of the building was on June 18, 1899.[71]

On August 30, 1898, B. C. Cox, one of the partners in H. Hulman & Company, died of a heart attack. His death did not come as a surprise, as for many years he had sought treatment for kidney disease. Since the forming of H. Hulman & Company, Herman Hulman had been grooming his son, Anton, as successor in management. After Cox's death, Anton took over Cox's duties, becoming the general manager of the company.

Under Anton Hulman's tutelage, H. Hulman & Company expanded their proprietary brands to include Rex, Dauntless and Crystal brands of baking powder. Effectively, Anton was a brand manager as the brands were expanded to include a variety of items including soups, fruits, vegetables, spices and cereals.[72] In 1905, H. Hulman & Company added the Farmer's Pride brand for jams, jellies, relishes and preserves.[73]

Herman Hulman remained the figurehead of the firm while Anton took over the day to day management of the firm. On November 10, 1911, Herman Hulman formed a new partnership with his two sons, Herman Jr. and Anton. Herman Jr. had not been actively involved with the firm. After his marriage, he settled initially in Oregon where he worked for a cousin. Upon returning to Terre Haute in 1889, he became involved with the liquor business in a partnership with John Boggs financed by his father. By 1898 the distillery wasn't doing well, and Herman Jr. was not interested in the business. Herman Hulman, Sr., bought back the distillery on February 22, 1898, dissolving the partnership. The property in which the liquor was produced was then repurposed as the manufacturing area for the baking powder line.[74]

4

Hulman & Company Middle Years

On January 10, 1900, Anton Hulman married Ada Grace Smith in Indianapolis at the home of a friend. After a honeymoon in Havana, Cuba, the couple settled in Terre Haute.[1] On February 11, 1901, the Hulman family expanded with the birth of Anton (Tony) Hulman Jr. He was raised in a home the couple bought on South Chestnut Street in 1902.[2]

The period of the early 1900s was a time of expansion for H. Hulman & Company. It was also a time of change in how American housewives obtained food for their table. Historically, Americans bought their food from peddlers, public markets or very small shops, often specialized, offering goods which could not be grown by the family. Most people maintained a garden and frequently also had some livestock, even in towns.[3]

Grocery stores were very much a neighborhood fixture. Housewives did the majority of the shopping. With limited ability to keep foods cool, they shopped daily. Without the use of the automobile, most housewives were further limited by the amount of goods they could carry. Grocers frequently provided credit for many clients, particularly in lower-income neighborhoods, and when the telephone became prevalent, they also took telephone orders.

A significant change in the product line carried by grocers was the development of cans and boxes. This led to one of the first mass distribution channels for consumer goods. By 1900, the American housewife could buy canned items such as soups, jellies and vegetables, including H. Hulman & Company proprietary brands.[4] This brought about consistency in the product and also began the branding of products. The development of branded products, such as Kellogg's toasted corn flakes and Van Camp baked beans, set into motion the beginnings of the grocery store which we know today.

By 1900, there were several chain grocery stores located primarily in the East and Midwest, most beginning as tea companies. Tea companies often had multiple shops. As they began adding additional products, beginning with sugar, their business model changed from a specialty store. The chain stores included A&P with 198 stores as well as a mail-order tea business and wagon routes,[5] and Grand Union Tea Company with 140 stores.

Although it may or may not have been recognized at the time, significant to H. Hulman & Company was the opening of a large warehouse in Brooklyn, New York, by Grand Union Tea Company. This allowed the chain grocery store, if they had multiple locations relatively near the warehouse, to gain efficiencies of scale. They could purchase in higher volumes, furthering the ability of the chain stores to supply their stores at a lower cost.[6] H. Hulman & Company and other wholesale grocers catered primarily to individual grocers. With the beginning of the development of warehouses by chain stores, the growth of chain stores would lessen the need for wholesale grocers.

As early as 1905, wholesalers were recognizing the threat of the chain stores and attempted to organize a boycott against large manufacturers selling to the large grocery chains.[7] By 1909, wholesalers and grocers had some success in convincing large manufacturers to sell them products at the same price as the large chain stores. Following the agreement, the large grocery chains, which by then numbering 257, brought legal action challenging the setting of prices. In 1911, the courts ruled that the setting of prices was an antitrust action.[8]

Herman Hulman, Sr., began the expansion of H. Hulman & Company with a branch in Matoon, Illinois, in the 1880s. In 1901, Anton Hulman, Sr., built a new building for the branch in Matoon and later added a small branch in Paris, Illinois. Expansion continued in 1905 when the company added a branch in Evansville, Indiana. As with other branches, the Hulmans constructed and owned the building.[9]

Pedestrians walking by the Evansville branch on the evening of July 31, 1909, heard some crackling. Given the hot weather of the day, they assumed it was caused by the weather. Around 12:30 a.m., a fire alarm was sounded as the Hulman building was ablaze. The fire, believed to have started on the second floor, was attributed to spontaneous combustion. Anton Sr. learned of the fire when the branch manager wired him, "Store is burning. Looks like total loss." The loss, including contents, was estimated at $100,000. H. Hulman & Sons continued operations in Evansville and the warehouse was rebuilt.[10]

On November 10, 1911, Herman Hulman, Sr., formed a partnership with his sons, Anton Sr. and Herman Jr., to own the business, with each partner owning a third of the company, H. Hulman & Sons. The real estate continued to be owned by Herman Sr. With the establishment of the partnership, Herman Sr. retired from active management of the business, and Anton Sr. assumed the mantle of the president.[11]

Anton Sr. continued the expansion of the firm; however, instead of internal growth, in July 1912 the firm expanded with the purchase of other wholesalers. This followed the pattern of many of the chain grocery stores who grew through the acquisition of independent stores or smaller chains. The first acquisition by Hulman was the Decker Wholesale Grocery Company in Brazil, Indiana.[12] Anton Sr. also addressed the need for a larger facility in Evansville by purchasing the property of Haas Grocery on Main Street. After relocating Haas Grocery to a building which he had built, the former Haas location was razed. On the lot, a five-story red-salt glazed brick building was built.[13]

Having lost on the legal front, the wholesalers and independent grocers in 1912 began a national political campaign to institute anti-chain-store laws on the basis that chain stores limited competition.[14] Despite the efforts of the independent grocers and wholesalers, the growth of chain stores, which offered lower-priced goods, had entered a substantial growth curve. For example, the Great Atlantic & Pacific Tea Company had grown to 480 stores in 1912. Atlantic & Pacific would soon try a new format, an "economy" store which offered a larger facility and more goods at a lower price. By 1915, the Great Atlantic & Pacific Tea Company had 1,817 stores and doubled again in the next two years.[15]

Herman Sr. died in 1914 at age eighty-two. His residence was left to Herman Jr. while the business and related real estate were left to Herman Jr. and Anton Sr. On December 26, 1916, Hulman & Company was incorporated as the successor company to H. Hulman & Sons. The stockholders included Anton Sr., Herman Jr., Adolph Meyer, Andrew Dempsey and James Conley. The business plan was "to continue the business heretofore and now conducted by Hulman & Company."[16]

With a strong history of supporting community needs, Anton Sr. and Herman Jr. contributed $30,650 of a $200,000 campaign to purchase property and build a new campus for Rose Polytechnic Institute. The amount contributed by the Hulmans equaled the cost of the property purchased. With this leadership gift, the school reached its goal within five days.

The day after the gift to Rose Polytechnic Institute, the Hulmans canceled a promissory note in the amount of $37,183.04 owed by the Catholic Cemetery Association with the funds having been originally used for Calvary Cemetery.[17] In 1857, members of St. Joseph's Catholic Church purchased three and one-third acres of land which was then part of Woodlawn Cemetery so that they could have burials in sacred land. This Catholic cemetery, St. Joseph's, was expanded over the next several years to a total of ten acres. In 1910, an additional seven acres were purchased to expand St. Joseph's Cemetery. The nearby residents responded complaining of additional lands in their neighborhood being dedicated to a cemetery.[18]

There were those in the Catholic community who were also opposed to the purchase. Their objection was the deteriorating condition of Woodlawn Cemetery after a new Protestant cemetery, Highland Lawn, was founded, with many Protestant families abandoning Woodlawn. Although not part of the Catholic doctrine, Catholics were also electing to be buried in Highland Lawn. In 1911, the Catholics decided to focus on establishing a new Catholic cemetery. The committee included Herman Hulman, Sr., who owned 104 acres on which the county poorhouse and a dairy were located.[19] After he donated the land to the Catholic Cemetery Association, Calvary Cemetery was established. The Catholic Cemetery Association gave a family plot to the Hulmans. Herman Hulman, Sr., was the first burial in the cemetery, having been transferred from St. Joseph's.[20]

The following day, Anton and Herman Jr. provided funds to ensure the expansion of St. Anthony's Hospital.[21]

When hostilities broke out in Europe in April 1914, the United States was in a recession resulting in high unemployment. As France and Britain turned to the United States for assistance, demand for war materials increased. Factories began working at full capacity. The economy was on the move again and employment was bountiful. The United States had over the years increased its workforce through immigration. World War I caused immigration from Europe to slow, resulting in a labor shortage.[22]

With the entry of the United States in World War I in April 1917, the cost of food skyrocketed, leading to riots in several major cities. This led to the establishment of the United States Food Administration on August 10, 1917, by President Woodrow Wilson. Its mission was to control food prices and eliminate speculation and wasteful practices in the food industry. As a food wholesaler, Hulman & Company was impacted by this agency. It was hoped that this agency would stabilize food prices, eliminate hoarding and share food with the United States' allies. To control the food supply, the export of meats, sugar and grains was under the control of the federal government, while food for consumption in the United States was under the auspices of a County Council of Defense.[23] In Vigo County, Anton Hulman, Sr., was nominated to be the local administrator. In accepting this voluntary, unpaid position, Hulman said, "If it is the wish of the authorities that I serve my country in that capacity, I am willing to do so."[24]

One of the regulations imposed by the U.S. government during World

War I was a prohibition against a business having more than one operation in a state. As a result, the branches at Evansville and Brazil, Indiana, and Paris, Illinois, were closed.[25] The warehouse in Evansville was leased for a ten-year period to Montgomery Ward.[26] Inventory in the Evansville and Brazil, Indiana, locations was transported to Terre Haute, while the inventory in Paris, Illinois, was transferred to Matoon, Illinois.[27]

Anton Sr. tried to balance the needs of Hulman & Company and his voluntary job as the Vigo County administrator. Due to the adverse impact upon his health, Hulman relinquished the position as well as the daily management of Hulman & Company. J. S. Ahlgreen was appointed the Vigo County administrator while Herman Jr. assumed the management of Hulman & Company.[28]

Hulman & Company actively supported the war effort both with the rationing of food supplies as well as the sale of war bonds. Each Hulman employee was given the option to purchase a $50 war bond by contributing $2 per week between October 27 and December 25, 1917. As a Christmas gift, Hulman & Company paid the remainder of the cost of the bond. Herman Jr. also developed a "war chest" to provide for the needs of overseas servicemen.[29]

Another impact of World War I upon Hulman & Company was the rise of union unrest as the result of inflation and widely fluctuating prices of food supplies.[30] Between 1915 and 1920, grocery prices on twenty-two items on average doubled while wages did not increase significantly Utilizing union wages, an hour of work bought 17 percent less food in 1919 than it did in 1913.[31] The impact upon Hulman & Company was that the company was unprofitable due to inflation impacting the cost of food.[32]

The company also watched as consumers flocked to chain grocery stores in an effort to reduce their food costs. This led to an explosion of chain grocery stores. As an example, A&P grew to 4,588 stores and had become the world's largest retailer.[33] Additionally, innovation by the chain stores lead to a new style of shopping. Historically, products sold were in cases which were accessed by store clerks. In 1916, the Piggly Wiggly chain introduced the self-service store in Memphis, Tennessee. This led to a lowering of costs at those stores which adopted self-service, as the stores were stocked by store clerks and checkout was done primarily by women at a lower wage. The chain grocery stores were quick to adapt this method of display and were followed by independent stores.[34]

One of President Woodrow Wilson's initiatives during World War I was to protect workers' rights to form labor unions.[35] In April 1917, the War Labor Conference Board was established with the mission of ensuring that labor was fairly compensated and was treated fairly as reflected in the opening declaration: "The right of workers, including common laborers, to a living wage is hereby declared." The board sought to ensure the subsistence of the worker and his family in health and reasonable comfort. It also provided for the right of labor to organize and collectively bargain with management.[36]

Although wages were higher in the larger cities, Anton Sr. decided to give his employees a wage increase of $1 per week in September 1917 so that the wages would parallel those of laborers in St. Louis and Chicago wholesalers. On September 22, 1917, Anton Sr. announced the company would recognize a teamsters' union. Shortly after the teamsters' union was organized at Hulman & Company, the Wholesale Packers and Handlers Union called for a strike and began picketing the company's facilities. On the day the strike was declared, Hulman & Company announced that the working day was being reduced to eight hours. Anton Sr. believed that the Wholesale Packers and Handlers Union had given him a set of demands which were impractical.[37]

The Central Labor Union executive committee attempted to engage the teamsters, engineers and printers in a sympathy strike. Before the strike began, management had agreed to modify the contract with the members of the Typographical Union. The new contract included a wage increase which would be in effect until May 1, 1919. When management also agreed to give all striking employees their jobs back, the strike ended. On December 2, 1917, the plant resumed normal operations.[38]

When the wage contract expired in May 1919, the Teamsters, Handlers and Packers union again demanded an increase in wages, a decrease in hours worked and elimination of a controversial rule of employment. The rule which angered the union was that "all employees must pay their bills. A repeated notice from tradesmen or boarding houses of unpaid accounts is reason for discharge."

Although Hulman & Company agreed to the wage demands, it did not agree to the change in working hours or conditions of employment, resulting in a strike being declared on May 1, 1919.[39] Management's response was that they would no longer recognize the unions but would operate on an open-shop basis. They offered the jobs back to the striking employees as long as the employee agreed to the company being an open shop. By May 13, over 60 percent of the employees had returned to their jobs. To supplement the workforce, the company also employed nonunion help during the strike.[40]

After the end of the war, the demand for goods continued to exceed the supply, and the firm continued to operate on very thin margins.[41] Nevertheless, in January 1920, management gave employees with five years of service and salaries of $1,352 or less per year one share of Hulman & Company stock. They also allowed employees with five years of service to purchase additional shares. Lastly, management declared and paid a dividend for 1919.[42] Most grocers, both chains and independents, as well as wholesale grocers were negatively impacted by the thin margins, and many operated at a loss during 1920 and 1921.[43]

In May 1921, St. Anthony's Hospital initiated a building campaign with a goal of $200,000. Heading the campaign was Herman Jr. The funds were raised with Herman and his associates contributing about 50 percent.[44]

The 1920s brought increased competition to Hulman & Company from chain stores, mail-order houses and door-to-door salesmen. Anton Sr. correctly believed the high prices during World War I were the impetus for shoppers to buy from chain stores. The company estimated that by 1926 about 25 percent of the buying in the Wabash Valley was at a chain store.[45]

Wholesalers, particularly in the South and Midwest began putting pressure on the state legislatures to pass anti–chain store legislation. Simultaneously, they frequently instituted campaigns to encourage consumers to support their local grocery stores. Anton Sr., who had resumed the reins of leadership of the company, initiated a "buy local" campaign. The company issued a bulletin entitled "FOREIGN OWNED as against HOME TOWN STORES." Beginning in June 1927, the company also started running weekly sales advertisements in the newspapers and experimented with the use of window advertisements to further promote the advertised sale items.[46]

As a response to the increasing competition from chain stores such as A&P, in May 1926, a group of 100 independent retailers formed the Independent Grocers Alliance with headquarters in Chicago, Illinois. By the end of 1926, more than 150 stores were operating with the trade style of "IGA." In 1927, IGA had its first proprietary product (flour). Independents joined the Independent Grocers Alliance rapidly, and there were over 1,500 locations in thirty-six states by 1929.[47] On July 6, 1927, Hulman & Company announced they had associated with the Independent Grocers Alliance and had been selected as the local headquarters.[48]

The banding together of independents also gave these stores the opportunity to carry private-label branded products, often manufactured by the wholesaler at lower prices than the nationally branded products, similar to the chain grocery stores. This enabled independent stores to compete on price with A&P and other independents on private-labeled items.[49] By the end of the 1920s nearly 60,000 independent grocers had joined cooperative buying organizations.[50]

After his early years of education at St. Benedict's School, Anton (Tony) Hulman, Jr., went east to attend the Lawrenceville School and Worcester Academy prior to enrolling at Yale University. After graduating from Yale, Tony Hulman joined the staff at Hulman & Company in 1925. As the only heir of Anton Sr., most felt that he would take over the reins of the company upon his father's retirement. But his father wanted to ensure that he understood the business and earned his right to manage it. Anton Sr. told his secretary, "Don't give Tony a place in the business. Let him work for it."[51] As a result, Tony started on the bottom rung of the business.

In the early 1920s, the use of a truck to move inventory from warehouses to stores within a city[52] had replaced the horse-drawn dray. Wholesalers with branch locations also shifted from shipping by railroad to truck.[53] Among his various duties, Hulman Jr. was one of the first drivers of a Clabber Girl truck. This gave him valuable experience interfacing with clients, learning what was valuable to them and how it impacted the company.[54]

On the morning of Wednesday, October 6, 1926, crowds gathered outside of the Assumption Church to catch a glimpse of Mary Josephine Fendrich, the daughter of one of Evansville's leading families, as she entered the church for her wedding to Tony Hulman Inside, the church was adorned with pink roses and blue delphiniums.

Mary Fendrich's wedding gown, imported from France by Madame Dreher of Chicago's Marshall Field's department store, was a knee-length dress with a fifteen-foot-long train. Her bridal bouquet measured three feet across made from lilies of the valley and pale lavender orchids.[55] Hulman wore a tuxedo with tails, gloves and white spats.[56] The reception was held at the Fendrich home.

Following the wedding and reception, Tony and Mary Hulman drove to Terre Haute where a reception was held for those Terre Haute residents who couldn't attend the wedding. Later the newlyweds caught a train to New York and sailed for Europe the following Saturday on the *Majestic* for a four-month honeymoon[57] touring England, France, Italy and Spain.[58] The *Majestic* was the flagship for the White Star Line and at the time was the largest ship in the world.

Upon their return to Terre Haute, the Hulmans settled into an apartment. Within a year, they purchased a home on 6th Street South where they would raise their family. Hulman commented on the home: "Thought I'd be there a few years and build a house later on. But to this day I'm still thinking the same thing. I'm still in the same house and it looks like I'll die in the same house." And he did—the Hulmans, despite their wealth, never built another primary residence in Terre Haute.[59]

In 1926, Tony and Mary Hulman also purchased their first boat, a dilapidated thirty-eight-foot fishing boat. They sailed it from Larchmont, New York, to Florida and then across to Bimini. Mary Hulman recalled the trip: "It was during prohibition so we spent most of our time in the local bar, but we got some fishing done too."[60]

Hulman & Company expanded in 1928, acquiring an interest in Ragon Brothers of Evansville which carried a similar product line. Upon the expiration of the lease with Montgomery Ward, the company moved back into the Evansville warehouse.[61] The company also started a fleet of delivery trucks, making both local deliveries as well as to the warehouses in Matoon and Evansville.

Responding to the political pressure from independent grocers and wholesalers, the Indiana state legislature passed a tax on chain stores. Compared with some other states, the Indiana tax was low. The charge was $3 per year for a single store, increasing to $25 per store for chain stores with more than twenty locations. This law was challenged and was eventually heard by the United States Supreme Court. The decision in the *State Board of Tax Commissioners versus Jackson* upheld Indiana's right to charge a different tax for chains than for single locations as it was a different type of store.[62]

As part of their product line, Hulman & Company would sell fresh produce in season. In 1925, the Atlantic & Pacific Tea Company opened a subsidiary, the Atlantic Commission Company, to source produce for its stores.[63] By 1929, the Atlantic Commission Company was contracting directly with farmers for their produce. The farmers liked the certainty of knowing their crops would be purchased at a given price and were willing to accept prices lower than market for this assurance. A&P benefited by not having to source the product through produce wholesalers and avoiding the wholesale commissions.

This created another mechanism through which A&P could bring produce inventory to their stores at a lower cost than their competition. Not only did they buy at lower cost, but the distribution system was also more efficient at getting the produce from the fields to the stores, resulting in fresher produce for the customer.[64]

Hulman & Company's business was like many of the other 13,618 wholesale grocery distributors in the United States. The vast majority of these companies had been around for generations and continued to be family owned. Approximately one-third of the grocery wholesalers distributed a broad general line of product. They would buy by the railroad car, store the product in their warehouses and distribute to the independent grocers when needed.

Despite the high number of wholesale grocers, there were already larger regional wholesalers in large cities whose market territory could stretch up to 500 miles.[65] The expansion of the regional wholesalers through acquisitions and the continued march of the chain grocery stores placed additional pressure on the smaller wholesale grocers such as Hulman & Company.

The world had changed significantly for Hulman & Company during Anton Hulman, Sr.'s, tenure. The growth of the chain stores altered the economic landscape and threatened not only the local merchant but also their suppliers. Technological improvements resulted in foods having a longer shelf life. The result was more innovation of the grocery store.

In 1930, Michael Cullen opened a supermarket in New York City. When this store opened, the average grocery store was about 600 square feet. This large grocery store sold products much cheaper than the conventional grocer, and the consumer responded by flocking to the store.[66] The opening of larger stores was soon pursued by both the independent grocer as well as the chain grocery stores. This put additional pressure on the small independent grocers as well as the wholesalers who supplied them.

By the fall of 1931, Anton Sr. felt that his son was ready to lead the company and handed over management responsibilities.[67] Anton Hulman, Jr., took the reins of the business when the country was in a severe economic recession which began in October 1929. Additionally, supermarkets were becoming larger, and independents were being consolidated into either other existing businesses or joining cooperatives. How would he respond to these management challenges?

5

Clabber Girl

Adding sodium bicarbonate and sour milk to dry ingredients changed the world of baking. Prior to this discovery, most bread was unleavened or leavened with yeast. The amount of acid in the sour milk impacted the level of rising. In the 1840s, cream of tartar was discovered to have the same reaction as sour milk to the sodium bicarbonate—the dough would rise. Substituting cream of tartar for sour milk also had the benefit of a more predictable level of rising and was the beginning of baking powder. Unable to control the chemical reaction, initially the two chemicals were in separate packets which the cook added to the other ingredients.

Baking powder took another step forward when Professor Eben Horsford of Harvard suggested replacing cream of tartar with calcium acid phosphate. In the early years of manufacturing calcium acid phosphate, the source of the calcium was bones treated with sulfuric acid. Horsford developed a process for manufacturing calcium acid phosphate, patented on April 26, 1856. Horsford and his partner, George Wilson, marketed the packets of calcium acid phosphate and sodium bicarbonate as Horsford's Bread Preparation. Horsford later discovered that cornstarch would allow the two chemicals to be mixed together at the factory.[1]

By the late 1880s baking powder was an established product, with Americans using an estimated 50 to 75 million pounds per year. Although it had gained acceptance in the marketplace, there was no uniformity of product. Many brands adulterated the product, and housewives were frequently not confident in the quality of the product being purchased.[2]

Among the companies making baking powder was the Atlantic & Pacific Tea Company. They began carrying the product in their stores in 1883. By 1885, a red box with the logo "A&P" began appearing on the grocery store shelves. This was the first product made and marketed by the Atlantic & Pacific Tea Company, beginning this company's transition from a tea and coffee retailer to a grocer.[3]

Hulman & Cox had been selling baking powder since 1869 when they started carrying the Royal Baking Powder line.[4] Although there were 600 different types of baking powder being manufactured and sold in the United States,[5] Herman Hulman continued the strategy of manufacturing some of the products sold by the firm when in 1879 he decided to formulate baking powder which could then be produced in the spice mill. The trade names "Dauntless" and "Crystal" were registered for the Hulman baking powder product.[6]

In 1897, the company unveiled a new baking powder formulation which they called "Milk." This baking powder was superior as it combusted twice, once when it was added to the ingredients and the second time when the cake or biscuit was baked.[7]

Herman Hulman and Gus Correll continued in their efforts to develop a formula for a faster-rising baking powder. Over a three-year period in the late 1890s, their experiments resulted in a formula they found satisfactory. They called this new product Clabber Baking Powder.[8]

Later to become controversial, the original label of Clabber Baking Powder was a kitchen scene. An older woman was seated holding a baby in her lap while a cat laid on the floor beside her. In the foreground a young girl was churning milk while two young children were nearby. With acceptance of Clabber Baking Powder, Hulman & Company soon discontinued the sale of the "milk" baking powder as its sales declined rapidly.[9]

A competitor complained to the Federal Food and Drug Administration in 1923 that the name, Clabber Baking Powder, was misleading, as the inclusion of "Clabber," a word for milk, implied that milk was part of the formulation. Hulman & Company responded by changing the name of the product to Clabber Girl Baking Powder.[10] The label for Clabber Girl Baking Powder was also changed so the young girl in the foreground was sweeping the floor rather than churning milk. The insertion of "Girl" into the label was an attempt to ensure the public knew there was no milk in the baking powder.[11]

As Tony Hulman took over leadership of the business, the country was in the third year of an economic downturn which would soon become much more severe. Although Hulman & Company dominated its territory, it had experienced stagnant sales as consumers abandoned the local grocers in favor of the chain stores. In this environment, Hulman decided to take Clabber Girl Baking Powder national.

Hulman remembered the decision to expand Clabber Girl's territory and the marketing strategy: "Of all the items we had, the baking powder seemed to have a little foothold of its own, seemed to repeat sales when it was given the opportunity."[12]

Among the advertising techniques used for Clabber Girl, Hulman followed the lead of Coca-Cola and Burma Shave with outside advertising of the product. Hulman continued, "We went out in the early days—I did myself—and we put up a lot of signs on barns and fences and every place down in Kentucky and Tennessee. In some places we'd get somebody to bake some cakes and go house to house and let them taste the cake."[13]

Cloutier believed they had approximately 100 men out, calling on the trade and putting up advertising signs along the highways in 1930. Another item generating sales was the offer of free product with the purchase of the product. The amount of product required to buy to get free product varied through the years, from four purchases for one down to two purchases for one and eventually one for one. Cloutier explained that they would do anything to get a carload shipment into a wholesaler.[14]

The advertising campaign generated an increase in sales, outstripping Hulman & Company's manufacturing capacity. In the early 1930s, Hulman added a pale yellow advertising sign on U.S. 40 approximately five miles east of Terre Haute, announcing, "Five Minutes to Terre Haute, the Home of Clabber Girl Baking Powder."[15]

With the focus on Clabber Girl, internal controls were established to track this product separately from other product offerings. The sales and advertising of Clabber Girl were also handled separately from the wholesale business. As sales increased, warehouses were set up at strategic points, and the plan for selling was revised from focusing on sales to grocery stores to focusing on wholesale grocers and chain store warehouses. The wholesalers then sold to the independent retailer who then sold to the consumer. Between 1931 and 1941, Clabber Girl became an industry leader.[16]

The impact upon Hulman & Company was the beginning of changing the focus of the company from a wholesaler. Before the start of the national campaign, Clabber Girl was a minor part of the Hulman & Company revenues. After the nationwide campaign, it became a significant part of the business.

Responding to the need for additional space to produce and store the product, Hulman & Company built a new six-story building in 1932[17] and purchased new equipment. It also meant they had to expand employment to handle the fulfillment of the orders.[18]

After his inauguration in March 1933, President Franklin D. Roosevelt declared a banking holiday. Roosevelt hoped that the banking holiday would allow time for Congress to pass new banking laws to prevent a run on banks. Unfortunately, it had the opposite impact. As there was no deposit insurance, a run on the banks ensued, with clients pulling their deposits out. This soon had the impact of stripping cash from the economic system. Companies resorted to paying their employees in scrip, and most retailers had to trade on credit.[19]

The Roosevelt administration also quickly passed the National Industrial Recovery Act intended to stabilize the economy and put the unemployed back to work. As part of this act, various industries were subjected to codes. For the wholesale grocery industry, the code was written by the National Association of Grocery Wholesalers, one of the two industry associations. The code favored independent wholesalers and retailers by imposing taxes upon the chain store operators. Not surprisingly, the chain grocery stores protested.[20]

In May 1935, the United States Supreme Court ruled that the National Industrial Recovery Act was unconstitutional, as it failed to define the purpose of the code. It further stated that Congress did not have the authority to delegate to an industry association the writing of the code.[21] This action revived the chain grocery stores, which had experienced lower customer traffic while the code was in place.[22]

The impact of the unconstitutional status of the National Industrial Recovery Act was short-lived. In June 1935, President Roosevelt signed into law the Robinson-Patman Act prohibiting chain stores from utilizing advertising rebates from manufacturers to lower their cost of sales. The result was an increase in the retail price.[23]

The Robinson-Patman Act combined with two other forces to place the independent grocer on a more even playing field. One of the impacts of the Great Depression was that many consumers needed credit to purchase food. Unlike the chain stores, independent grocers had historically extended credit to their clientele. The second was that the cost of operating a car to drive to the chain store had become a luxury for most families—and they were shopping closer to home. The impact upon chain stores was significant as consumers returned to buying at the independent grocers.

Just like his father, Hulman had to deal with unionization attempts at his company. It began with a bitter strike at another Terre Haute business, the Colombian Enameling Stamping Company, on March 23, 1935. By June 11, the situation had become so inflamed that a mob attacked the company's offices. Tensions continued to rise, and by mid-July, Columbian Enamel had guards armed with shotguns and submachine guns protecting the property. On Sunday, July 21, a massive demonstration was held at the Vigo County courthouse. The tensions between labor and management bled over to the larger Terre Haute community.[24] The union posted pickets around the Hulman facilities as they attempted to organize.[25]

The Great Depression also changed the products consumers bought, which in turn impacted the scope of products carried at Hulman & Company. Instead of prepared foods, consumers either grew or bought fresh produce and returned to canning. Cloutier said, "You could drive out through the countryside here and see people with peaches and apples upon the rooftops of their sheds and their barns and everything, drying out." During the height of the Depression, Cloutier believes the sale of fruit jars, lids, and sugar peaked. As quickly as they could get in a train car of fruit jars from Ball Brothers, the orders would be fulfilled and shipped out to grocery stores.[26]

With a legacy of philanthropy handed down from Herman Hulman, Sr., Anton and Tony Hulman established the Hulman Foundation with $5,000 on December 13, 1940, to "promote educational, literary, scientific, religious, and charitable purposes."[27] Among the first donations of the Hulman Foundation was $1,000 to establish the Purdue University Sanitary Research Board in November 1945.[28] In September 1941, Anton Sr. and Tony Hulman donated a residence to St. Margaret Mary's Church to be used by the church's nuns.[29]

In 1941, the Teamsters organized a strike over wages, negatively impacting Hulman & Company's coffee operation. During the strike the competition tried to get some of the business. In order to reward those customers who stayed with Hulman & Company during the strike and to potentially get some old customers back, Hulman decided after the strike was over to lower pricing on coffee for a two-week period. This would allow clients to stock up during the two-week period on the product being advertised.

After the entry of the United States into World War II, the federal government enacted wage and price controls with an announcement freezing all prices as of March 24, 1942. Unfortunately for Hulman & Company, the sale price of coffee to their customers was to expire on that day. The prices were to have gone up the following day. Hulman & Company representatives went to Washington armed with copies of their sales letter sent out two weeks prior to the date of the initiative and catalog pages with the temporary pricing structure. Despite their pleas to the federal government, they were not given any leeway on pricing. If they sold coffee, they had to keep the sale price throughout the war.

Additionally, the grading of coffee changed. Although the federal government had frozen the cost of imports, the new grading structure meant that to keep the same quality, a higher grade of coffee bean needed to be purchased.

The result was that the industry was paying more to produce the coffee and couldn't pass along the price increases to the customer.

Hulman mulled the issue over. Coffee had not been a significant product for Hulman & Company. Given the increase of the cost of producing the product without being able to pass these costs along, Hulman elected not to put any effort into it. By the end of the war, Hulman's coffee business was nonexistent.[30]

World War II created other impacts on the production and distribution of Clabber Girl. Like other companies, Hulman & Company was impacted by the rationing of items such as tires, gasoline, and truck parts. The company also experienced a decrease in the sales force as people entered the armed forces.[31]

According to Cloutier, Hulman & Company's largest problem was the rationing of tin for cans. Prior to World War II, Hulman & Company made its own tin cans into which Clabber Girl was packed. With limitations on tin, the company needed to utilize paper cans for packaging of Clabber Girl.[32] Wanting to control the packaging side of the business, Hulman & Company purchased equipment to make the cans. One of the challenges was attaching the metal lid to the paper can. Unlike metal cans which have a precise width, a can made of paper can be influenced by temperature and moisture.[33] Additionally paper cans were harder to fill and required more employees to try to get the same volume of product out.[34]

After World War II ended, packaged cake and biscuit mixes were introduced to the market and became very popular with housewives due to their convenience. After taking a look at expanding into this product, Hulman decided not to participate. Of the decision, Hulman said, "We felt like being content with the baking powder."[35]

Although Hulman decided not to enter the packaged cake and biscuit mix industry, expansion of the Clabber Girl Baking Powder brand occurred when Hulman & Company purchased the baking powder plants of two competitors. One company acquired was the K. C. Food division of Jakes Manufacturing Company in North Little Rock, Arkansas, in 1950. The larger acquisition was Rumford Chemical Works in Rhode Island, a subsidiary of the Heyden Chemical Corporation, in 1949 for $2.5 million.[36] Rumford Baking Powder and Hearth Club Baking Powder were distributed by Rumford Chemical Company in the eastern seaboard area and New England where Clabber Girl sales were weak. The impact of the acquisitions was to take Clabber Girl to a national basis and to improve profitability.

At the time of the purchase, Rumford Chemical Works made pyrophosphate and sulfuric acid in addition to baking powder. Hulman & Company had no interest in anything other than baking powder, so Hulman divested

Hulman at his desk at Hulman & Company, Terre Haute, Indiana. The gentleman in the picture is Hulman's grandfather, Herman Hulman (Martin Collection Community Archives, Vigo County Public Library).

the chemical works. After purchasing the baking powder operation of Jakes Manufacturing, they transferred the operation of Rumford Baking Powder to the North Little Rock facility which was built in 1947.[37]

In 1953, Hulman & Company celebrated its 100th anniversary. As compared to the celebration held with the opening of the Hulman building in Terre Haute, it was a quiet affair held at the Terre Haute House. Entering the hotel, celebrants heard a calliope playing. On display was the bicycle ridden by Herman Hulman, Jr., in the 1880s, an elaborately decorated wagon used by H. Hulman & Company in the late 1800s, and the Marmon Wasp, winner of the 1911 Indianapolis 500.[38]

Hulman described the offices at Hulman & Company: "We always seemed to keep our office in the same old place because it's sort of a luck charm piece. Sort of like the old crossroads grocery store, only just a little advanced."[39] His office was dominated by a gigantic oak desk which Hulman described as cluttered.[40]

Prior to World War II, wholesalers started building one-story warehouses which were more efficient in fulfilling orders, lowering the costs of handling the product.[41] Historically, wholesalers had operated in multistory warehouses similar to the one operated by Hulman & Company. With diversification of the family assets well under way, Hulman chose not to build a one-story warehouse for Hulman & Company.

By 1998, Clabber Girl Baking Powder had a 65 percent market share of the U.S. market, and the product had been introduced into Europe, Asia and Africa. Ultimately, Hulman & Company exited the wholesale business in 1995.[42]

6

Tony's Early Adventures

Terre Haute, Indiana's seventh-largest city in 1900 with a population of 36,673, was filled with optimism for the new century. It had abundant natural resources including coal and access to natural gas to fuel industrial growth. Terre Haute was also the home of two of the nation's largest distilleries, and Terre Haute Brewing was the seventh-largest brewer nationally. It also had three glass companies providing bottles for these industries as well as the local Coca-Cola bottler, and mason jars. Rounding out the industrial base were three foundries.[1]

Tony Hulman, Anton and Grace Hulman's only child, was born on February 11, 1901. The Hulmans were among the leading families in Terre Haute. Tony had an extended family including uncles Herman Jr. and Theodore and their families. His early childhood was spent in Terre Haute. At an early age, he showed athletic ability—and a love for adventure and speed.

When Hulman was ten, seventy-five miles down the road they were running the first Indianapolis 500. Hulman's father knew one of the founders of the Indianapolis Motor Speedway, Carl Fisher, from his bicycle racing days. Creating additional interest, Frank Fox, a Terre Haute resident who owned the local Pope-Hartford automobile dealership, participated in the inaugural race placing twenty-second in a Pope-Hartford.[2]

Hulman showed an early love for speed. At age eleven, he and a friend, Dave Bronson, were riding to Turkey Run State Park on their Banger motorbikes. He skidded on some gravel and lost control. Both boys were pinned beneath their motorbikes, and before they could get it off, Hulman suffered burns to his legs. When he was twelve years old, Hulman bought a motorcycle and took it to the Vigo County fairgrounds in Terre Haute. After watching some motorcycle races, he decided to try out the track. To eliminate dust, the track had been watered down making it slick. Hulman crashed his bike through a wooden fence.³

At age fourteen, Hulman entered a motorcycle race at the track in Terre Haute. His childhood friend, Dave Bronson, recalled, "Tony and I used to take the motorcycle out to an old dirt track on the side of town and practice racing, and one Saturday Tony went ahead and entered himself in a race. He was only fourteen and I guess he was a little young at that. Anyway, his dad got wind of it and yanked him out an hour or so before the start."⁴

After spending his early school years at St. Benedict's in Terre Haute, he studied at the Lawrenceville School in New Jersey for three years and Worcester Academy in Massachusetts for one year. He was involved in athletics at both schools. At Lawrenceville, he played intramural basketball and baseball, but he excelled at track events. He was considered among the best young track stars with a wide range of events including pole-vaulting, broad-jumping, high-jumping, shot put and hurdles.⁵ In 1919 he was named "best school-boy vaulter in the U.S."⁶ Hulman later remembered, "As a schoolboy at Lawrenceville (NJ) and Worcester academies, I participated mostly in track and besides the individual honors for pole vaulting and high hurdling, I was named to the mythical Amateur Athletic Union League."⁷

His education continued at Yale where he studied engineering at the Sheffield Scientific School. A good student, he was a member of Tau Beta Phi and the Torch Society.⁸ The Torch Society was founded in March 1916 to honor the ten outstanding juniors for their achievements at Yale.⁹

He also continued to participate in athletics and was voted the best all-around athlete at Yale, winning seven letters. He excelled at track events, and in his freshman year he won ten medals for pole-vaulting and high-hurdling. As a rising sophomore, he participated in a meet where Yale and Harvard competed against Oxford and Cambridge in Boston.¹⁰ He was also on the varsity rowing crew and the track team.¹¹

Hulman also participated in collegiate football at Yale. Remembering those days, he said, "I read recently that the undefeated 1923 team I played on was about the best team Yale ever had."¹² The 1923 team benefited from a strong freshman team of 1920 (then seniors) and 1921 (then juniors) as well as the transfer to Yale of Century Milstead at tackle, Marvin (Mal) Stevens and Widdy Neale (halfbacks) and Lyle Richeson at quarterback.¹³ Hulman played offensive end backing up Shep Bingham.¹⁴ For his efforts, Hulman earned a Yale letter and was named to the All-Big Three team (Harvard, Yale and Princeton).¹⁵

6. Tony's Early Adventures

Before returning to Yale for his senior year, Hulman again participated as a member of the team representing Harvard and Yale in a biennial international competition against Oxford and Cambridge in Wembley, England. During this meet, he won the high-hurdle event.[16] After the conclusion of the meet, Hulman toured the continent including London, Amsterdam, Vienna, Budapest, Paris and Berlin. He also visited his ancestral home, Lingen. While in Germany he wrote to his mother, "In Berlin we bought six steins of real, honest-to-goodness beer for a cent."[17]

While in Lingen, he bought a police dog which accompanied him back to Terre Haute. Upon arriving home, his fiancée, Mary Fendrich, recalled, "He was wearing white English knickers. I thought he was a wow!"[18]

He had met Mary Fendrich on an earlier trip home from Yale. Driving his Duesenberg, Hulman had stopped at Atlantic City, New Jersey, where Mary, then a teenager, was with her family on vacation.

Hulman returned to the gridiron for his senior year and again played offensive end. He also was an All-American member of the Yale football team in 1924. For the second year, Yale was undefeated and won the Big Three championship (Yale, Harvard and Princeton).[19]

Hulman graduated from Yale in 1924 with a degree in engineering.[20]

His father introduced him to speedboat races. Hulman fondly remembered going to Miami Beach and being on the very fast speedboat owned by Carl Fisher, one of the founders of the Indianapolis Motor Speedway and a key developer of Miami Beach. He also enjoyed time with his father on the Wabash River, where his father reportedly had the fastest boat.[21]

7

Racing Resumes

If the experience in Europe was indicative, Hulman's decision to buy the Speedway would not be the white elephant some thought it might be. When World War II hostilities ended in Europe in May 1945, Europe had many of the same issues that faced America ... a war which limited the innovation of new racing cars, aging drivers and, unlike America, the massive destruction of infrastructure caused by multiple years of war.

The European racing structure was always different than that in the United States, with the majority of races being road races. The resumption of racing in Europe began on September 9, 1945, with three races in Bois de Boulogne Park in Paris.[1] By the spring of 1946, Grand Prix races had returned to Marseilles, Nice and Paris in France; Geneva, Switzerland; and Milan and Torino, Italy. Given the lack of new racing cars, the races were run with the 1.5 liter voiturette formula cars popular before the war.[2]

In the United States, the resumption of racing was primarily on dirt tracks, which had dominated the racing circuit since its inception. The board tracks, popular in the 1920s, had disappeared during the Great Depression due to the cost of construction and maintenance. Maintenance of a board track was expensive due to the pounding by the cars as well as the weather. Racing teams were dominated by private groups, most of whom depended upon racing for their livelihood.[3]

With preparations for the resumption of racing at the Indianapolis Motor Speedway under way, the entry date for the running of the 1946 Indianapolis 500 was May 1. At the close of the entry period, the Speedway had received fifty entries,⁴ including Rudy Caraccioli, the famed Mercedes team Grand Prix racer who had won numerous races prior to World War II. With an understanding of how racing celebrities could increase interest in races, he had been specifically invited by Hulman and Shaw.

When Caraccioli arrived in Indianapolis, Shaw introduced him to the Indianapolis 500 fans as "the best driver in the world—and I'm not kidding." Unfortunately, Caraccioli's Mercedes race car did not clear customs, and it appeared he would not be driving in the race. After touring the track with Shaw, Caraccioli said, "It's a wonderful track, those banked curves. I've a little Mercedes, a tinier car than these around here that would be just right for those. Top speed, say, of about 160." Rumors floated around the track that perhaps he would be given a ride in a French car. If not, Caraccioli said he hoped to get an entry for the 1947 race.⁵

With renovation work continuing on the racetrack, Speedway management announced that practice would be held from May 5 through May 10 between the hours of 4:30 p.m. and 7:30 p.m. Qualifying runs would be made on May 19, 25, and 26, and on Tuesday, May 28.⁶

In conjunction with qualifying, owners and drivers were asked by Speedway management to sign documents where they would drive the cars entered for the prize money reflected on the entry blanks. In a forerunner of things to come, some entrants signed and some refused. The *Indianapolis Star* indicated that a secret drivers meeting was held on May 17 and wondered if there would be a demand for additional prize money.⁷

On the first day of qualifying, Speedway management announced that the minimum qualifying speed would be 115 miles per hour for four laps. The fastest thirty-three cars would start the race. The tradition of having the car placed in terms of the qualifying speed on each day of qualifications was established. This meant that if you had a qualifying speed on the first day of qualifying which was in subsequent qualifying days exceeded by another car, you would not be bumped.

For the first day of qualifying, approximately 20,000 spectators were at the Speedway when veteran Indianapolis racer, Cliff Bergère, won the pole position with an average speed of 126.47 miles per hour. Bergère's familiarity with the course might have been an advantage as he had driven more miles in competition than any other driver.⁸

The next day of qualifying, 60,000 went to the Speedway. Indianapolis had a traffic jam caused not only by people trying to go to the Speedway but also a home show at the Indiana State Fairgrounds, a baseball game at Victory Field located about three miles east on 16th Street, and people going to the Riverside Amusement Park, which was also on the west side of the city. Ominously the roads leading to the track were clogged with spectators trying to get into the track through the narrow gates. After battling the traffic, the spectators were disappointed as there were no qualifying runs for the day. At first it was strong winds which kept the race drivers in the garages, and later, rain.[9]

Qualifying on May 26, Ralph Hepburn thrilled spectators by shattering the qualifying record speed previously set by Jimmy Snyder in 1939 at 130.138 miles per hour. Hepburn had been in fourteen prior races, with his best finish being a second place behind Wilbur Shaw in 1937. Hepburn's qualifying speed was nearly four miles per hour faster than Snyder's at 133.944 miles per hour.

At the conclusion of qualifying, only twenty-five cars qualified for the race. Several teams still trying get their pre–World War II cars into racing form asked for additional time. Although Speedway management had originally planned to use the time for practice and driving trials, they agreed to add four more hours of qualifying between 1 and 5 p.m. on Monday, May 27.[10]

Caracciola obtained a ride from Joel Thorne and took the car out for a test drive. While going 115 miles per hour, he crashed in the southeast turn, sustaining serious injuries when he was thrown from the car.[11] Probably saving his life was the hard army helmet provided by Colonel Arthur Herrington, head of the AAA Contest Board. Racers in Europe were not required to have hard helmets for racing, so upon arrival in Indianapolis, he had only his cloth helmet.[12] He initially was taken to Methodist Hospital in Indianapolis for treatment. For long-term recuperation, Hulman took him to Lingen Lodge, Hulman's retreat outside of Terre Haute.[13]

The lodge was located on 800 acres of rolling hills which had been in the Hulman family for a number of years. In 1938, Hulman decided to build a house on the property as a family retreat. Hulman recalled, "At that time most of the young people in the city liked to have a nice place to go and it was almost a municipal lake. We gradually built a house and got it private again. It's a lovely place to just go out to and entertain now and then." The lodge, which contained Hulman's collection of sports and photographic memorabilia, overlooks a twenty-two-acre lake. One special room of the house included hand-carved panels and fireplace decorations from the Standish Castle in England which Hulman had purchased from the William Randolph Hearst collection.

In a 1961 interview with Fred Cavinder of the *Indianapolis Star*, Hulman recalled his concern about the demand for the 1946 race: "I remember when we were building the first stand in the paddock. I suppose it held maybe 4,000, with boxes and rails around. I remember walking along a few days before the race and wondering how in the world there'd ever be enough people interested enough to pay $10 or $15 a seat. We did really worry if there'd be anybody there that first time."[14]

Popular Mercedes-Benz driver Rudi Carriciola getting ready to take a few laps in the Joel Thorpe racer. Thorpe is in the wheelchair. Carriciola would be seriously injured in a crash (Indianapolis Motor Speedway).

In a May 1977 interview, Hulman expanded upon his concerns about the ability to fill the demand for tickets. "But in that time we did build a steel and concrete paddock across from the starting line and also the old G grandstand had fallen down and we had to build one to replace it. I remember walking past that new paddock stand and I thought it was the biggest thing I'd ever seen. I couldn't believe we'd ever fill it up on race day. We were so worried that first year that the grandstands we did have might burn down before the race, so every night Wilbur would get out the fire hoses and sprinkle them. We kept them pretty well soaked because we thought if we'd sold tickets in the grandstand and if it had burned down before the race, we'd go broke."[15]

By race day, the field of thirty-three was filled. Despite the age of the cars, interest in the race was substantial. The Indianapolis Speedway Housing Bureau responded to the need for housing, sending hundreds of visitors to private homes as the hotels had been sold out for weeks in advance. Fans lined up along 16th Street waiting to get into the track when the gates opened at 7:00 a.m. The *Indianapolis Star* described the scene: "Tent oasis offered beer, cold drinks and hot dogs to race fans already on hand—hours in advance—for the opening of the Speedway gates."

Hulman worked hard to promote the Indianapolis 500 to celebrities and business leaders. Notable spectators at the 1946 race involved in the automobile industry included a contingent from Firestone Tire & Rubber (Harvey E. Firestone, Raymond Firestone, and Roger Firestone) who arrived in Indianapolis on their private Pullman car, and representing Ford Motor Company, Henry Ford II and Benson Ford. Jack Dempsey, the boxing legend and former heavyweight champion, and famed aviator Lieutenant General Jimmy Doolittle were also in attendance.[16]

To accommodate the crowds, Indiana senator Homer E. Capehart and Representative Louis Ludlow petitioned the Office of Defense Transportation for permission to have the New York Central Railroad run trains from Union Station to the Speedway at fifteen-minute intervals. Train service continued to be limited due to a shortage of coal.[17]

With expected attendance of 175,000 and the traffic jam on the second day of qualifying when the Speedway had 60,000 fans, it should not be a surprise that traffic trying to get to the race was badly snarled on race day. By 6:00 a.m., traffic was already lined up on 16th Street to Central Avenue, some five miles to the east. Captain Audry Jacobs of the Indianapolis Police Department believed nearly 200,000 people traveled to the Speedway, including those using the public transportation system. Jacobs commented, "The cars came faster than they could be handled at the Speedway gates."[18]

Despite the indications of interest in the race, Hulman remained concerned. He had been staying with Fred Holliday, a steel man who also owned one of the race cars.[19] As they started the journey to the track on a beautiful spring day, Hulman became increasingly concerned. In 1958, he recalled, "I was halfway down Kessler Boulevard, riding along with a friend of mine, and there wasn't a soul. My heart sank."

But he was not to be disappointed. He continued his tale:

> Then we hit one of the cross highways, and it was so mobbed we could not get across. I never saw anythin' like it. Those cars were stacked up for miles and the radios were blarin' and eatin' and drinkin' and playin' cards. I remember there was a two-headed cow being shown.
> We tried another way around and ran into the same thing. Finally we went through a field and tried shootin' up the shoulder of a road about 2 miles from the track. "Where the hell do you think you're going?" someone shouted. And then they were all on us. "To the races, we got tickets," we said. "Well ain't that just too bad, so have we," they roared back. I started breaking out in perspiration because it was close to startin' time, and then a policeman came over. I finally had to tell him I had an interest in the track so he let us go ahead.[20]

7. Racing Resumes

Introduced at the 1946 race and subsequently becoming an Indianapolis 500 tradition, the race parade included fourteen cars dating back to an 1896 model of an electric-powered automobile. Harkening back to earlier times, the passengers in the 1896 horseless carriage were attired in period outfits, with the ladies wearing enormous hats with ostrich feathers while the men wore linen dusters and brown derbies.

Hulman also harkened back to the 1919 Indianapolis 500 race, with James Melton, a leading tenor with the New York Metropolitan Opera, singing "Indiana," more popularly known as "Back Home Again in Indiana." This tune was written in 1917 by lyricist Ballard MacDonald, with the melody composed by James F. Hanley.[21] The song was popular with Hoosier troops serving in World War I. After Howdy Wilcox won the 1919 race driving a car owned by Indianapolis 500 co-founder Jim Allison, the massed band followed the car down the straightaway playing the tune.[22] Under Hulman, the singing of "Indiana" has become a traditional part of the pre-race festivities.[23]

Opera star Melton told the story of one of his first appearances at the Indianapolis 500: "It was one of my first years of the 500. Of course, I was nervous. I heard a fellow say that no one was interested in all that pomp and preliminaries. They just wanted to see the race get underway. So, I'm singing right along, doing my best not to make this mistake, with 2 or 300,000 people standing by. Just as I got to the last line, some mechanic jumped the gun, fired one of the cars. Well, when that engine burst into its song, I jump straight up in the air. That's when I did it: I sang the last line from *My Old Kentucky Home*."[24]

The age of the racing cars was an issue. Since few new cars had been built during World War II, most cars were between six and eight years old. Attrition during the race resulted in only nine cars finishing. With so few cars running, Wilbur Shaw asked Billy DeVore, who had dropped out of the race because of throttle problems, to rejoin the race. DeVore rejoined the field even though his car could only go ninety miles per hour. As a result, he was rewarded tenth place.[25]

Shortly after the purchase of the Speedway, Shaw and Hulman traveled to Florida. While there, they visited with Rickenbacker who offered some advice: "I want to tell you a little advice about that Speedway. I've been there since 1927 and if you boys are gonna make it go, never get the prize money over $75,000 a year because if you do, you'll be a flop."[26] Despite Rickenbacker's admonition to Hulman of keeping the prize money to less than $75,000, Hulman had different ideas. By offering the biggest purse in auto racing, he reenergized the sport of auto racing. In turn, this attracted racers, sponsors and spectators.[27]

The race was won by George Robson with an average speed of 114.82 miles per hour. Robson had participated in the 1940 and 1941 races. Total prize money was estimated at $105,000.[28] An Indianapolis clothing store awarded a trip around the world to race winner Robson.[29]

Because of the traffic issues, Hulman received over one thousand letters of complaint after the race. Years later, Hulman recalled one of the letters: "I remember one told me how he came to the race the night before and camped at the ball park and didn't get in to the race until it was over. By the time he put more water in his radiator he had to turn around and go home."[30]

One of Hulman's priorities became improving ingress to the track for the 1947 race. Speedway management developed a plan to double the number of lanes into the track and hired Harry Tousley's construction firm, which had constructed the new grandstands, to make this modification.[31]

A June 1946 article in the *New York Times* praised Hulman:

> There is no question but that Hulman made a wise choice in selecting the able Shaw as his right arm in these endeavors. Rickenbacker had lost the pulse of today's drivers and Shaw is of their generation in thinking. In many concerns, such as the garages, Shaw and Hulman worked together to restore the Speedway's lock on the racers' loyalty. Hulman assured the racing team managers and mechanics that the garages were their property for so long as they bring cars to race. As a result, several have installed permanent machinery, benches and other auxiliaries.
>
> Likewise, as tire concerns, automotive parts manufacturers and others saw Hulman opening his pockets to improve the Speedway and make the annual race a first-class venture, they too contributed to a sizeable purse.[32]

Robson would not be at the Speedway to defend his title in 1947. He was killed in a wreck at the Atlanta Speedway on September 2, 1946, while driving the car in which Floyd Roberts won the Indianapolis 500 in 1938 and Cliff Bergère placed third in 1941. The force of the wreck also killed George Barringer, whose car had been driven to victory by Wilbur Shaw in 1938.

In an era when cars were restored after crashes, even fatal ones, to see another day of racing, Bergère, owner of the car, took the mangled racing machine back to his garage where he proceeded to dismantle it with an acetylene torch. He commented, "Two of my best friends had been killed in that thing and that's two too many."[33]

1947

By 1947, the influence of technology used in World War II began to be felt by the Speedway in terms of equipment and drivers. Led by companies such as Offenhauser Engineering and Thorne Engineering, two government contractors who transitioned to building race cars, many of the aircraft innovations developed during World War II started to be used in race cars, including high-octane gasoline, fuel injection, disc brakes, hydraulic shock absorbers and radial tires.[34]

The void created from the retirement of many of the pre–World War II race drivers was filled with servicemen primarily from California. After having fought in battles, they missed the adrenaline rush, which could be replaced by action on the racetrack.[35]

In the years immediately following World War II, most of the racing teams were small private companies depending upon racing for their livelihood. One of their goals was to increase the prize money. As a result, in 1946, a group of owners and drivers based on the West Coast, led by Joel Thorne, formed the American Society for Professional Automobile Racing (ASPAR). They had success with many promoters in increasing the purse and approached the Indianapolis Motor Speedway management. Duke Nalon, a driver for the Novi team, recalled that the 1947 entry blank had the same guaranteed prize money as that from 1946—$75,000. Nalon later recalled, "We wanted more prize money."[36]

Speedway management had a decision to make and either of the obvious options would not end in a win-win for both sides. The first option was to acquiesce to the drivers' demands. Although this would permit the race to go forward in 1947, it risked the long-term viability of the Speedway to be self-sustaining. There were still many items which needed to be addressed in terms of the physical renewal of the track. If management declined to increase the purse, they risked having a field that wasn't full on race day, and many of the well-known drivers wouldn't participate, hurting the brand.

Ultimately, Speedway management declined ASPAR's request, as their business model was different from that of other promoters. Most promoters used dirt ovals located at state or county fairs owned by third parties. The promoters did not have the fixed overhead of the ongoing maintenance of the track. As a result, they were able to increase the purse to the drivers and car owners to 40 percent of the gate. But the Indianapolis Motor Speedway had all of these fixed cost.[37] Shaw, who traveled in the off-season to promote the Speedway, met with ASPAR leadership on a trip to the West Coast to explain the differences between the Speedway operating model and that of the promoters but was unsuccessful. He also pointed out that the Indianapolis 500 had the biggest purse in auto racing and that the total prize money, including a bonus payment, for the 1946 race was $115,450.[38]

When the deadline for the submission of entries arrived on April 15, the Speedway had received thirty-five entries for the 1947 race. They did not include entries from ASPAR members. Believing they had bargaining strength as they represented some of the most popular drivers of the day, ASPAR threatened to boycott the Indianapolis 500 unless Speedway management agreed to their demand of a guaranteed purse of $150,000.[39] The drivers also expected support from Shaw who had been an active participant in the 1937 boycott by drivers related to the ousting of Howdy Wilcox II from the starting lineup. Shaw's reaction to the ASPAR demands was, "We'll race without them."[40]

The ASPAR drivers, frustrated by the apparent intransigence of the Speedway management, waged a public relations campaign to promote their cause and convince the public that without their participation in the race, the Indianapolis 500 would not be run. Representing Speedway management, Wilbur Shaw, who had met with Hepburn, responded, "I have told Ralph that the purses will be increased just as fast as possible. There was an increase of 22 per cent after the race last year. This is the same coercive type of thing that happened to 15 major speedways and they're all out of business except one. They went bankrupt."[41]

At a meeting of the AAA Contest Board held at the Indianapolis Athletic Club on May 7, 1947, Speedway management and other interested parties spent five hours trying to negotiate an agreement with ASPAR representatives. Although a tentative agreement was reached where the prize monies would be increased as the gate allowed, there was still the issue of the entries of the protesting drivers. At the meeting, ASPAR appealed directly for the AAA Contest Board to declare this an emergency, thus being able to require the reopening of the application filing.

The AAA Contest Board denied the request. Representing the AAA Contest Board, Arthur Herrington explained the decision: "The contest board today was requested by ASPAR to order entries to the Indianapolis Motor Speedway race on May 30 reopened. In justice to the 34 who filed their entries by the official closing date of April 15, 1947, the request is denied. In accordance with the usual procedures, post-entries may be accepted provided all entrants or their agents sign a waiver of post-entry."

With the refusal by the AAA Contest Board to reopen the application period, ASPAR member Jim Frantonne filed an application for a competing race at the Langhorne Speedway on May 30. This was quickly denied by the AAA Contest Board on the grounds that their by-laws prohibited two races on the same day. Afterward Hepburn, as president of the ASPAR drivers, declared, "A majority of outstanding racing automobiles and their drivers in America will not participate in the race on May 30."[42]

In order to stimulate interest in the qualifications, Shaw announced special qualifying prizes of up to $10,000 when the time trials opened on May 17. "This is the first time cash prizes have been offered for qualifying runs and we believe the additional money will provide incentive for the drivers to provide more thrills than the fans have ever derived from the preliminary activities."⁴³ This offer of special qualifying prizes would quickly become a sticking point in the negotiations with the ASPAR drivers.

When the time trials started in mid–May, pressure on the ASPAR members increased as they had no viable racing options on Memorial Day. Following the action on the track during qualifying, they realized the field would be strong without their participation. Ted Horn had taken the pole driving the Maserati in which Wilbur Shaw had won the Indianapolis 500 in 1939 and 1940. Other qualifiers on the first day included Cliff Bergère, Mauri Rose and Merrill (Doc) Williams.⁴⁴

Seeing that their efforts had not succeeded, the ASPAR drivers indicated a willingness to drop their demands if they could participate in the time trials. Unfortunately, since the deadline for entries had passed, the drivers could participate only if all of the entrants in the race agreed to their participation. Negotiations continued between ASPAR officials and Speedway management. There were two sticking points. The first was that to get the agreement of the entrants into the race, ASPAR participants needed to agree that no ASPAR team could take the spot of a team which qualified at a minimum 115 miles per hour time trial speed. The second requirement was that the ASPAR drivers would not participate in the special qualifying purse.⁴⁵

ASPAR driver Nalon recalled of Shaw, "He refused to arbitrate anything with us at all." With a week remaining before the race, negotiations led by journalists from the *Indianapolis Star* continued between Shaw and Hulman representing the Speedway and Rex Mays and Hepburn representing ASPAR. The crisis was averted when Hulman agreed to provide the ASPAR drivers a separate purse for qualification runs if they placed between first and fifth. Hulman also agreed that the ASPAR drivers starting positions would be assigned according to qualifying speed rather than at the end of the field. With a solution apparently at hand, Hepburn announced that between fifteen and nineteen cars were ready to make qualifying runs.⁴⁶ Nalon continued, "If it wasn't for Tony Hulman, we probably wouldn't have had a race here. But he agreed to pay the prize money."⁴⁷

With a settlement reached, the ASPAR drivers were ready to begin qualifying. Reminiscent of the failure of Ralph DePalma to send his entry form by the deadline for the 1916 race, the AAA Contest Board required that all of the drivers and team owners who had qualified for the race agree to the ASPAR drivers being given the chance to qualify.

Even though an agreement had been reached between Speedway management and ASPAR representatives, Shaw believed the Speedway had no right to ask the entrants to sign the waiver permitting the ASPAR drivers to qualify. The entry form clearly stated that all applications needed to be submitted to the Speedway by April 15.[48] In fact, the Speedway office had stayed open until midnight rather than the normal close of business of 5:00 p.m. on the 15th in case there was a last-minute entrant.[49]

The prolonged negotiations to avert a strike by the ASPAR drivers resulted in a great deal of acrimony between ASPAR and the entrants into the race. Speedway management believed if an ASPAR representative approached the qualified drivers, their efforts to obtain the concurrence of the entrants would fail. The solution appeared to be a neutral third party, Bill Fox, the *Indianapolis News* sports editor.[50]

For an intense forty-eight hours, Fox worked to obtain the necessary waivers. In the end, there were seventeen ASPAR drivers with cars ready to participate in the qualifying trials. Of the thirty-five original entrants, twenty-one had qualified for the race.[51] The ASPAR drivers and cars showed up at the Speedway, but by and large their cars were not prepared for the race. By the closing of qualifications, only four additional drivers had made the field.

(Left to right) **Hulman, Wilbur Shaw and Pop Myers meet at the Indianapolis Motor Speedway office in 1947 (Indianapolis Motor Speedway).**

ASPAR appealed for additional qualifying time which was granted for two additional days to end on May 28 at 4:00 p.m.[52]

At the drivers' meeting before the race, the ASPAR drivers pleaded for yet more qualifying time. Speedway management agreed to continue the qualifications for an additional hour beginning at 6:00 p.m. subject to the qualifying cars obtaining the waiver of the other participants in the race. Four cars attempted to qualify, with two, Mel Hanson and Emil Andres, making the field. But by the end of the extended qualifying time, only sixteen of the waivers had been received. This left Hanson and Andres unable to be part of the field unless the remaining twelve waivers were obtained.[53]

By the start of the race, the needed waivers had been obtained and thirty cars participated in the 1947 Indianapolis 500. Watching the race as a guest of Hulman was movie star Clark Gable, a racing enthusiast.[54] The race turned into a duel between teammates Mauri Rose and Bill Holland. With Bill Holland in the lead and Mauri Rose in second place as the race was nearing 500 miles, team owner Lou Moore flashed an EZY sign to his two drivers. As he later explained, "I wanted both of them to slow down and Holland slowed down more than Rose did. They were so far ahead there was no reason for either of them to take a chance." The race was won by Mauri Rose.[55] Ironically, the top five finishers were all teams which had submitted entries by April 15.[56]

1948

When the track opened in May 1948, there was a very unusual entry—a six-wheeled racing car. The car was brought to the racetrack by Billy DeVore who hoped that the four wheels in the back would result in better traction in the turns.[57] This car, powered by a four-cylinder engine with 270 cubic inches of displacement, qualified on the second weekend of qualifications with an average speed of 123.867 miles per hour.[58]

The pole position was won by Rex Mays with an average speed of 130.5 miles per hour. On the second day of qualifying, veteran Indianapolis driver Ralph Hepburn was on the track in a car which just two days before had been crashed by Cliff Bergère. After the crash, Bergère and car owner Lew Welch parted company. Hepburn, whose Indianapolis driving career started in 1925, had raced in fifteen Indianapolis 500s. For Hepburn, this car represented a return to racing at Indianapolis after he had missed the 1947 contest due to the ASPAR dispute. While on the track, Hepburn lost control of the car. The crash resulted in severe head and chest trauma which Hepburn did not survive.[59]

Although Hulman was the owner of the track, he was not well known to the personnel at the Speedway. In 1948, he was to appear at a broadcast from the Pagoda. Unfortunately he forgot his credentials and was unable to get to the broadcast spot. He recalled, "I didn't get up there either so I just sat down and decided I'd stay there until someone came along and identified me. I got in too late ... I missed the broadcast."[60]

Wilbur Shaw returned to the track at the beginning of the 1948 race to pilot the pace car, a gray Chevrolet Fleetmaster, at the start of the race.[61] The 1948 race will be known as the year that Mauri Rose won his third Indianapolis 500. His teammate Bill Holland took second place but was more than a lap behind the winner.[62]

In September 1948, Hulman took time out from his busy duties at Hulman & Company to go tuna fishing off the coast of Nova Scotia. For the previous twelve years, Hulman had enjoyed big-game fishing for tuna, marlin, broadbill and swordfish off the coasts of Cuba, Jamaica, the Florida Keys and the Bahamas. Over several days with fishing guide Tommy Gifford, they bagged bluefin tunas weighing in at 772 pounds, 642 pounds and 587 pounds. Hulman explained that a bluefin tuna "is too temperamental to bite on the same thing all the time." What was the key to his success? Pork rinds. Hulman explained, "Done up like a fish and carefully bleached, the pork produces a motion in the water that's irresistible to a blue fin who is a little off his feed. We just had a little rind to experiment with but if we'd had a lot of it, we could probably have sold it for almost any amount of money."[63]

1949

By 1949, in order to pass the rookie driving test, the Speedway rookies needed to successfully negotiate the track at 95, 105, 110 and 115 miles per hour. Byron Horne had successfully completed the first three phases of the rookie test when he took to the track to pass the final phase at 115 miles per hour.[64] Losing control of the car in the southwest corner, Horne smacked the wall. He was taken to Methodist Hospital in critical condition,[65] with injuries to the chest, a broken jaw, broken left leg and cracked right leg.[66]

There was a crackle in the air when Nalon completed the first lap of his qualifying run. A bolt of lightning came from thunderheads to the northwest. Nalon, driving the Novi that others were unable to handle, took the pole position with an average speed of 132.939 miles per hour.[67]

Earlier in the day, with an estimated 60,000 on hand to witness the first day of qualifying, too many spectators piled into Grandstand B, the oldest at the Speedway, near the first turn. Due to the weight, two boxes of the grandstand collapsed, injuring thirty-four, one with a serious head injury. Most of the injured were treated and released at the infield Speedway hospital, Methodist Hospital or Indianapolis General Hospital. Only five were admitted.[68] People in the stands remembered hearing a cracking sound and then the sensation of falling. Mauri Rose was qualifying at the time, leading to speculation that the collapse was due to people trying to see him entering turn 1.[69] Since the action on the track was suspended while victims of the grandstand collapse were being taken to the hospital, qualifying was extended until 6:45 p.m.[70]

After inspecting the grandstand following the collapse, Fire Chief Roscoe A. Turner declared, "There are a lot of rotten spots in the timbers underneath. New supports must be put in under the entire row of boxes. Unless this is done, the stand will not be safe."[71] The Speedway grounds crew responded with rebuilding a portion of the grandstand.

Some Indianapolis residents who were in the right place at the right time witnessed the first television broadcast in Indianapolis. On May 28, WFBM-TV tested its equipment with live shots from the Indianapolis Motor Speedway for forty minutes. Televisions weren't commonplace in residences, but people gathered around televisions in storefront windows, including L. S. Ayres, the Indianapolis department store which sponsored the telecast.[72]

WFBM-TV had announced they would be broadcasting a special program, "The Crucible of Speed" produced by Firestone Tire & Rubber, on race day. It was a promotional film and included famed Indianapolis winners Ray Harroun, Ralph DePalma and Cliff Bergère talking with Johnny Moore, the head of Firestone's Racing Division about the improvements in the automobile since the first race in 1911. It also featured some clips from various races, including Shaw's crash in 1941 as well as his 500-mile tire test at the Speedway in November 1944. It would be followed by forty minutes of coverage from the Indianapolis Motor Speedway on race day.[73]

Indianapolis was also abuzz with the presence of movie stars, Clark Gable and Barbara Stanwyck, in town for the filming of *To Please a Lady*. The film featured Gable as a race car driver, with the final three weeks being filmed in Indianapolis. Although he did some of his own driving, race car driver Bud Rose was used as a double during the action filmed at the Indianapolis Motor Speedway, where speeds during the racing scenes reached 100 miles per hour.[74]

Two days before the race, mechanic H. C. "Cotton" Henning discovered sand in the crankcase of Ted Horn's car, which was confirmed by some engineers at the Allison Division of General Motors.[75] It was discovered prior to any damage being done to the engine. Henning reported they had gotten all of the sand out of the crankcase.[76] He said, "I'm sure someone was paid to put sand in the car. I can't prove it but there's no other explanation of it. I'll ask the Speedway management and state police to investigate."[77] In response to the sabotage, many of the team owners had mechanics sleeping with their cars in the garage area. Additionally the Indianapolis Motor Speedway hired the Pinkerton Detective Agency to investigate.[78]

In 1949, Hulman returned to the waters off of Nova Scotia as a member of the four-person team representing the United States in an international tuna fishing contest. The U.S. team scored 4,530 points, defeating Cuba by 1,308 points and bringing the championship to the United States for the first time.[79] Hulman returned to the international fishing tournament three more years and recalled, "I was on the U.S. Tuna Team competing with 14 or 15 countries in tuna-fishing competition staged by the government of Nova Scotia. In 1952, my last year, I was team captain."[80]

1950

After five years of ownership of the Indianapolis Motor Speedway, Hulman got a personal tour of the track from a different vantage point—in a race car driven by Wilbur Shaw. Sonny Kleinfeld reported that as the speed approached 120 miles per hour, Hulman, who was known to zip along in his personal automobile, was yelling to Shaw to let up on the speed and then knocked Shaw's foot off the accelerator. After the harrowing trip around the Speedway, Hulman swore he never wanted another tour of the track by race car.[81]

Of the rookies at Indianapolis in 1950, two from California garnered a lot of attention. Bill Vukovich, the 1950 AAA National Midget Car champion, arrived in Indianapolis without a ride. His friends in the racing world urged him to at least pass his rookie test. He did so in Wilbur Shaw's "pay car," the Boyle Maserati in which Shaw won the Indianapolis 500 in 1939 and 1940. Although passing the rookie test, Vukovich failed to qualify for the race.[82] The other rookie, Walt Faulkner, smashed the one-lap and qualifying records held by Ralph Hepburn. In front of 50,000 spectators, Faulkner, also an experienced midget driver, established a new lap record of 136.013 miles per hour, going nearly a mile and a half faster than Hepburn's record. The new qualifying record was 134.343 miles per hour.[83] Faulkner had passed his rookie test for the Indianapolis Motor Speedway just three days earlier.[84]

Johnny Parsons won a rain-shortened race with an average speed of 124.002 miles per hour. The day had been overcast, and drizzle began to fall. The result was three minor accidents. The conditions at the Speedway quickly deteriorated. What had been a drizzle became a steady rain and then within thirty minutes became a downpour. Chief Steward Tommy Milton in consultation with Referee Earl Cooper decided to call the race after 345 miles due to the slickness of the track. At the time the race was called, twenty-three cars were still running.

Parsons' mechanics didn't expect his car would finish the race. Minutes before the start of the race, a hair-line crack had been spotted in the engine block. Another interesting twist is the car had just been sold to Jim Robbins by Ed Walsh, Jr. A part of the agreement for sale was that Robbins wouldn't be eligible for any of the earnings of the car during the race.

Although it was clear that Parsons had won the race, upon review of the tabulation tapes, Chester Ricker, chief timer and scorer, discovered that Tony Bettenhausen, who originally appeared to finish second, really finished fifth. This resulted in Mauri Rose being declared the second place finisher.[85]

8

The Vukovich Era

As the racetrack was opening in 1951, Clarence Cagle and his grounds crew were very busy trying to ready the track for the upcoming speed trials and also the race. But there were issues to overcome. The short-term challenge to be addressed was the buckling of the track at the expansion joints caused by temperatures in the nineties. Cagle was on a roller trying to smooth the track prior to its being opened for practice.

The second challenge was the completion of the new grandstand under construction, especially since the tickets for the seats had already been sold and there was no alternative comparable seating available. This was a massive project as the Speedway was relocating Little Eagle Creek which flowed underneath the racetrack as part of the project. The Speedway had hired H. D. Tousley Company to replace Grandstand A located on the main straightaway just before the cars enter turn 1 at a cost of $600,000. The grandstand had seating for 13,500 spectators, including 3,300 seats on the upper level with the remainder on the lower level.[1]

Although Cagle liked to get major construction projects completed in the fall to ensure that weather and other unforeseen forces couldn't cause delay, he was not successful in 1951. The local ironworkers union had declared a strike, being dissatisfied with the fifteen-cent-per-hour increase in wages granted under an escalator clause in the existing contract with the Indianapolis chapter of the Builder's Contractor Association. The seats in this grandstand were already sold, but the grandstand was only 75 percent complete.[2] Additionally, construction debris was on the main straightaway and needed to be removed prior to the track being opened for practice.[3]

8. The Vukovich Era

Conversations at the Speedway centered on the hoped-for increase in speed. Firestone had developed a tire using a new compound. When Jack McGrath and Chet Miller tested the tires at the Speedway, Firestone technicians were pleased with the results. The tires seemed to reduce the draft in the corners, resulting in improved speeds averaging between 128 and 132 miles per hour. One Firestone technician said, "The tires held much better in the turns and, as a result, the drivers were able to negotiate the turns at increased speed. A number of tires were run on the track until completely worn out to check tread wear performance. Based on the test results, we expect a marked tread wear performance and an increase in speed in the 1951 race." After watching some of the testing, Wilbur Shaw, who had tested tires for Firestone at the Speedway in 1944, predicted the new tires would "increase the speed of racing cars up to 4 miles an hour."[4]

Speedway aficionados welcomed back Duke Nalon who had been severely

Hulman sitting on the wall with racing flags in 1951. Notice the wooden Pagoda built in 1926 by original track owners Fisher, Allison, Wheeler and Newby (Indianapolis Motor Speedway).

burned during the 1949 race when he crashed after his rear axle broke and the fuel cell ruptured upon impact. The Speedway crowd was delighted when Nalon took the pole position.[5]

Missing from the Speedway was perennial contender Bill Holland, who was suspended by the AAA Contest Board for running in unsanctioned races. In the prior four years, he had won the race in 1949 and he finished second three times.[6]

Broadcasting of the race was taken over by local radio station WIBC. Mutual Broadcasting Company had withdrawn from the broadcast after the race's sponsor of the previous races, a piston ring company, was unwilling to pay the sponsorship, fee which had increased 50 percent to $30,000. With WIBC heading the broadcast team, race fans throughout the nation would be introduced to Sid Collins, who in subsequent years would become known as the voice of the Indy 500. Although Mutual Broadcasting Company did not broadcast the race, its 300 affiliate stations were interested in race coverage, which was provided through feeds from WIBC.[7]

Lee Wallard won the race setting a new track record, completing the 500 miles in under four hours. When he finished, he was more than two laps ahead of the nearest competitor, Mike Nazarek.[8] Among the rookies in the race were future Indianapolis 500 winners Bill Vukovich and Rodger Ward.[9]

1952

Mauri Rose, the winner of three Indianapolis 500s, announced his retirement after his car's wheel collapsed and the car overturned during the 1951 race.[10] The next year, Howard Keck, the team owner, begged him to reconsider his decision to retire. Keck told him he had a car which would revolutionize racing and he could become the first driver to win four Indianapolis 500s. Rose reportedly said, "You know how many times I've heard that?" When it became apparent that Rose was not going to reconsider driving the new revolutionary car, Keck hired Bill Vukovich.[11]

In May 1952, tensions were high as the labor unions had struck the oil refineries. Oscar L. Chapman, head of the Department of the Interior, expressed concern that rationing might be necessary. The Midwest was the most impacted area of the United States, with Indianapolis, Chicago and Detroit being particularly hard hit.[12]

Despite the potential for gasoline rationing, Speedway officials did not think the strike would have an impact on the race. Wilbur Shaw said, "All the fuel needed for practice, qualifications and the race is already on hand. It would be of little use for any other purposes because of the unique blending for the racing cars." He also believed rationing would have little impact upon the race fan as railroad travel provided an alternative way of getting to Indianapolis. He said, "Even if gas is rationed, 'dyed in the wool' race fans will find some way of getting here."[13]

The greater Indianapolis area used an average of 900,000 gallons of gasoline per day. The Rock Island refinery on the northwest side of Indianapolis in Zionsville, Indiana, had a capacity of 250,000 gallons daily. A breakthrough in the strike appeared to happen on May 7 when the union at the Rock Island refinery agreed to an eighteen-cent-per-hour increase in wages. But on a national scale, the unions rejected the federal government's request they go back to work.[14] In order to break the strike, President Truman threatened to invoke the Taft-Hartley Act.[15] The threat appears to have worked as by May 14, the union had tentatively agreed to a fifteen-cent-per-hour increase in wages plus differential work. They had been demanding an increase of twenty-five cents per hour.[16]

The Speedway was not immune from union organizing activities. A representative of one of the local Teamsters unions approached mechanics, drivers and owners about forming a union. His efforts failed to gain traction. One of the mechanics pointedly indicated he wasn't sure how this would work since each of the groups had different concerns. Wilbur Shaw said of the organizing activity, "Never before has the relationship between the car owners and drivers with the Speedway been at a higher level. We are not surprised at the lack of interest displayed in the efforts of union organizers because everything possible is being done in the best interest of the racing fraternity without the expensive advice of outsiders."[17]

On the first day of qualifications, spectators were amazed at the car taking the pole. The Cummins Diesel Special was powered by a diesel engine. Cummins Engine Company, with operations in Columbus, Indiana, used the Indianapolis Motor Speedway to test their engines. With a history dating back to 1919, the company had focused on marine and stationary engines. During the Great Depression, they repositioned the company to focus on automotive and industrial engines. Their first entry in the Indianapolis 500 was in 1931. This car was the first car to go the distance without a fuel stop. They returned to the Speedway in 1935 with two entries. One of the diesel-powered cars was sidelined by an accident on lap 81 and the other finished eighteenth. In 1950, Cummins was back at the Speedway and their entry finished thirty-third. Due to their testing program at the Speedway, Cummins had successfully developed a small turbo-charged diesel engine with good acceleration and fuel mileage.[18] With Freddie Agabashian at the wheel, the Cummins Diesel Special had a qualifying time of 138.010 miles per hour for the four laps.[19]

Vukovich was back at the Speedway in the Fuel Injection Special, a four-cylinder rear drive car with a 270-cubic-inch Offenhauser engine. In his qualifying run on the second weekend of time trials he set a new lap record—138.212 miles per hour.[20] His car was the revolutionary car promised by Keck to Mauri Rose if he would reconsider his decision to retire.[21]

The Fuel Injection Special driven by Vukovich was clearly the car to beat. The race turned into a duel between Vukovich and Troy Ruttman. Ruttman led the race for 44 laps, and Vukovich led the race for 150 laps. Vukovich had a nineteen-second lead with eight laps to go when his steering shaft broke and the car slid into the wall. Ruttman won the race with an average speed of 128.922 miles per hour. Remarkably, his car had caught fire in the pits and he was down to the last set of tires when he took the checkered flag.[22] Ruttman's share of the $230,000 purse was $61,743.18.[23]

Hulman along with some other American and South American businessmen were involved in the establishment of the Cabo Blanco Fishing Club, a resort for deep-sea fishermen, by S. Kip Farrington, Jr. In February 1952, Hulman spent several days fishing off Cabo Blanco, Peru, where he caught three black marlin in four days. But that was just the beginning of his catches. He also bagged a 762-pounder on the fifth day of fishing, and believes that he had a 1,000-plus-pound marlin which got away on the sixth day of fishing. He rounded out the trip by bagging a 918-pound marlin on the seventh day of fishing and concluded the trip with an 837-pounder on the final day of fishing. Farrington described Hulman's performance as "the most unbelievable catch in fishing history."[24]

1953

As the Speedway opened in 1953, seventy-six of the eighty-three car owners had signed a petition to ban the use of nitromethanol as an additive. Nitromethanol, a mixture of nitrogen, hydrogen and oxygen,[25] was used primarily to increase the speed during qualifying. It was not widely used during the race, as fuel efficiency was negatively impacted and there was a limitation on the amount of fuel that could be used during the race. The Speedway regulations required all registrants sign the petition and set a deadline of May 4 for submission of the signed petition. On May 4 there were seven car owners who had not signed the petition. Without all of the car owners signing the petition, the use of "pop" continued at the Speedway.[26]

Safety experts had been encouraging drivers to use fire-retardant chemicals on their driving suits, but most resisted. A fiery crash by Al Griffith sent the drivers to soak their driving suits in fire-retardant solvent. Griffith had

8. The Vukovich Era

been entering turn 1 when his tire hit a slight bump in the Speedway pavement. Losing control, he smashed into the wall and his car erupted in fire. In addition to a broken pelvis, he suffered second- and third-degree burns over 40 to 50 percent of his body.

Some additional safety items were added during the early practice sessions at the Speedway. Some tire-balancing weights had been found on the track surface which if hit by another car could become airborne. If the bolt struck someone, it could cause serious or deadly injuries. As a safety measure, AAA officials required the bolting of the balancing weights to the tire rims. Additionally, some teams were storing bulk fuel in their garages. Remembering the 1941 fire which destroyed some of the garages on race day, Wilbur Shaw banned this practice and threatened to confiscate any bulk fuel found in the garages.[27]

On the last day of practice prior to qualifications beginning, the "Dean of the Speedway," Chet Miller, took the Novi out for a test. This Novi had a history, having been the same car in which Hepburn died and Nalon had received critical burns. Miller lost control of the Novi in the southwest turn and suffered a fatal basal skull fracture and brain hemorrhage. Miller had begun his driving career at Saginaw, Michigan, in 1924 and made sixteen appearances at the Indianapolis 500. His best finish at the Speedway was third in 1938 behind Floyd Roberts and Wilbur Shaw.[28] Prior to going to Indianapolis for the 1953 race, he told his wife he would retire from racing after the Indianapolis 500. At the time of his death, he held the one-lap record of 139.6 miles per hour and the four-lap record of 139.034 miles per hour.[29]

The first day of qualifications were postponed due to rain. Although qualifying didn't start until mid-afternoon the next day due to the track being wet, Vukovich took the pole position with an average speed of 138.392 miles per hour.[30] On race day, Vukovich was the favorite to win the race of the estimated 200,000 people expected to attend.[31]

He did not disappoint. Despite an extremely hot day, Vukovich led for all but two laps of the race, with an average speed of 128.74 miles per hour. The heat, which reached an estimated 130 degrees on the track, took its toll. It contributed to the slow pace of the race, and only twelve cars were running at the conclusion. Additionally, driver Carl Scarborough died of a heat stroke.[32] To combat the heat, Vukovich poured three quarts of water down his back at every pit stop.[33] For his efforts, Vukovich's share of the purse was $89,497.[34]

Race fans unable to attend the Indianapolis 500 could listen to the race on the newly formed Indianapolis Motor Speedway Network which Hulman and Shaw had put together the previous winter. All five Indianapolis radio stations (WIBC, WFBM, WISH, WXLW and WIRE) joined together for the broadcast to twenty-six affiliate stations. WIBC sports anchor, Sid Collins, was the Voice of the Indianapolis Motor Speedway. This first broadcast included the Armed Forces Network. Over time, the Indianapolis Motor Speedway Network would televise the race. The broadcast was sponsored by Indianapolis-area Ford dealers.[35]

1954

As the Speedway opened in 1954, the bus drivers' union in Indianapolis was on strike. Expecting a lengthy strike, Indianapolis officials were making alternative plans including use of train shuttles to get spectators to the track should the strike continue. Paul Shick, president of the Board of Public Safety, said, "Our interest is to see that traffic moves as smoothly and safely as possible. With the prospect that the Indianapolis Transit System may still be shut down, we will do our best to expedite the use of all other facilities to handle the vast volume of traffic."[36]

After having eighty-three cars entered for the 1953 race, entries dropped to sixty-five cars for the 1954 contest. Rodger Ward hypothesized that part of the drop might be a lack of qualified drivers. He believed the owners did not want to entrust cars with a cost of $25,000 each to an untested driver. In a related action, the rules on the driver test were changed by the AAA Contest Board to require prior experience in driving the Indianapolis type cars. A driver seeking a test needed to be recommended by a zone supervisor of the AAA Contest Board. One of the requirements for getting the recommendation was that the AAA official "will recommend only drivers with actual racing car experience in competition."[37]

The transit strike continued for the first day of qualifications. Speedway officials expected traffic jams around the track and were planning to stop activity on the track for about an hour to allow spectators to cross over the track. For those not planning to go to the track for qualifications, Indianapolis radio station WIBC interrupted its regular broadcasting for periodic updates, and there was a national hookup between 5:30 and 6:30 p.m.[38]

Despite the transit strike, on a beautiful Indianapolis day, an estimated crowd between 100,000 and 125,000, the largest for qualifying day, watched Jack McGrath take the pole, setting a new record of 141.033 miles per hour.[39] McGrath's car was a brand new Kurtis Kraft 500 C roadster with a 270-cubic-inch Offenhauser engine.[40]

The nitromethanol controversy returned to the Speedway in 1954. Ten cars which used "pop" during qualifications suffered from damaged crankshafts. Russ Snowberger, an owner/mechanic, explained the issues surrounding the use of "pop": "Everybody is abusing crankshafts. Those engines aren't built for

Hulman with Wilbur Shaw holding a bouquet which includes a small racer at the bottom in 1954. Within six months, this partnership, which brought the Speedway back from the brink of destruction, ended when Shaw was killed in a plane crash (Indianapolis Motor Speedway).

the use of nitro. They're made to turn 4500 to 4700 RPMs. It's crazy to make them turn up to 6100 RPMs with nitro. Sure you get the added speed but you wreck your engine doing it." Snowberger believed many car owners were using nitromethanol as a defensive measure. He said, "One car owner wants that extra 2 miles per hour to get his car in the field and so what does he do? He uses nitro and everyone else starts using nitro too. Now you can see with the result is. A big mess of cracked crankshafts caused by engines doing more than what they were built to do." Unfortunately, the maker of the engines, Meyer-Drake, only had two replacement crankshafts on hand. One owner complained, "Meyer's factory makes enough money from us supplying the engines. Why in the devil can't he have replacements on hand? What kind of deal is that?"[41]

Race day 1954 was very hot, with temperatures in the high eighties. In a race in which relief drivers would be used by most teams, Bill Vukovich drove the entire race.[42]

Prior to qualifications, Jep Cadou, Jr., sports editor for the *Indianapolis Star* mused that he thought it would be impossible for anyone to come from the middle of the field and win the race. Vukovich took umbrage to this and stated he didn't think starting position made a difference in winning the race.[43] Starting the race in 19th position, Vukovich steadily worked his way to the front of the pack. He was in seventh place at the 50-mile mark and in fourth place at the 100-mile mark. He gained the lead on the ninety-second lap[44] and went on to win his second consecutive Indianapolis 500 with an average speed of 130.84 miles per hour. He joined the exclusive club of Wilbur Shaw (1939 and 1940) and Mauri Rose (1947 and 1948) in winning back-to-back Indianapolis 500s.

Despite the high temperatures, it was a very fast race in spite of a rain, wind and dust storm which kicked up late in the race slowing the speed. The top five finishers beat the record speed for the race of 128.922 miles per hour established by Troy Ruttman in 1952.[45]

In October 1954, Hulman was elected to the board of directors of Indiana National Bank, then the nation's forty-ninth-largest bank, based in Indianapolis.[46]

The Hulman-Shaw leadership team, which had brought about the resurgence of the Speedway, was disrupted by a plane crash into a farmer's field about three and a half miles north of Decatur, Indiana, on October 30. The three people aboard the plane, Wilbur Shaw, Indiana artist Ernest Roose who painted portraits of Indianapolis 500 winners, and the pilot Ray Grimes, were killed. They had traveled to Detroit, Michigan, where Shaw had test-driven a new 1955 Chrysler Imperial. Ironically, after the test drive, Shaw had commented, "This is safer than flying."[47]

9

The Crisis in Auto Racing

Auto racing has always been inherently dangerous. Although most people recognize the danger for the drivers, less recognized is the danger faced by spectators. What starts out as a fun excursion can become a tragedy in a fraction of a second. On Long Island, spectators gathered on the public roadways to witness the Vanderbilt Cup races in the early 1900s, risking life and limb to see the action on the track as the racers passed by.

Due to the dangers of road racing, this form of racing lost favor with the American public. The Vanderbilt Cup was canceled after a spectator was killed in the 1906 race. It returned in 1908 after William K. Vanderbilt II built the Long Island Motor Parkway where crowds could be better controlled. Although safer for spectators, road courses had less visibility for spectators and eventually declined in popularity.

When the Indianapolis Motor Speedway was built in 1909, the prevalent style of racetrack was a one-mile dirt oval at state or county fairgrounds, traditionally used for horse racing. The visionary of the Speedway, Carl Fisher, believed that a larger course than one mile provided a better test for the automobile and would lead to improvements in quality. The four founders of the Indianapolis Motor Speedway, Fisher, James Allison, Arthur Newby and Frank Wheeler, wanted the track surface to be something more substantial than a dirt track. Believing the cost of either a concrete or a brick track would be prohibitive, they decided upon a composition track made of layers of crushed stone and asphaltum oil packed down by heavy rollers and built upon a foundation of clay.[1]

The first automobile races at the Speedway were held in late August 1909. Automobile manufacturing was concentrated in the Midwest, resulting in a significant rivalry between Indianapolis and Detroit. Multiple teams including a forty-person Buick contingent as well as teams from Dayton-based Stoddard-Dayton and Indianapolis-based National and Marmon were involved. The three-day race schedule included races of varying lengths culminating in a daily featured race.

The featured race on the first day of racing, August 19, 1909, was the Prest-O-Lite Trophy race, a 250-mile event.[2] By the time of the running of the Prest-O-Lite race, the track had taken a beating, particularly in the corners, from the heavy automobiles. The first fatalities at the Indianapolis Motor Speedway occurred when Wilfred Bourque, driving a Knox automobile, tried to sneak a peek at a car approaching from behind driven by Jap Clemens. Hitting a hole in the pavement, Bourque lost control of the vehicle. When the auto hit a ditch on the outside of the track, the car flipped end over end before coming to rest against a fence post. Both Bourque and his riding mechanic, Harry Holcomb, were killed.[3]

After the conclusion of the Prest-O-Lite Trophy race, won by Bob Burman driving a Buick, the AAA Contest Board was very concerned about the breaking up of the track, particularly in the corners, as well as the design of the track which had ditches on the outside. When the AAA Contest Board threatened to cancel the remaining two days of racing, Fisher assured the AAA Contest Board the track would be repaired overnight and that heavy boards would be placed over the ditches.[4] With these assurances, the AAA Contest Board agreed to the resumption of racing at the track subject to the proposed repairs being made.

Although the next day of racing did not have any serious wrecks, on the third racing day Herb Lytle, driving an Apperson, hit a rut causing him to lose control of the automobile on the forty-first lap during the featured 300-mile Wheeler-Schebler Trophy race. The automobile ended up in the in-field with no major injuries to either the riding mechanic or Lytle.

Johnny Aitken, a member of the Indianapolis-based National Motor Racing Team, was leading the Wheeler-Schebler Trophy race at 105 miles when his vehicle experienced a cracked cylinder head, ending his day of racing.[5] Upon returning to the pits, Aitken commented that if the race continued, somebody would be killed. His prediction soon came true. At 175 miles, Charlie Merz, another National Motor team member, blew a tire. The car became airborne for 100 feet, taking out a row of fence posts. The car then bounced on its tires and flipped over, causing the death of his riding mechanic, Charles Kellum, and two spectators watching the race from behind the barrier created by the fence.[6]

9. The Crisis in Auto Racing 81

The carnage continued when Bruce Keene, driving a Marmon, hit a hole on the southeast corner of the track. He lost control of the car and hit a pedestrian bridge, injuring Jim Schiller, his riding mechanic. With this mishap, Fred Warner, the AAA Contest Board starter, called an end to the race.[7]

Rumors quickly began circulating throughout Indianapolis that there would be no more races at the Speedway.[8] The Speedway partners realized that the choice of crushed stone and asphaltum for the surface resulted in a serious safety issue. They announced that the track would be improved and that the final weekend of racing in the fall of 1909 was canceled.[9]

The partners met with Park Andrews, the architect who designed the Speedway. They needed a more stable surface and considered repaving the Speedway with either brick or concrete. Andrews estimated that the cost of paving the track with concrete would be $110,000. Although the cost of paving with brick would cost an estimated 50 percent more, bricks would be longer lasting and provide better traction, which could translate into increased speed.

Before making a decision about the paving materials, the partners conducted a test of paving with brick. Several hundred yards of brick were laid on the Speedway's surface. The partners called upon Johnny Aitken, a National Motor driver, to run high-speed tests over the bricks. In an additional test, they anchored Aitken's car and had Aitken run the car at full throttle causing the auto's tires to churn. The bricks held up well during the tests, resulting in the partners' decision to repave the Speedway with brick.[10] The paving of the Speedway was completed in December. Upon the return of racing to the Speedway in May 1910, the racetrack held up well.

Over the next several years, as auto engines became more powerful, Speedway management would lower the cubic inch of displacement limits on the automobiles in order to limit the speeds obtained by the racers. Following the 1915 race, Speedway management lowered the engine displacement to 300 cubic inches, which followed the standard set on the European continent.[11] When in 1920 the 300-cubic-inch-of-displacement engine provided too much speed to safely navigate the racetrack, Speedway management lowered the maximum displacement to 183 cubic inches.[12] In 1923, the engine displacement was decreased to 122 cubic inches,[13] followed in 1926 by 91.5 cubic inches.[14]

Eddie Rickenbacker, who purchased the Indianapolis Motor Speedway in 1927, had as a priority making the Speedway safer. His first actions included rebuilding the retaining walls and changing the angle of the curves.[15] Rickenbacker, who had owned a Sheridan dealership and also represented General Motors on a safety tour, wanted to encourage automobile manufacturers, who had not entered the Indianapolis 500 since 1920, to participate. For the 1930 race, he banned the use of superchargers and changed the specifications of the autos.[16] The decision by Rickenbacker to encourage semi-stock cars in the race probably saved the fabled track. Prior to the decision, the cost of owning and maintaining a racing vehicle had spiraled upward.[17]

Despite Rickenbacker's focus on safety, during the early 1930s the race became much more dangerous. During the six-year period between 1930 and 1936, nine drivers and six riding mechanics died, compared with four drivers and two riding mechanics in the eighteen years between 1911 and 1929.[18]

An analysis of the underlying causes pointed to the inexperience of first-time drivers. Rickenbacker instituted a rookie driving test requiring driving of a hundred miles on the track before being allowed to practice and attempting to qualify for the race. The outside corners of the track were also reworked. When the track was built, there was a forty-five-degree lip on the racetrack. This was removed and a second retaining wall was built at a ninety-degree angle to the track. Additionally, the inner retaining wall was removed and a safety apron was installed.[19]

After a hiatus from racing during World War II, accidents increased significantly. Part of the problem was the lack of experienced drivers. Many participants in the races prior to World War II had retired from the sport.[20] An additional issue was that most of the race cars were between five and eight years old.[21]

By the 1950s, the AAA Contest Board was responsible for many different types of auto racing. In addition to the Championship series which included the Indianapolis 500 and many 100-mile races run on dirt fairground tracks, the Contest Board was also the sanctioning body for sprint cars generally run on half-mile tracks, midgets generally run on quarter-mile tracks, and stock cars. AAA, whose primary focus was on automobile safety, was subject to criticism whenever there was a racing accident. It didn't matter if the race was sanctioned by AAA or not.[22]

Racing deaths had been a frequent occurrence since resumption of racing following World War II. In 1947, Ralph Hepburn died of a basal skull fracture driving a Novi V-8 at the Indianapolis Motor Speedway.[23] Ted Horne, the 1947 racing champion, died in 1948 after being ejected from his car at the DuQuoin, Illinois, dirt track. The following year, a two-page spread in *Life* magazine sensationalized the death of Rex Mays at the Del Mar, California, racehorse track. He had been ejected from his vehicle and was then run over by a trailing racer.[24] Many race cars involved in wrecks were rebuilt and used again. In 1953, Chet Miller's ride was the Novi V-8 crashed by Ralph Hepburn in 1947 at the Indianapolis Motor Speedway. In a strange twist of fate, Miller crashed the car in approximately the same place as Hepburn and also died from a basal skull fracture.[25] The 1953 Indianapolis 500 champion, Bill Vukovich, said of

9. The Crisis in Auto Racing

Miller's death, "He made a mistake. He got killed. That simple. You don't make a mistake in this place. Some days you eat the bear. Other days the bear eats you."[26]

Vukovich, born in Alameda, California, was raised in Fresno, California, where his stepfather had a vineyard.[27] Vukovich, an auto mechanic, owned a small auto repair shop in Fresno,[28] but his passion was auto racing. In 1950, he won the AAA National Midget Championship. Like many drivers, winning at the midget or sprint car levels was a stepping stone to the National Championship racing circuit.[29] By 1951, he was driving at the Indianapolis Motor Speedway. In 1953, he qualified on opening day when others avoided the track because of threatening rainstorms. In an act of hubris, he drove his final qualifying lap in a driving rainstorm to grab the pole position.[30]

The weather for the 1953 race was very hot. By 10:00 a.m., the temperature was eighty-eight degrees.[31] It is estimated the track temperature was 130 degrees.[32] Vukovich would establish himself as the race leader very quickly and led in all but five laps of the race.[33] After winning the race, Vukovich returned to California. Unlike the majority of competitors, he wasn't in need of additional winnings. In the racing circuit, the race driver shared the winnings with the car owner and crew and took home approximately 40 percent. For winning the 1953 Indianapolis 500, Vukovich won $89,496. He also won a Ford Sunliner automobile, a wristwatch, a year of free meals from an Indianapolis restaurant, a tool set, a cocker spaniel puppy and a case of Ideal dog food.[34]

In 1954, Vukovich did a hat trick, winning a second Indianapolis 500 on a very hot day, joining an elite group of drivers to win back-to-back races. Most drivers on the circuit participated in other races. After winning the 1954 Indianapolis 500, Vukovich entered the 100-mile championship at the California State Fair. His qualifying speed was 3.5 seconds slower than the remainder of the field, and he didn't qualify for the race. His failure to run in the remainder of the National Championship circuit was a disappointment to the organizers of the remaining races who depended upon the Indianapolis 500 winner to be a draw at the gate. But Vukovich hated the dirt tracks on which all of the remaining races were run. He explained, "You get really tired out there over a hundred miles. Or else the car does. You make one slip and you're done. You couldn't pay me enough to get me on that circuit."[35]

The 1955 Championship racing season was very bloody and brought things to a head for the AAA. The deaths started on March 20 at the Langhorne Speedway, a dirt track outside of Philadelphia, where the 1954 "500 Rookie of the Year" Larry Crockett was killed after he hit a rut on the racetrack. Then on May 1 at the Larry Crockett Memorial[36] race, run also at the Langhorne Speedway, "Iron Mike" Nazaruk hit a rut on the course and his car became airborne. The collision with a tree was so violent that his helmet was ripped from his head and his driving suit was shredded.[37] Ironically, Nazaruk had won the race at Langhorne Speedway when Larry Crockett was killed. In a period of two months, the Langhorne Speedway had claimed the lives of two of the participants in the 1954 Indianapolis 500.[38]

As practice opened at the Indianapolis Motor Speedway for the 1955 contest, there were three pacesetters. Jack McGrath set a lap record at 141 miles per hour in a Hinkleheld. Jimmy Bryan, winner of the 1954 National Championship, had a new Kuzma. Vukovich, who had both a new car and was working for a new car owner, rounded out the front leaders.

In 1954, Vukovich had driven for the Keck team. His crew chief, Jim Travers, was developing a streamlined car similar to the one developed by Mercedes-Benz which was very successful in European races.[39] The new race car was also to have a new three-liter V-8 supercharged by a Rootes-type blower engine.[40] When it became apparent to Travers that the engine wouldn't be ready for the race, he suggested to Keck that an Offenhauser engine be substituted. Keck refused. Keck then offered his team to Lindsey Hopkins, an Atlanta, Georgia, sportsman and Coca-Cola stockholder. Hopkins accepted. Vukovich's new ride was a year-old Kurtis-Kraft.[41]

On the final day of practice prior to the qualification rounds, Vukovich served notice of the speed of his car when he completed a lap at 141.2 miles per hour. Vukovich was the fifth driver to go over 140 miles per hour during the practice laps.[42]

On the first day of qualifying, May 14, 1955, Indianapolis was cold and windy. Throughout the day, winds ranged from thirty-one to thirty-six miles per hour, too strong for qualifying attempts.[43] If there weren't any qualifying runs, the Speedway faced the possibility of having to refund the spectators' tickets. Late in the afternoon, Joe Cloutier, Speedway treasurer, approached Travers trying to pressure him for Vukovich to attempt a qualifying run. "Look, somebody's got to get out there and make some laps. I've got sixty thousand of 'em sitting in the grandstands at a buck apiece. Unless somebody does some qualifying I'm in the tank for refunds. The last thing I need—and you guys need—is me passing out sixty thousand rain checks."[44] Despite Cloutier's plea, Vukovich did not make a qualifying run that day.

Instead, Jerry Holt, a twenty-six-year-old graduate of Arsenal Technical High School, became the first Indianapolis resident to sit on the pole since Bill Cummings in 1937. Holt's speed during the qualifying run was 140.045 miles per hour. Also qualifying on the first day was Tony Bettenhausen.[45]

The next day, the wind had died down and the speedsters were out qualifying. Vukovich set the early pace qualifying at 141 miles per hour.[46] Three

Joe Cloutier, Hulman's right-hand man, sitting on a wall at the Speedway. Cloutier was the trusted adviser for Hulman in his various business dealings and upon Hulman's death in 1977 took the leadership role at Indianapolis Motor Speedway (Indianapolis Motor Speedway).

hours later, McGrath shattered the record. His first lap was at 143.793 miles per hour, two miles per hour faster than any previous recorded lap at the Speedway. McGrath said of the ride, "It was the most hair-raising ride I ever had. I'll guarantee you I was scared." McGrath shattered the record set by Vukovich with a speed of 142.58 miles per hour.[47]

Two minutes before the closing of the track on Monday, May 16, Manuel Ayulo took his car out for a practice run.[48] Ayulo served as both the chief mechanic and driver for Peter Schmidt. His car, equipped with an Offenhauser engine, had developed lubrication problems. Ayulo had worked through the night on the engine and didn't rest before getting into the race car. He had completed two laps with an average speed of 139 miles per hour. Roaring down the straightaway on the third practice lap, witnesses said that he never made a turn going into the corner. He smacked directly into the retaining wall and was severely injured.[49]

The next day, Ayulo died from his injuries. It was believed that part of the steering system had failed, leading to the crash.[50] Since the Speedway had opened, thirty-seven drivers and mechanics and seven spectators had died.[51]

In Europe, two-time champion Alberto Ascari was driving in a Grand Prix race in Monaco on May 22. While braking on a narrow part of the course bordering the Bay of Hercules, the brakes of his D-50 Lancia locked up. The car sailed over the low wall into the water. Skin divers, stationed in the bay in case there was an accident, rescued Ascari.[52]

Four days after returning to his home in Milan, Ascari went to Milan's Autodome to visit with some drivers in town for the Supercortemaggiore, a 1,000-kilometer road race to be run over the weekend at Monza. After eating lunch with a friend, Ascari borrowed Eugenio Castellotti's Ferrari to "work some kinks out of his back." On the third lap, the car picked up speed on the straightaway. The car failed to negotiate the Vialone, a left-hand turn. Ascari was ejected from the car as it flipped end over end, and he died in the back of an ambulance.[53]

The 1955 Indianapolis 500 developed into a duel between McGrath and Vukovich. On the fortieth lap, smoke began rising from McGrath's tailpipe, and on the fifty-third lap, McGrath's day was over.[54] Shortly thereafter, Vukovich was involved in a multi-car crash.

The Vukovich crash began when Rodger Ward, driving an old Kuzma dirt track car, caught a breeze coming out of the southeast turn. Unable to control the race car, he hit the wall coming out of the second turn. Despite the spinning action of Ward's car, Johnny Boyd and Al Keller were able to avoid it; however, their evasive action ultimately resulted in Vukovich's crash. Keller, a rookie, driving an old Kurtis-Kraft, attempted to avoid the melee by using a hand brake, but the car's brakes locked up causing his car to careen back across the track from the inside grass. Boyd, not able to avoid Keller's car, took evasive action but ultimately was hit, losing two front wheels and rolling over.[55]

Vukovich, leading the race by nearly a lap, clipped Boyd's car, slammed into a footbridge, and then sailed over the retaining wall upside down.[56] Vukovich's car went as high as twenty-five feet in the air before smashing to earth. It bounced about fifteen feet and landed on three parked cars before scraping a utility pole, flipping on its back, and bursting into flames.[57]

Brock Yates, covering Vukovich's attempt to win the Indianapolis 500 for the third straight time for *Car and Driver* magazine, described his learning of the wreck in his book *Against Death and Time*: "Another yellow flag. This time Vandewater was at the edge of the track, waving frantically. The cars slowed as they passed. Several drivers were gesturing toward the backstretch. Others were tapping the tops of their helmets, indicating that somebody was upside down. I looked for the blue Hopkins [Vukovich's car]. It did not come by. Travers looked worried. He stared at the stopwatch in his hand. The pace car was out on the track, leading a pack of cars now lumbering by at 50 m.p.h. The stands were silent. Someone gestured behind me. I spotted a pall of smoke rising in the distance, apparently near the exit of the second turn. A man in a suit with an AAA armband came up to Travers. He was obviously an official. He moved close to Travers and whispered in his ear. Travers reeled back, clearly disturbed. He moved to Coon and spoke softly. Coon dropped his head, then looked back at the rising smoke. A man came up and said, to no one in particular, "Four cars. Vuke's upside down, outside the track. Car's on fire. Looks bad."[58]

It was bad. Vukovich died of a basal skull fracture probably in the first millisecond of the flip.[59] Vukovich's death was the second time in Indianapolis 500 history when a 500-mile race winner had been killed during a race. In an eerie coincidence, Vukovich's death was similar to that of Floyd Roberts in 1939. Roberts had won the 1938 contest. Both Roberts and Vukovich were killed in almost the same spot in similar accidents.[60]

In the final laps of the 1955 Indianapolis 500, another crash occurred when Cal Niday lost control of his Kurtis-Kraft car in the fourth turn. He slammed into the wall and then careened across the track ending up in a ditch. He survived serious injuries including third-degree burns on his right leg, a frontal skull fracture and a crushed chest.[61]

The winner of the 1955 Indianapolis 500 was Bob Sweikert. An interesting tale behind Sweikert's winning is that his chief mechanic, A. J. Watson, had left the car engine in a thousand pieces when he rushed to California for the birth of his child. He left Sweikert a note saying, "Have the crew put the chassis together. You build the engine." Sweikert built the engine and won the race.[62]

Two weeks later, the Grand Prix race at Le Mans, France, was held. Begun in the early 1920s, it was the longest-running road course race. Organized by the local auto club D'ouest, the race was both a test of an auto's endurance and speed. The 8.4-mile road course used public roads closed for the running of the race. Over 300,000 spectators would go to Le Mans for the race.[63]

The Le Mans race is unique as it is a twenty-four-hour race rather than a specific length (such as 500 miles). Due to the length of time, it is run by twenty-six teams comprised of two drivers,[64] with the drivers alternating four-hour shifts. During the race, an estimated 2,500 miles would be driven by a team.

The 1955 Le Mans race began with a foot race to the race cars at 4:00 p.m. The drivers leaped into the cars and drove off toward the Dunlap pedestrian bridge.[65] The favorites included the Mercedes-Benz team of Juan Manuel Fanzio and Stirling Moss, the Jaguar team of Mike Hawthorn and Ivor Bueb and the Ferrari team of Eugenio Castellotti and Count Paolo Marzotto.[66]

The early race was a two-car duel between Hawthorn, a member of the Jaguar team, and Lance Macklin, driving an Austin Healy. Hawthorn had just passed Macklin when he noticed his pit crew signaling to come in for refueling. In an attempt to make the entrance to pit row, Hawthorn slammed on the brakes. Following closely behind, Macklin took evasive action to avoid the quickly slowing Hawthorn. Pierre Levegh, closely trailing in a Mercedes, wasn't able to avoid the quickly slowing car. The force of the impact caused Levegh to lose control of his car which slammed into an earth embankment. Levegh was killed instantly while the force of the impact caused his car to explode. The front half of the car sailed into a tightly packed group of spectators gathered near the start/finish line across from the pits. The ensuing fireball and shrapnel from the car resulted in approximately eighty spectator deaths.[67]

Ironically, Alberto Ascari, who had died in Milan days before the Indianapolis 500, had been involved in trying to find the cause behind the mysterious explosions such as occurred at Le Mans. He theorized that metal fatigue was responsible. International News Service writer Charles Amadir wrote,

> Two years ago I had completed test-driving a powerful racer entered in Mexico's Pan American speed marathon. Two hours later, I stood on a hill and saw the same car explode in a roaring swish, hurling shrapnel pieces over the jungle hillside. It exploded in a ball of fire to release a force equivalent to a detonated bomb. The late Alberto Ascari, Italian ace, gathered a piece of this metal and started a laboratory study. He gathered the pieces of the metal. Detailed examination showed barely visible scratches. Ascari, killed last month in an Italian race when his powerful car exploded, wrote me that the scratches were splints in the metal, bursting the car's body like a punctured balloon. The metal had blown outward, he wrote, and fuel flooding the engine had caught fire. The fire was not the first to happen.[68]

Ascari had planned to meet with investigators conducting experiments on jets which he believed had encountered the same fate as exploding race cars.[69]

9. The Crisis in Auto Racing

The wrecks in auto racing in which 91 died and 106 were injured between January 1 and June 30, 1955, resulted in an outrage against auto racing. One primary cause was that the racetracks were inadequate to cope with the speeds of the modern race cars. They were either road courses run on narrow roads, dirt tracks which were subject to holes and ruts, or specially built tracks, such as the Indianapolis Motor Speedway, designed when auto speeds were much lower.

Juan Fangio, an Argentinian driver who barely missed crashing into Levegh's car at Le Mans, said, "Organization of the race must be changed. It no longer corresponds to the current speed of motor racing." Italian driver Luigi Villoresi also felt that the solution might be a reduction in speed. He said, "A limitation of speed will not be a detriment to progress in the automotive field, even though it may damage the spectator aspect of the competition. Let's revise the rules and let the thrill lovers resign themselves."[70]

As the controversy over auto racing raged, Indianapolis native and 1955 pole setter for the Indianapolis 500, Jerry Hoyt, was critically injured in a race in Oklahoma City. His racer hit the wall, flipped in the air landing upside down, and then bounced in the air landing right side up.

Sweikert hypothesized about the cause of the wreck: "I was leading the race and Jerry was second. The track was rough and full of holes. And when we headed into the third turn, we were looking right into the sun. Jerry apparently hooked one of the holes in the track with his right rear wheel that spun the front around and he rolled over."[71] The next day, Hoyt died because of a severe brain injury. He was the fifth Indianapolis 500 driver to die in 1955.[72]

On July 13, 1955, Senator Richard L. Neuberger from Oregon called for the U.S. Senate to outlaw the sport of auto racing. The response from the Indianapolis racing community was immediate. Jep Cadou, Jr., sports editor for the *Indianapolis Star*, wrote in a blistering article, "Senator Neuberger seems convinced that he is a better judge of what is good for race drivers than race drivers are. He adopts the all-too-familiar attitude that the government knows better what is right for the people that then people know themselves."

Cadou continued:

> We have known race drivers, mechanics and car owners on close terms. They all realize that auto racing is a hazardous business and that people are going to be killed and injured. Why, then do they participate in auto racing? For a living, of course. Men drive race cars for exactly the same reasons that other men engage in other "hazardous" occupations, for financial gain.
>
> Men in other professions take great risks. Construction workers on skyscrapers, sand hogs, motion picture stunt men, airplane pilots, professional soldiers—all of them take the calculated risk of their life. Why doesn't Senator Neuberger call for legislation to outlaw these professions?

Cadou called upon the two Indiana senators, Homer E. Capehart and William E. Jenner, to vigorously oppose the initiative taken by Senator Neuberger.[73]

After having vigorously defended the auto racing community from Senator Neuberger's initiative, the next day, Cadou went after the racing community, in particular the race promoters. In his "Calls 'Em" column, Cadou wrote,

> It is time for some of the people in auto racing to wake up to and realize that the sport is in mortal danger of extinction unless they take prompt and effective steps to put their own house in order. The sad and brutal fact is that all too many auto races still are run on tracks which are absolutely and beyond doubt unfit for racing.
>
> We are not going to attempt to single out any specific track. The facts—and the casualty lists—speak for themselves.
>
> The tragic fact is that we already have lost five of the top 500-mile race drivers this year as a result of crashes. Two were at the Indianapolis Motor Speedway and neither could be attributed to the condition of track. Whether the condition of the track was the primary factor at fault in the other three deaths is debatable—but at least there are definite contentions that it was.
>
> Who is responsible for auto races being run on bad tracks? Four groups must be charged with the principal responsibility—AAA officials, promoters, car owners and drivers. But, any really constructive action to bring about better racing conditions, safer tracks and less casualties must come mainly from the first two groups. In too many cases, AAA officials have done only a half-hearted job of policing the tracks on which the "500" drivers run elsewhere. Too many of them have regarded racing as only a social event instead of a grim life-and-death matter. And, too many promoters have shaved costs here and there at the expense of permitting the drivers to run under hazardous conditions.[74]

The public also expressed outrage with Senator Neuberger's proposed ban of auto racing. Don Strobel of Batesville, Indiana, wrote to Jep Cadou,

> Auto racing is generally considered by many as a bloody sport and there are bad accidents it's true. However, one point which I would like to bring out is why driving an automobile on the highway hasn't been outlawed. Jerry Hoyt, a popular driver and a good one, was the 92nd fatality this year in auto racing. There were around 400 people killed both on Memorial Day and on Fourth of July besides thousands maimed or injured on the highways. Yet, pleasure driving goes on with no one but the Safety Council caring or worrying much about it.[75]

Although Senator Neuberger's bill did not materialize, the sentiment against auto racing caused AAA to act. On August 3, Andrew J. Sordoni, AAA president, released the formal announcement which said, "Upon completion of the schedule of events already undertaken for the year 1955, the American Automobile Association will 'dissociate' itself completely from all types of automobile racing in the United States." He explained the rationale.

It was the feeling of our Executive Committee that automobile racing, as now conducted in this country, is not compatible with one of the main objectives of the AAA and its affiliated clubs in the day-to-day promotion of street and highway safety.[76]

In making the announcement, Sordoni said, "Racing has unquestionably become a popular spectacle in the United States, but there is serious question that racing contributes any material way to better cars or better parts for cars."[77]

Arthur Herrington, chair of the AAA Contest Board, said, "There is no question that the LeMans race is the cause of the order. The AAA fears the legal liabilities connected in a remote possibility that something similar might happen here. I think our safety regulations are better than those in Europe but those are my personal opinions only." He also predicted that racing would go to "heights higher than previously reached."[78]

Joseph Cloutier expressed his reaction to the announcement which was reflective of that of Indianapolis Motor Speedway management. "The announcement came as a complete surprise to us. We have no immediate answer to the new problems that may confront us. We do intend to proceed as in the past with the 500-Mile Race and we assume that by race time there will be organized a regulatory body that will take the place of the AAA's contest board."[79]

The next day, officials at the Indianapolis Motor Speedway announced that the AAA exit from auto racing would not impact running of the fortieth Indianapolis 500 mile race in 1956. Hulman said, "I don't see any reason why the AAA action should affect the 500." Understanding that racing needs a sanctioning body, Hulman continued, "I don't know exactly what angle it will take but there will have to be some form of organization. This will probably just mean there will be a different sanctioning group."[80]

Both the National Association for Stock Car Auto Racing (NASCAR) and the Sports Car Club of America (SCCA) expressed an interest in becoming the sanctioning body for the Indianapolis 500. At the time of the AAA announcement, the Sports Car Club of America was the only sanctioning body for auto racing in the United States that would qualify for inclusion in the Federation Internationale Automobile (FIA), the sanctioning body for international races including the Indianapolis 500.[81] Colonel Herrington indicated he would contact the top officers of the Sports Car Club of America to discuss the possibility of that group assuming the sanctioning body responsibilities for the Indianapolis 500. Herrington believed although the Indianapolis 500 could operate for one year without a sponsoring association, on a long-term basis one was needed to take over the duties of the AAA Contest Board. He said, "There has to be some sort of umpire. I fully expect auto racing to go on to even greater heights. We've been through worse things than this in the past."

People involved in the Indianapolis racing community were concerned that Bill France, Sr., president of NASCAR, would try to take over the top drivers in the AAA contest world as well as the tracks. NASCAR had recently built a two-and-a-half-mile track at Daytona Beach which could be in competition with the Indianapolis 500.[82]

Jep Cadou, Jr., expressed his opinion about the AAA Contest Board withdrawing from auto racing in his "Calls 'Em" column on August 5:

> Yesterday was a black day for auto racing but the blow struck at the sport by the American Automobile Association need not prove a fatal one. For quite a while now, the Contest Board which supervises auto racing has been practically a stepchild of the AAA. Most auto racing men have long believed that it was the 500 mile race which kept the AAA Contest Board alive instead of vice versa. Disbanding of the Contest Board impresses us as a vicious and unwarranted slap at a group of men who have given their time and energy generously to the sport through the 54 years of the board's existence.[83]

Cadou predicted that the void left by the departure of the AAA Contest Board would be filled quickly with leadership provided by the Indianapolis Motor Speedway. He wrote, "Surely there will be some form of new sanctioning body set up under the guidance of the Indianapolis Motor Speedway and with the cooperation of other tracks on the championship circuit to handle what has been AAA championship racing."[84]

Bill Fox, sports editor with the *Indianapolis News,* strongly voiced his opinion that the new sanctioning body should be acceptable to the Federation Internationale Automobile. "If the 500-Mile race is to expect foreign drivers and cars, any racing group in the country that sanctions races must be affiliated or recognized by the Federation Internationale Automobile. The problems confronting the entire structure of big car racing now, in this country and in others, are great ones but they are not beyond solution. Increased safety measures for all involved in the sport are important avenues of approach now."

The departure of the AAA Contest Board from racing was the type of problem solving Hulman enjoyed and where he was effective. Hulman immediately stepped up to fill the void. On August 5, Hulman; Bob Estes, a West Coast car owner; Tom Marchese, a Milwaukee promoter; and George Ober, a magistrate for the town of Speedway, Indiana, met at the Indianapolis Motor Speedway offices located at 729 North Capitol Street in Indianapolis. At this meeting, Hulman expressed his desire that the National Championship series, including the Indianapolis 500, would continue. He also felt that the establishment of a farm system of midget and sprint cars would help to develop drivers who could eventually race in the Indianapolis 500. The midget and sprint car races would also provide another source of income for the drivers.[85]

After this preliminary meeting, Hulman arranged for a meeting to take the first steps toward creating a new sanctioning body, to be held at the Indiana State Board of Health auditorium. Hulman said, "No attempt will be made to extend a personal invitation to anyone but we expect a representative turn-out from every section of the country. Racing is sure to continue as it has for the last 54 years and we are hopeful that a new organization will be formed which will enhance the future of competitive racing for everyone. The annual 500 mile race, which has been one of the outstanding fixtures on the world sports calendar since 1911, will be run for the 40th time next May 30."[86]

Two hundred and sixteen people attended the organizational meeting held on August 10, 1955. A steering committee of seven individuals was selected to establish the new organization whose purpose was "to take over all rule enforcement, disciplinary action and such control as will be necessary for an orderly and continuous transfer of these activities from the American Automobile Association."[87] The seven individuals included Hulman, Estes, Marchese, and Ober as well as Herb Porter, a mechanic; Duane Carter, a driver; and Colonel Herrington, an engineer and industrialist.[88]

The new association was named the United States Auto Club (USAC). Donald Davidson, Indianapolis Motor Speedway archivist, related the story as told by John Cooper of the naming of the organization: "We went outside for break and we stood underneath this tree next to the door. Somebody suggested that since we had been running under the title of American Automobile Association, why not just call it The United States Automobile Association. Sam Nunis, the East Coast promoter, said 'No, don't call it an association. People think it's a union. We're more of a club.' Somebody else suggested 'Then how about the United States Auto Club?' And that is basically how it came about. Right under that tree."[89]

On Friday, September 16, the United States Auto Club was incorporated as a nonprofit with the Indiana secretary of state.

John Cooper also told the origin for the logo for the United States Auto Club: "I was with Tony Hulman and his assistant Kenny Grimm, and we happened to notice on the wall this very attractive shield, underneath of which were the words United States Tuna Team. Tony was a member of the seven man United States championship team which beat Brazil in 1949. We basically copied the shield for the USAC logo."

The offices for USAC were initially at the Indianapolis Motor Speedway offices in downtown Indianapolis. The staffing included Duane Carter, the first director of operations; John Cooper; Lenora Adam (Duane and Arza Carter's babysitter); and Mari Hulman (Hulman's daughter). The first president of the organization was J. Morton Swango, a Terre Haute attorney. Soon afterward, Herrington assumed the duties of the office.[90]

Herrington, previously the chair of the AAA Contest Board, was very familiar with the racing community. Active in motorcycle racing, Herrington attended the Indianapolis 500 from 1911 through 1921. In 1922, he headed the pit crew for Jimmy Murphy. In 1923 and 1924, he headed the pit crew for Peter DePaolo who won the Indianapolis 500 in 1924.[91] In 1931, Herrington joined with Walter Marmon, principal of the Marmon Motor Car Company, to form Marmon-Herrington Company Inc. to build trucks.[92]

After the formation of the United States Auto Club, Hulman expressed his disappointment and anger at the American Automobile Association: "It was not a very nice thing to do, all the work we did for AAA, and what good did it do us? Maybe we should have gotten out of AAA a long time ago. Now we've got to look out for our own interests."[93]

10

USAC's First Years

Hulman's program of upgrading the Speedway facilities resulted in a new look in 1956. For the first time, the Speedway corporate offices were moved from downtown Indianapolis to the Speedway grounds. The 7,200-square-foot building, located at the corner of Georgetown Road and 16th Street, was built by Tousley Construction Company for $125,000. It contained not only the offices for the building but also a museum.[1]

As practice for the race got under way on May 13, two racers quickly set new track records. Sam Hanks' new one-lap record of 144.346 miles per hour was quickly shattered by Tony Bettenhausen who drove the two-and-a-half-mile track at 144.951 miles per hour.[2] With speeds continuing to escalate and members of the racing community speculating when the 150-mile-per-hour record would be set, there was talk that Speedway management was thinking of setting new specifications for the engines to be used in the 1957 race. There were two trains of thought. By changing the specifications to encourage more stock engines, some felt there would be greater diversity than the Offenhauser engine then dominating Indianapolis racing. The other train of thought was that the spectators didn't care if there was diversity in the engines.[3] What was important to race fans was the speed at the track and breaking records.

When qualifications got under way, an estimated 125,000 fans saw Pat Flaherty take the pole while establishing a new qualifying record of 145.596 miles per hour and a one-lap record of 146.056 miles per hour. By the end of the first day of qualifying, seventeen cars were in the field.[4]

Indianapolis was experiencing a very wet May. The second weekend of

Chief Steward Harlan Fengler on the left at the track in 1953. Fengler became the chief steward in 1956 and served through the 1973 race (Indianapolis Motor Speedway).

qualifications was hampered by rain. At 6:00 p.m. on the final day of qualifying, the field was filled, but there were twelve cars lined up to attempt qualifying runs. In his first year as chief steward, Harlan Fengler announced that qualifications could continue for an additional two hours until sundown at 8:00 p.m. Spoiling the additional time was more rain, causing qualifying to be called after fifty-seven minutes.

This led to a controversy over the end of qualifications. Most upset was chief mechanic Jean Marcenac of the Novi team. Paul Russo, one of his two entries, had qualified for the race. But the second entry, driven by Eddie Russo, did not have the opportunity to qualify. In frustration, Marcenac announced that the Novi entry wouldn't run in the race. After a four-hour conference, Indianapolis Motor Speedway and USAC officials decided against extending the remaining sixty-three minutes to the next day.[5]

The rains continued to come down resulting in massive flooding of the Indianapolis area, considered to be the worst since 1913. In that year, flooding caused a postponement of the running of the third Indianapolis 500. In the

View down the straightaway showing the flooding in 1956 which nearly delayed the running of the race (Indianapolis Motor Speedway).

1956 flooding, approximately 2,000 families had to be evacuated from the western part of town as both White River and Big Eagle Creek flooded.[6]

Being located on the west side of Indianapolis, the Speedway was also experiencing flooding. Water cascaded over the banks of Dry Run Creek flooding the grandstands on the main straightaway. Water was seeping under the barrier but failed to reach the track. The infield was mired in mud. The rains, which would have eliminated any additional qualifying if they had been scheduled, caused the Novi team to reconsider their decision to pull their qualified racer from the field. Team owner Lew Welch subsequently announced that Paul Russo would participate in the race.

But the question gripping Indianapolis was whether the race would be run as scheduled on Memorial Day. Hulman responded, "Preparations for the 40th annual 500-mile race at 10 a.m. (CST) Wednesday are proceeding according to schedule. The Speedway management definitely is not considering the

Hulman in front of the Pagoda and race crowd in 1956 (Indianapolis Motor Speedway).

possibilities of a postponement."⁷ Hulman later revealed that "it rained so hard for two days before the race, we thought we'd have to quit."⁸

The track was relatively easy to dry as flooding had not reached it. The most challenging aspect of getting the facility ready for the race despite the flooding was getting the tunnels dry. As there was not any drainage at the bottom of the tunnels, Clarence Cagle's crew was busy pumping hundreds of thousands of gallons of water.[9] As promised by Hulman, by Memorial Day, the Speedway was ready to greet the race fans.

The rains ceased by Memorial Day. Although the infield continued to be very soggy, the race was run as scheduled. In a crash-marred race in which five were injured and eight cars were eliminated, Pat Flaherty won with an average speed of 128.480 miles per hour.[10] Flaherty had dominated the race but considered himself lucky to win. Flaherty explained, "I had just taken the flag when the engine went back to idle. I pushed on the gas, but nothing happened. The throttle shaft between the pedal and the injectors had broken. If that happened a couple minutes sooner, I'd never made it to the victory lane."[11]

This race was the last for the Pagoda, the Speedway landmark built in 1926, which had been declared unsafe for occupancy of more than sixty people. The Speedway announced that the Pagoda would be replaced by a new five-story structure.[12]

1957

When the Speedway opened in 1957 for practice, it sported a million dollars' worth of improvements including the new Pagoda. The new structure was constructed of steel, concrete, glass and tile. The ground floor, to be used by race officials including the timers and scorers, had an area ninety feet long and twelve feet wide. The second through fifth floors were twenty feet by twelve feet. The second floor was dedicated to the broadcast staff. The third and fourth floors were for Hulman and Speedway management, while the top floor was for the safety officials.

The Pagoda wasn't the only improvement to the Speedway facilities. The Tower Terrace was constructed to provide additional seating directly behind the pits. Access to the pits was also improved and upgraded. A new retaining wall and a fifteen-foot-wide grass strip were constructed,[13] providing the first separation of the access road to the pits from the racing track in the world.[14] The pits, traditionally ending at the start-finish line, were expanded, providing each team with a pit area stretching thirty feet rather than the previous twenty feet in length. A three-lane-wide tunnel under the track on the backstretch provided much-needed additional ingress to the infield.[15]

With 100,000 seats available at the Speedway, demand for tickets exceeded the Speedway's capacity. In a 1957 interview with Don O'Reilly of the *Indianapolis News*, Hulman lamented, "I should be jubilant, but I almost dreaded coming down here this week, because it makes me feel so bad when friends cry on my shoulder with their request for additional tickets."[16] In response to the demand for tickets, at the last minute, Cagle's crew constructed 4,000 temporary bleacher-type seats on the north side of the Tower Terrace.[17]

Popular driver and winner of the 1956 Indianapolis 500, Pat Flaherty wouldn't be participating in the 1957 race. He had been critically injured in a wreck at the Illinois State Fairgrounds in August 1956 when his car hit the outside barrier and flipped twice. Flaherty suffered a severely broken right arm when it was crushed by the roll bar of his car. He also suffered a broken left shoulder and broken jaw. His arm had not healed sufficiently for him to rejoin the racing fraternity.[18]

Prior to the start of qualifications, there were twelve crashes, all of which occurred in the corners. Speculation abounded about the causes. One frequently mentioned cause was the lighter-weight chassis. Others felt that a "groove" hadn't been established around the track, and until the groove was established, it was unsafe to run on the Speedway at high speeds. One chief mechanic speculated that the cause might be the smaller engines. He believed that since the smaller engines limited the speed on the straightaways, drivers were pushing harder through the turns.[19]

On May 15, Keith Andrews, a participant in the 1955 and 1956 Indianapolis 500s, lost control of his car coming out of the fourth turn. The car skidded for 755 feet and hit the retaining wall with such force that it broke through the six-inch concrete barrier. The force of the crash drove the tail and fuel cell of the car into the cockpit. Andrews died of a broken neck by the force of the crash, which drove him into his steering wheel.[20]

In front of an estimated crowd of 130,000, Pat O'Connor won the pole position with an average speed of 143.948 miles per hour. Qualifications were called early due to rain; however, nine racers qualified for the race on the first day.[21]

Sam Hanks, a veteran driver of the Speedway with thirteen previous starts, led 141 of the 200 laps in the race. He won the race with an average speed of 135.601 miles per hour. His previous top finish was second in 1956.[22] Hanks had promised himself that if he won the Indianapolis 500, he would quit racing. This was reaffirmed in the winner's circle. Hanks said, "I'll be here next year but strictly as a spectator."[23]

Jep Cadou, Jr., the *Indianapolis Star* sports editor, speculated that Hanks would make a good addition to the Speedway staff. Cadou praised Hulman for leading the Speedway after the death of Wilbur Shaw but also acknowledged that Hulman was a very busy man with multiple business interests. Cadou wrote, "The need for a top-flight driver to be the 'front man' for the Indianapolis Speedway Corporation has become increasingly and sometimes glaringly apparent since the death of Mr. Shaw in an airplane accident in 1954."[24]

1958

Pat Flaherty returned to the Speedway in 1958 hoping to pass a medical exam so that he could return to racing. He had undergone a bone graft on his shattered arm, and the cast had been removed only ten days before. He was examined by three Indianapolis orthopedic surgeons who did not agree to his returning to the Speedway. They were concerned the muscle had atrophied and about the possibility of a re-fracture of the bones during the race.[25]

The first day of qualifications for the 1958 race was very exciting for the spectators. Dick Rathmann set a new qualifying record of 145.954 miles per hour while Ed Elisian set a new one-lap record of 146.508. Joining Rathmann and Elisian on the first row was Jimmy Reece with a qualifying speed of 145.396 miles per hour. All three race cars had A. J. Watson in common. He was the chief mechanic and builder of the Zink Specials which were the rides for Elisian and Reece. And he had built the car in which Rathmann qualified.[26]

Watson built the Rathmann car in his spare time with the financial support of Henry Blum. He entered it in the race as the Watson Special without a driver. When he arrived in Indianapolis, Watson was a part of the Zink team and had been the chief mechanic for the winners of the 1955 and 1956 races. Most people at the Speedway didn't think the car had much chance of getting into the race.

Meanwhile Lee Elkins of Kalamazoo, Michigan, had entered the McNamara Special in the race. He, too, didn't have a driver but was planning to hire one when somebody got fed up with their ride or had an engine fail. While at the track, Elkins and Watson started talking. Elkins decided to buy the Watson Special for $10,000 plus the $500 entry fee, but Elkins would need to provide the engine. As it happens, Elkins had an engine from a dirt-racing machine which he put into the car. He hired Floyd Trevis as his chief mechanic and Dick Rathmann as the driver.[27]

At the beginning of a race, there is frequently a rush of racers to the first turn as drivers try to get a position at the front of the pack, resulting in frequent crashes. At the driver meeting held the day before the race, Hulman implored the drivers not to rush to the first turn. It was a long race, and being the fastest to the first turn wouldn't guarantee victory. He said to the drivers, "Let's really, honestly try to get through that first turn all right—and every other turn."[28]

Hulman's words of caution had little impact. The start of the race which began in the pits has been described as one of the sloppiest in Speedway history. While jockeying for position, the front row of racers passed the pace car driven by Sam Hanks on the initial pace lap. It took two additional pace laps for the field to get properly aligned. When the green flag dropped signaling the start of the race, the racers made it through the first turn in fine shape.

As the cars came into the third turn, the jockeying for position continued. The resulting crash involved fifteen racers, eight of whom were eliminated from the race. At the center of the crash were Dick Rathmann and Ed Elisian. Rathmann pointed the finger of blame at Elisian who passed him going into the turn "about 25 miles an hour too fast." Elisian meanwhile retorted that Rathmann "shut off right in front of me." Witnesses indicated that Elisian's car spun just after it had passed Rathmann's car. In order to avoid Elisian's car, Rathmann attempted to squeeze by on the inside but was unsuccessful, starting the multiple-car crash. Elisian's car nearly broke Rathmann's car in two in the crash. Unbelievably neither Rathmann nor Elisian sustained serious injuries. But also involved in the crash was Pat O'Connor who hit Jimmy Reece's car. O'Connor's car overturned coming out of the third turn and caught fire. Speedway medical officials believe that O'Connor was killed instantly.

With an average speed of 133.791, the race was won by Jimmy Bryan in the same car that Sam Hanks drove to victory in 1957.[29]

In his first year as chief steward, Harlan Fengler was a familiar figure in the racing fraternity. He was a veteran of the board tracks and had been the riding mechanic for Harry Hartz in the 1922 Indianapolis 500. In 1949, Fengler returned to the track and in 1953 became a referee.[30] Fengler's investigation indicated that Elisian's actions had caused the wreck and he planned to seek sanctions by USAC.[31] USAC concurred with Fengler's analysis, and Elisian was suspended by USAC for excessive risk taking.[32]

Speedway management also addressed the issues of the start of the race. Fengler indicated that although the start was sloppy, it wasn't a factor in the crash. "We finally got them straightened out before the green flag dropped so that they were lined up properly. I don't think the confusion had anything to do with the pileup."

Hulman promised that Speedway management would review the starting procedures for the 1959 race. For the 1958 race, the pace lap started from the pits rather than from the track. Sam Hanks, who had been hired by Hulman as director of racing, believed that going back to having the start on the racetrack rather than from the pits would be better.[33] Hulman agreed, stating, "This is the way the Speedway was originally built and this is how we ought to keep it. If you bank a turn and get clear up, all you'd get would be a motordrome and pretty soon you wouldn't need drivers. You could just start the engines and let the darn things roll around automatically."[34]

Hulman preparing for a drive around the Speedway in the HOW racer. His son-in-law Elmer George is adjusting Hulman's helmet and was the normal driver of the car (Indianapolis Motor Speedway).

1959

After the disastrous race in 1958, safety was one of the top priorities of the Speedway and USAC as the Speedway celebrated its fiftieth year of racing.

It was a muted celebration as most racing fans think of the Indianapolis 500 whose fiftieth year would be celebrated in 1961.

When the winning car of the 1957 and 1958 campaigns arrived at Indianapolis for the 1959 race, it was equipped with two new features. Air jacks had been installed on the car to improve the lift time during tire changes. The jacks could lift the car in a half second, and it was believed that this improvement could lead to a twenty-seven-second pit stop. The second change to the car related to safety. Chief mechanic for the car, George Salih, talked of the installation of a double bumper, also called a nerfing bar, to prevent a car from running over the back of another. "A lot of our fatalities recently have been that type of accident. This is built so that both bars are lower than the center of the wheel. We think it might save the life of the driver hitting our cars as well as our own." Pat O'Connor was killed when another car ran up over the back of his racer in the 1958 race.[35]

On a lighter side, there was a new driver at the Speedway. After paying $41 for the license and benevolent fees, Hulman borrowed his son-in-law's HOW racer for a spin around the track. This was his first experience piloting a race car at the Speedway. After driving several laps, Hulman had a new appreciation for the skill of the race car drivers at the track. He said, "Oh, golly. This is not nearly like what I thought it was. It's kind of rough out there. I think this was the beginning and the end of my career as a race car driver." Part of the issue was that he was unable to find the groove. Upon realizing this, Hulman recounted, "Finally, I said to myself 'For Lord sakes, this isn't the groove where I am.'"[36]

The track also saw the return to racing of Duane Carter whose last race was in 1955. He had retired from active racing to become the competition director for the newly formed USAC.[37] After three years in this position, he had been fired because of his "one-man rule" management style.[38]

On the second day of practice, Jerry Unser lost control of his car after completing several laps at 133 miles per hour. It slid broadside into the outside wall. The force of the impact ripped open the fuel cell. As the car continued to slide back across the track, the fuel flowed down into the car's underpan and then into the cockpit. The car, then ablaze, hit the inside wall broadside before coming to a rest.

Unser was rushed to Methodist Hospital with third-degree burns over 35 percent of his body, principally his legs and left arm. He had also suffered a broken neck.[39] Although racing officials had encouraged drivers to wear fireproof driving suits, few did. Unser had been wearing street clothes for the practice lap. Seeing the horrific burns Unser sustained, many drivers went to get their driving suits dipped in fire-retardant materials.[40]

Thrilling the spectators at the Speedway at the conclusion of the first week of practice were three drivers—Rodger Ward, Jim Rathmann and Dick Rathmann—exceeding 144 miles per hour. This led to increased interest in qualifying, where hopes were high that new speed records would be set.[41] Three days later, Jim Rathmann roared around the track at 147 miles per hour. The excitement over his speed was tempered by the news that Jerry Unser, who had been transferred from Methodist Hospital to Robert Long Hospital on the campus of Indiana University Medical Center for treatment of uremia by an artificial kidney, wasn't responding to treatment.[42] Unser would succumb to his injuries on May 17. At the time of his death, Unser was the USAC stock car champion.[43]

As often happens after serious racing crashes, new rules were implemented to provide better protection for the drivers. After Unser's death, Speedway management required drivers to wear long-sleeved shirts which had been treated with fire retardant.[44] USAC, which already required a firewall between the engine and the cockpit, considered requiring a firewall between the fuel tanks and the cockpit.[45]

On the first day of qualifying, Johnny Thomson, the current reigning sprint car national champion, set a new track record for one lap (146.532 miles per hour) and four laps (145.908 miles per hour) to take the pole. He had begun driving race cars in 1938, and his first appearance at the Speedway had been in 1953.[46]

The Speedway fraternity suffered the loss of another driver when rookie Bob Cortner lost control of his car and hit the wall. The force of the impact slammed him first into the steering wheel and then back against the roll bar, shattering his helmet. He was rushed to Methodist Hospital with a skull fracture, a broken jaw and facial fractures[47]

The disastrous start to the 1958 race had been on Hulman's mind. For an eight-month period, Hulman sent surveys to spectators at the 1958 Indianapolis 500 soliciting their views on the starting of the race. They indicated that race fans would prefer a traditional start to the race. In February 1959, Hulman told the *Indianapolis Star*, "I don't know just yet how we'll work it out, but we're going to have to do something to keep them from dashing up from the back rows."[48]

At the pre-race drivers' meeting, both Chief Steward Fengler and Hulman emphasized safety. The track had experienced six crashes since opening on May 1 claiming the life of two drivers. Also fresh in their minds was the disastrous crash at the beginning of the 1958 race. Fengler promised to black flag any driver who got out of position prior to the start of the race, one of the key contributors to the 1958 crash. For emphasis, he added, "If you don't believe me, just test me." Hulman also emphasized the need for safety when he said, "The eyes of the world are upon you. The public expects you to conduct yourself as gentlemen. Gentlemen, you are."[49]

Although there were five crashes during the race, none were serious. With an average speed of 135.857 miles per hour, Rodger Ward won with a twenty-three-second margin over Jim Rathmann. Contributing to the victory were air jacks which had been installed on his car. This enabled his pit crew to perform all three pit stops in seventy-three seconds. As a comparison, Rathmann's pit stops consumed eighty-six seconds. Ward's victory was the third time in five years for an A. J. Watson–built car. The other two were Bob Sweikert's car in 1955 and Pat Flaherty's car in 1956. Watson had also built runner-up Jim Rathmann's car.[50]

1960

Opening day for practice is always a balancing act for Speedway officials trying to limit the speeds at the Speedway and the desire of the racers to test their vehicle. Until the Speedway has had several cars go around it at moderate speeds and seasoned drivers at high speeds, USAC officials would prohibit high-speed testing. This was both to make sure the track was clear of dust that could have blown on it as well as to begin to lay down a groove which is composed of oil and rubber.

In a break with tradition, Hulman opened the Speedway for practice on a Sunday in 1960. Speedway rookie Richard (Red) Amick took to the track on the first day of practice. Although he had been warned by Chief Steward Fengler to keep his speeds down, he was driving at 129 miles per hour on the track upon which dust had blown. With the track being slippery from the dust, he lost traction. Although he was uninjured, Speedway officials prohibited him from driving the car again on opening day as a consequence of this speedy run. Amick later acknowledged his error: "I was running faster than I should have been. The car felt real good and I guess I was just too eager to get going, that's all."[51]

On the first day of qualifying, an estimated 80,000 spectators were treated to a speed duel. Jim Rathmann set a new speed record. A mere ninety minutes later, Eddie Sachs gained the pole position with another speed record of 147.251 miles per hour for one lap, at 146.592 miles per hour for four laps. It was a busy day of qualifying with sixteen cars making the field.

Significant was that five of the six first starting cars were built by master mechanic A. J. Watson, which included the front row of Sachs, Rathmann, and Rodger Ward, with Len Sutton and Troy Ruttman in the fifth and sixth positions respectively.[52]

10. USAC's First Years

Speculation was growing about when the 150-mile-per-hour speed barrier would be broken. On the final day of qualifications, the estimated crowd of 70,000 was awed by rookie Jim Hurtubise when he set a new track record of 149.601 miles per hour for one lap and 149.056 miles per hour for the qualifying run. Remarkably, Hurtubise had been a USAC driver for less than nine months, having first driven in the Hoosier Hundred the previous year.[53]

In 1960, the Indianapolis Motor Speedway hosted its first Pro Golfers Association golf tournament. Just as when Hulman was unable to get into the Pagoda in 1948 for an interview, he wanted to see the professional golfers play but forgot his credentials. He asked a newspaper man, "Say, how can I get over there to see the golf boys?"[54]

In the carburetion day tests, Jimmy Daywalt was unhappy with his car. His mechanics had done significant work to it, and Daywalt was unable to get it up to a speed he felt was competitive. Having achieved a speed of only 137 miles per hour during the tests, Daywalt decided to give up his spot in the field of thirty-three, explaining, "I want to win the race if I'm running, not merely fill out the field." This provided a challenge for Speedway officials. The rules regarding the race stated that the driver who qualified the car had to run the first lap unless he was ill, injured, or otherwise disabled. They had two choices: allow the Bryant team to hire a backup driver or let the first runner-up into the race.[55] Speedway officials ultimately allowed the Bryant team to hire a backup driver.

One of the long-standing traditions of people with plans to watch the race from the infield was to build a makeshift seating tower. Some of these were quite elaborate. Two of the people building a makeshift tower in the infield in 1960 included Fred H. Linder and his brother-in-law William A. Shortridge. Their multitiered tower, built of pipe and boards, rested on top of a two-ton truck, rising some thirty feet into the air. It was anchored to the truck by guy wires at about eight to ten feet. They sold seats in their makeshift tower for $5 or $10 each.

An estimated seventy-five people were on this makeshift structure at the beginning of the race. In an attempt to see the race cars coming around the second turn on the pre-race lap, people stood up and leaned toward the action. With the guy wires being too low to effectively anchor the structure, the makeshift tower toppled to the ground as spectators below ran for safety. Two people, Linder and William C. Craig, died of broken necks, and eighty-four others were injured. The injured were initially taken to the Speedway infield hospital and then transferred to other Indianapolis-area hospitals as their condition warranted. The deaths were the first to spectators at the Speedway since 1938.[56]

Ironically, in a 1959 *Indianapolis Star* article, Clarence Cagle had talked about these make-shift stands: "We make them take them down if they don't look safe. Sometimes they do it gladly, sometimes they resent it."[57]

The 1960 race turned into a repeat of the speed duel between Rodger Ward and Jim Rathmann of the 1958 race, which Ward won. On the eighty-sixth lap of the race, Eddie Russo lost control of his car in the southeast turn and crashed into the outside wall. Critically injured, he was taken to Methodist Hospital with internal bleeding from either a broken spleen or a torn liver as well as head injuries.

In the race which saw the lead change twenty-nine times, Rathmann led for ninety laps and Ward led for fifty-nine laps. On the 197th lap, Ward noticed that his car's right front tire was worn through to the cord. He made the decision to ease up on the speed rather than risking blowing the tire. He said, "I thought I would probably go right through the cord and crash, so I figured I'd better settle for second money." Rathmann's margin of victory was 12.67 seconds.[58]

Hulman joined with 15 other Indianapolis businessmen including Tom Binford, Howard Fengler, Rodger Ward and Frank Dickie in the establishment of the Indianapolis Raceway Park in nearby Clermont, Indiana. This racing facility was the first built for multiple types of racing, with tracks for midget, sprint cars and drag cars. The facility was built on 267 acres, with drag racing beginning in 1961.[59]

11

The Golden Jubilee Race

Hulman was at the track on May 1 when it opened for its golden jubilee celebration of the Indianapolis 500 race in 1961. In recognition of this milestone, Ford Motor Company supplied thirty-three golden Thunderbird pace cars.[1] The talk around the track centered on the speeds of the automobiles. A mere fifty years before, the race was won by Ray Harroun with an average speed of 74.602 miles per hour. Would this be the year when the 150-mile-per-hour barrier was broken?

When practice started, USAC officials set an informal speed limit of 135 miles per hour for the first two days of practice. Despite the informal speed limit, Jack Turner went 140 miles per hour and Johnny Boyd recorded a speed of 139 miles per hour in practice. Both drivers were waved off the track because they were "running too fast."[2]

As qualifications approached, drivers were concerned about having time to practice and tune their machines. Although the track was scheduled for seventy hours of practice before qualifications began, significant rains in the Indianapolis area resulted in only thirty hours being available. Chief Steward Fengler addressed the drivers' concerns, indicating that qualification time would be made available when the track was suitable and after there had been thirty minutes of practice. He also stated that "if at all times during posted qualification time there has been a car at the line properly presented for qualification for its first time and any entrant has his car in line properly presented for the first time when posted qualification ends, qualification time will be extended until there is not a car at the line properly presented for the first time."[3]

The rains also impacted the construction of paddock seating. The Speedway had demolished the existing grandstands where the new paddock seating would be located. Unable to begin the construction because of rain, the resulting vacant space created a wind tunnel. With gusty winds whipping between the grandstands, drivers would feel their cars move several feet. Driver Johnny Boyd said, "It isn't really enough to make you lose control, I don't think, but it's plenty to surprise you." The other impact was the rainwater collecting in the track tunnels providing access to the infield. The grounds crew had been busy pumping water from the track tunnels. Despite their efforts, on May 8 only one exit gate was available.[4]

Dick Rathmann had agreed to drive the Jim Robbins Special. He took the Novi, which had been sold by Lew Welsh to Andy Granatelli, for a practice run and recorded a lap at 148.26 miles per hour. On May 11, Rathmann announced he was switching from the Jim Robbins Special to the Novi.[5] But this was not to happen. Robbins did not agree with the switch and said, "I have an iron-clad contract with Rathmann. I gave him $1,000 in advance and I don't think he can drive the Novi. I can make him sit here on the pit wall on race day if I want to, even if we don't get a car into the race. This contract even keeps him legally from taking a ride in another car."[6]

Needing a driver for the car, Granatelli decided to let Ralph Liguori take the Novi for a practice session. Liguori lost control of the car, hitting the wall on the northeastern part of the Speedway on his first run. Although he escaped with second-degree burns on his face and neck, the damage to the chassis was extensive, including a bent frame and a broken transmission.

Car owner Granatelli said, "It's no reflection on Ralph but this wouldn't have happened if Rathmann had been running it at 155 miles an hour. We had the car all set up for Rathmann to run 150 plus and it tuned and carbureted for 6,400–8,400 revolutions per minute. Ralph punched the throttle down at 4,000 r.p.m., lugging the engine. In the course of lugging, he just unloaded it. He didn't build up to speed gradually like you have to. He just got on it too quick. But I don't blame him because I didn't warn or tell him. I had no idea he would try to punch the throttle through the floor. He was just getting overenthusiastic to impress us."[7]

The next day, tragedy struck at the Speedway. Popular driver Tony Bettenhausen died of a broken neck when Paul Russo's car, which he was driving, had a bolt snap and he lost control. The car climbed the three-foot retaining wall before cartwheeling along its top for 325 feet. It ultimately landed upside down and caught fire.[8] At the time of the crash, Bettenhausen was going 149 miles per hour.[9]

With twenty-eight previous crashes, Bettenhausen had built a reputation

11. The Golden Jubilee Race

of indestructibly. In a 1959 interview with the *Indianapolis Star*, Bettenhausen commented on the crashes, "I'll never worry about those flips as long as I can keep counting 'em."[10] At the time of the interview, he had flipped his car twenty-seven times. Over a driving career which began in 1941, Bettenhausen had won twenty-one 100-mile championship races, more than any other driver, and was the national champion in 1951 and 1959. Despite his driving successes, he was frequently jinxed by mechanical issues and had never won the Indianapolis 500, logging 1,904 laps in the effort.[11]

On May 15, Andy Granatelli decided to withdraw the Novi from the race. He explained that delays in receiving the needed transmission shaft would preclude adequate practice time before the final weekend of qualifications. He also indicated that Rathmann was the first man to be able to really drive the Novi. He said, "As far as I'm concerned, Rathmann is the man for the machine. I sincerely believe he would go 152 or 153 miles an hour."[12] Indicating that the car would be back for the 1962 race, Granatelli announced he had already signed Dick Rathmann to drive the Novi.[13]

Despite all the prognostication of potentially breaking the 150-mile-per-hour speed barrier, this failed to happen. The average of the thirty-three cars in the lineup was 145.302 miles an hour, which was the fastest in Speedway history. Eddie Sachs was sitting on the pole for the second consecutive year. Despite having won the pole, Sachs was not the favorite to win the race. Rather, Rodger Ward was the experts' favorite. Others who might figure into the race included rookie Parnelli Jones, Jim Rathmann and Don Branson.[14]

Jep Cadou, Jr., sports editor of the *Indianapolis Star*, believed the rookie of the year might be Parnelli Jones. With a reputation as a successful sprint car driver, Jones first appeared at the track in 1960 and was offered four or five different rides. Rather than accept an offer, he spent countless hours watching and analyzing the experienced Speedway drivers as they maneuvered around the track. Immediately after the Indianapolis 500, Jones joined USAC and went on to win the Midwest Sprint Car Championship. In the summer of 1960, Jones returned to the Indianapolis Motor Speedway. During an unofficial practice, he recorded a lap speed of 134 miles per hour.[15] His hours of watching had paid off in his ability to handle the track.

At the drivers' meeting before the race, Hulman shared with the drivers his anxiety at the start of the race. He said, "I'm always fearful in the early part of the race. We're all tense at the beginning. I don't think you're going to win it right at that time."[16]

The pre-race festivities celebrated the fabled track's history. As the crowd roared in approval, Ray Harroun, the 1911 winner, returned to drive the Marmon Wasp. Eddie Rickenbacker, who had driven for the Speedway's original owners as the head of the Prest-O-Lite team in 1915 as well as the owner of the track between 1927 and 1945, returned to drive a 1914 Duesenberg. Earl Cooper, winner of the 1924 Indianapolis 500, drove a 1919 Stutz.[17] Of the thirty-eight men who had won the Indianapolis 500, twenty were still alive in 1961. Harroun always attended the race, stating, "Only a broken leg or the Grim Reaper could keep me away."[18]

The race turned into a duel between A. J. Foyt and Eddie Sachs. Sachs was leading the race with only three laps to go when he made a pit stop due to excessive tire wear. His pit stop allowed Foyt to win the race with an average speed of 139.131 miles per hour, a new track record.[19] Sachs later said, "I saw the tire was wearing out on the 194th lap. I just couldn't stand it any longer. I didn't want to make a permanent retirement."[20]

The 1961 race was broadcast on the world's largest radio network, the Indianapolis Motor Speedway Network. When it began on Memorial Day 1952, it had just twenty-six stations. By 1961, over 400 stations in all fifty states would carry the broadcast live, and the Armed Forces Radio Service Network would broadcast it around the globe. It was estimated that 100 million people listened to the 1960 race.[21]

At the fifth annual USAC dinner held at the Indianapolis Athletic Club in early May, Hulman was among the award recipients. Accepting the Continental Casualty Award for "persistent efforts to make the Indianapolis Motor Speedway a symbol of safety in automobile racing," Hulman said, "Our intentions are always to do everything in the world for the safety of the drivers."[22] Hulman also received high praise from George Souder, the 1927 winner of the Indianapolis 500. Souder said, "The auto racing world—in fact all the fans, too, should erect a monument to Tony Hulman. He's done more to advance the safety and pleasure factors of auto racing than any other man in the business."[23]

12

Breaking the 150 Mile-Per-Hour Barrier

The quest for a 150-mile-an-hour lap continued in 1962. Underpinning these hopes was the repaving of the main straightaway in the fall of 1961. With the exception of a yard-wide strip of bricks at the start-finish line, this concluded the paving of the Speedway first begun by Eddie Rickenbacker in 1939 when he paved the corners.[1]

Considerable effort was put into the paving of the main straightaway. With a goal of having a surface as skid resistant and safe as possible, the Speedway hired Roadways Inc., an Indianapolis bituminous paving contractor, and a sales engineer from the American Bitumuls & Asphalt Company to develop a mixture that would meet the specifications for the track established by Clarence Cagle. After a series of tests, the Cincinnati Paving Design Laboratory of American Bitumuls & Asphalt Company developed a special slag surface comprised of 36.4 percent of ¼[qm] minus slag, 29.8 percent of slag sand, 29.8 percent of silica sand and 45 percent limestone dust. Chevron asphalt made up 10 percent of the final paving mixture. Approximately 450 tons of the material were used to cover the 50-foot-wide by 2,200-foot-long surface. It was hoped the new pavement would help increase speeds.[2]

Also increasing the hope for a 150-mile-an-hour lap was the return of the Novis with drivers Jim Rathmann and Parnelli Jones. In practice on May 3, Jones thrilled race fans setting a 148.515-mile-per-hour pace, increasing the speculation that the 150-mile-per-hour barrier would soon be broken. Car owner J. C. Agajanian only increased the speculation when he said about Jones' run, "He's not running too fast through the corner." Agajanian expressed confidence that Jones would break the speed barrier.[3]

On the first day of qualifications, the *Indianapolis Star* reported that a consensus of twelve experts from the Speedway predicted that this would be the year the 150-mile-per-hour barrier would be broken.[4] The estimated crowd of 150,000 was thrilled when Parnelli Jones won the pole position with both a new one- and four-lap record. He set a blistering pace of 150.729 miles per hour for one lap, and the four-lap qualifying try had an average speed of 150.370 miles per hour.[5] In recognition of Jones' breaking the 150-mile-per-hour barrier, Phil Hedbeck, president of Bryant Heating and Cooling, put 150 silver dollars in Jones' helmet.[6] For the day, nineteen racers qualified with an average speed of 147.769 miles per hour, which was higher than 1961 pole holder Eddie Sachs' qualifying run of 147.481 miles per hour.[7]

When qualifications ended, the Indianapolis 500 had the fastest field in history with an average speed of 147.330 miles per hour. This was the first year under Hulman's ownership that not a single minute of qualification time was lost due to rain. But speeds were depressed on the final weekend as Indianapolis was experiencing a heat wave, making high-speed runs very difficult.[8]

Jones was the obvious hands-on favorite to win the race in his second outing. Setting the pace, he led for the first 59 laps and was in front for a total of 123 laps.[9] Despite a brake line breaking on his car on the seventy-fifth lap leaving him without brake fluid, Jones continued to drive and ultimately drove 312 and a half miles without brakes, averaging 143 to 144 miles per hour.[10] In order to stop the car in the pits, his crew would grab on to the side of the car and slide on the rough concrete.[11]

The race was won by Rodger Ward with an average speed of 140.292 miles per hour. His teammate, Len Sutton, finished second. It was the first one-two finish since 1948 when Mauri Rose and Bill Holland took the top two slots.[12]

1963

When the track opened for practice in 1963, there was a new challenger, the Lotus-Ford. Colin Chapman, the English builder of Lotus cars, had installed a Ford Fairlane engine, resulting in a car significantly lighter than the other cars at the track. Not only was the car lighter, which should improve miles per gallon, but it also had a smaller, fifteen-inch tire instead of the sixteen-inch/eighteen-inch combination commonly used. To provide more traction around the track, the fifteen-inch tire was also an inch wider.

After testing the smaller tire, A. J. Foyt was convinced it would allow him to go about two miles per hour faster than an eighteen-inch tire.[13] This only increased the consternation among the other drivers and owners that the Lotus-Ford cars had an unfair advantage.

Particularly upset by the appearance of the Lotus-Fords was the Offenhauser contingent, which filed a protest. There were rumors of some drivers circulating a petition in the garage area and threatening not to run unless the fifteen-inch tire was banned. Although these drivers were unable to get a critical mass of interest in signing the petition, the uproar over the fifteen-inch tire resulted in a ninety-minute meeting of the drivers, car owners and mechanics. They decided to ask Firestone Tire & Rubber Company, which had developed the tire, to withdraw the new tire from the race.[14]

Firestone's response was quick. A spokesman for the company said,

> We have no intention of withdrawing the 15-inch tire from the 1963 500-Mile Race. First of all, it was our obligation to meet the requirements of these smaller cars who had requested small tires and therefore it is necessary to make this smaller tire wider because of the smaller diameter and more revolutions per mile. Firestone feels that all tires in this year's race will be the best ever in performance in any of our experience here in 35 years.[15]

After setting a new unofficial track record at 152.027 miles per hour using the fifteen-inch tire, Parnelli Jones said, "You can run quicker like the Lotus-Fords have done on 15 inch tires."[16] This comment resulted in a sudden flight to the fifteen-inch tire. Although Firestone Tire & Rubber Company had plenty of fifteen-inch tires, the problem was they required new wheels. Ted Halibrand, who machined the wheels for race cars, indicated he was unable to meet the sudden demand for the smaller-sized wheel. Believing he could supply about 50 percent of the race cars, he said,

> This is a tribute to American ingenuity and manufacturing know-how. We were in good shape until everyone wanted to try the new 15-inch Firestones. Our contract with the foundry has been filled for the 16-inch fronts and the 18-inch rears. And then overnight I asked them to stop their current work and cast me some more new magnesium wheels of the 15-inch size.[17]

After Firestone rejected the request to ban the fifteen-inch tires from the race, one of the organizers of the protest meeting, car owner Robert C. Wilke, said, "We will just have to race them and beat them."[18]

The Indianapolis 500 field was the fastest ever, with five drivers qualifying at over 150 miles per hour, including the pole sitter, Parnelli Jones, at 151.153, Jim Hurtubise at 150.357, Don Branson at 150.188, A. J. Foyt at 150.615 and Paul Goldsmith at 150.163.[19] The hands-on favorite to win the race was Parnelli Jones. Reflecting on the prior two years, Jones simply said, "We hope to do it this year."[20]

Understanding the importance of promotion, Hulman announced that the winner of the race had been invited to appear on the *Ed Sullivan Show* the following Sunday. Many drivers were less than enthusiastic as they already had commitments to drive in either a stock car race at the Illinois Speedway or a sprint car race in Ohio. Hulman's son-in-law, race car driver Elmer George, retorted, "See that you don't win it if you can't go."[21]

In a very controversial race, Parnelli Jones won the Indianapolis 500 with an average speed of 143.137. During the race, his car developed a crack in the oil tank, spilling oil on the track.[22] Two racers in particular were very upset. Eddie Sachs and Roger McCluskey charged that they spun in oil from Jones' car. McCluskey said, "I had to clean my goggles every straightaway because he was throwing so much oil." Sachs believed that the oil leaking from Jones' car was a hazard for every car on the track.[23]

Chief Steward Fengler considered black-flagging Jones. But he opted to consult with J. C. Agajinian, the car owner, and Johnny Pouelsen, the chief mechanic. In the consultation, Agajinian and Pouelsen indicated that the car had stopped losing oil. Fengler couldn't see any sign of further oiling of the track and chose not to black-flag Jones.[24] He explained, "You can't take this race away from a man on snap judgment." He also reminded the drivers that other cars were also losing oil.[25]

Compounding the issue was the black-flagging of Jim Hurtubise. On a pit stop, he stopped his Novi with such force that the oil flowed out of a breather. A USAC official took a long time to decide to release the car. As Hurtubise returned to the track, on the main straightaway, he was black-flagged again. The car was ruled out of the race because of an oil leak. At a press conference after the race, Andy Granatelli, owner of the car, took the engine up to 8,000 rpm for several minutes. Hurtubise had been black-flagged when there was no oil leak![26]

1964

When the Speedway opened in 1964, Henry "Smokey" Yunick had a new race car design. Yunick, a master mechanic with many innovative racing car designs, had created a car which in some ways resembled a motorcycle with a side car. Rather than the driver being in the cockpit of the car, he sat in a sidecar with only a brake, throttle and steering wheel. The theory behind the car was that the weight of the driver and sidecar counterbalanced the weight of the racer, thus improving tire wear.[27]

Yunick wasn't the only one with an innovative design at the Speedway. Mickey Thompson, who first introduced the rear engine stock car to the

Speedway, had developed a car where there was steering of three wheels for rear-engine cars. He explained the thought process behind the new design: "As a race car goes through the turns the right rear wheel begins to curl and the full surface of the tire is not in contact with the pavement. This means you lose traction, have more tire wear, build up more heat and require more power to come out of the turns at a decent speed. To offset this, I hit on the idea of steering with one of the rear wheels."[28]

Additionally, Meyer-Drake had modified the Offenhauser engine so that it was made primarily out of aluminum. It was a V-8 and weighed 399 pounds with fluids compared to the Ford double overhead cam aluminum engine believed to weigh between 410 and 415 pounds.[29]

On the first day of qualifications, an estimated 225,000 people watched as Jimmy Clark, a Scottish sheep farmer, took the pole with an average speed of 158.828 miles per hour—nearly seven miles an hour faster than the previous pole winner. It was a big qualifying day with sixteen cars making the field, including nine rear-engine cars and seven roadsters.[30]

Controversy erupted at the Speedway when USAC refused to certify Paul Goldsmith for the race. Goldsmith had been suspended by USAC for driving in a NASCAR-sanctioned event at a stock car race in Riverside, California. The race had been approved by the Federation Internationale Automobile (FIA). There was an agreement between USAC, NASCAR and the Sports Car Club of America in which drivers would be recognized by each racing association if their events were approved by FIA.

The underlying issue was a new agreement, reached in 1963 to be effective for the 1964 racing season. USAC believed the agreement began immediately and had ordered Goldsmith not to participate in the Riverside race. When he ignored this order, USAC suspended him from participation in USAC races.

As a response to Goldsmith's suspension, the Automobile Competition Committee for the United States (ACCUS) of the Federation Internationale Automobile threatened that no foreign drivers would be permitted to race at the 1965 Indianapolis 500 unless Goldsmith was reinstated for the race.[31]

Spilling of oil, which had been controversial during the 1963 Indianapolis 500, continued during the run-up to the 1964 race. On May 22 during a practice session, the track was closed due to excessive oil leakage. Although there were others whose cars leaked oil, the biggest contributors to this problem were Rodger Ward's Kaiser Aluminum Special whose leakage closed the track for one hour and thirty-three minutes and Johnny Rutherford's Racing Associates Special which closed the track for one hour and seventeen minutes for cleanup.

Oil spills were a big problem for the Speedway. If oil seeped into the track, the Speedway's maintenance crew would be unable to get it up. Clarence

Cagle said of the oil leakage, "If we don't get this thing under control, we are going to have the slimiest mess you have ever seen around here."³²

Always looking for ways to promote the race, Speedway management negotiated with Music Corporation of America to broadcast the race through a pay-for-view closed-circuit telecast. In preparation for the telecast shown in 108 theaters in 101 cities, a broadcast studio was constructed for this one-time sporting event. It included six concrete and steel towers from twenty-five to fifty feet high. On top of the towers were five-by-seven-foot platforms. The race was covered by twelve cameras, three videotape recorders, eleven broadcasters and a twenty-by-sixty-foot control room. In all, seventy-eight people were part of the broadcast crew.³³

Attending the broadcast in Chicago, Corbin Patrick, a reporter for the *Indianapolis Star*, watched as a Ford Mustang convertible, introduced in March 1964, led the field of thirty-three racers through the pace lap. On lap 2 of the race, there was a fiery crash in the fourth turn of the Speedway when rookie driver Dave MacDonald lost control of his car. Upon hitting the wall, his car burst into flames. Unable to avoid MacDonald's car, Eddie Sachs was one of seven cars involved in the crash. Sachs died at the Speedway while MacDonald died at Methodist Hospital of fire inhalation several hours later. Also suffering burns were Parnelli Jones, Bobby Unser and Ronnie Duman. Starter Pat Vidan red-flagged the action on the track, and it took nearly two hours to clean up the wreckage.³⁴

Through the early part of the race, the pole sitter, Jimmy Clark, led the pack. His car started vibrating when the suspension started collapsing. The underlying problem was the stickier Dunlop tires which began chunking with the buildup of heat during the race.³⁵ Under the cloud of this tragic race, A. J. Foyt was victorious.

MacDonald's car was running on gasoline rather than the less volatile methanol. After the race, one participant said, "They saw what gasoline will do. I'll bet you'll never see gasoline in another race car out here again."³⁶

The controversy over gasoline increased when popular driver Jim Hurtubise suffered severe burns to the face and hands a week later at a race in Milwaukee. In November, Bobby Marshman suffered fatal burns while testing a car in Phoenix. One of the reasons for using gasoline rather than methanol was better mileage. Cars using gasoline needed only one pit stop for fuel rather than two pit stops for methanol. Rather than ban the use of gasoline, USAC responded by instituting a rule requiring two pit stops at the Indianapolis 500, effectively equalizing the use of methanol.³⁷

In early September 1964, the Speedway played host to four young British musicians. The Beatles were on their first American tour and played two sold-

12. Breaking the 150 Mile-Per-Hour Barrier

out concerts at the Indiana State Fair. The Beatles stayed at the Speedway Motel on the grounds of the Indianapolis Motor Speedway.[38] George Harrison recalled, "As we were leaving, on the way to the airport, they took us around the Indy circuit, the 500 oval, in a Cadillac. It was fantastic. I couldn't believe how long the straightway was; and to be on the banking, and see all of the grandstands, was great."[39]

1965

After a very difficult 1964 race, Speedway fans were delighted with the return to the track of Jim Hurtubise. He had returned to racing participating in a 300-mile race at the Indianapolis Raceway Park.[40] Racing fans had their hearts in their throats when Hurtubise lost control of the car after his throttle stuck during a practice session at the Speedway. As he slid down the outside wall, both of the right tires collapsed, which potentially could have caused the fuel tank to explode.[41] In response to the fiery crash which killed Sachs and MacDonald during the 1964 Indianapolis 500, both Firestone and Goodyear had developed rubberized fuel cells to protect the fuel cell from ripping.[42] Thankfully, Hurtubise's car had new fuel cells. Firestone's fuel cell engineer, Del Cline, said, "If Jim had been using regular fuel tanks, his car probably would've exploded."[43]

The tire wars, which had begun in 1964 when Goodyear returned to the Speedway, heated up in 1965. Goodyear had withdrawn from Indianapolis 500 racing after the 1922 race, ceding the track to its rival, Firestone. The company returned to the track in 1964, but withdrew after having difficulties with its racing tire and released those using its product, enabling them to run on other tires. In 1965, Goodyear was back at the Speedway and was very confident of its racing tire. Jim Loulan, chief engineer for race tire development, said, "We feel our racing tire has double the wear of Firestone. Right now we have our tires on 50 per cent of the cars on the track and we feel we'll hold that percentage in the race itself." Firestone's Jim Thiese retorted, "We believe, and think the drivers agree, that we have the finest racing tire ever built."[44]

Unfortunately, the right front Goodyear tire on Gordon Johncock's car developed a chunking problem during a practice session, and he switched to Firestone tires. After qualifying, A. J. Foyt, Billy Foster and Don Branson also experienced chucking problems during practice sessions. USAC rules required the equipment with which a car qualified to be used during the race. This prohibited Foyt, Foster and Branson from changing to Firestone tires. With the inability to change tire manufacturers, pressure was on Goodyear to determine the cause of the chunking problem and provide a solution.

One of the underlying contributing factors to chunking can be the thickness of the tires. Goodyear tires had a thickness of 7/32 while Firestone tires had a thickness of 5/32.[45] But the underlying problem wasn't the thickness of the tire. Goodyear engineers discovered that a "blade fold" during the manufacturing process led to the tire failure.[46] Goodyear began manufacturing replacement tires, and Loulan assured everyone the tires would be fine. Much to Goodyear's chagrin, Chief Steward Fengler ruled that the Goodyear tires had been buffed to wear off a bit of the tread and were ineligible. In response, Goodyear provided additional tires. Rather than having them machine buffed, they had drivers run on the tires for twenty to thirty laps to achieve the same effect.[47] The problem was resolved.

On the first day of qualifying, a rear-engine Lotus-Ford dominated the front row. A. J. Foyt took the pole with an average speed of 161.233 miles per hour. Joining him in the front row were Jimmy Clark and Dan Gurney.[48] The emergence of the V-8 rear engine, originally developed in 1961 by Cooper-Climax, underscored the age of the Offenhauser engine. The Offenhauser engine, originally developed by Leo Goosen for Louis Meyer in the 1930s, had been the primary power plant for the Indianapolis open cockpit racing cars since 1947. The rear-engine V-8 could produce 425 horsepower while the Offenhauser engine had a production capacity of 400 horsepower. Also contributing to faster speeds was the lighter weight of the rear-engine car.[49] Louis Meyer, aware that the Offenhauser engine was no longer competitive, had a pair of experimental engines developed during 1963–1964.[50]

The race was won by Jimmy Clark, the first foreign driver to win the race since Dario Resta in 1916, with an average speed of 150.633 miles per hour. The race confirmed the dominance of the rear-engine car.

Flooding had always been an issue for the Speedway, caused not only by the creek which runs through the property but also by the surrounding land which is a floodplain. In 1965, the Speedway undertook a major project to address the flooding issues in turn 1 by creating "Dry Run," which runs under the main grandstand.[51]

Hulman was honored by the milk industry in 1965 for the tradition of the winning driver drinking milk at the ceremonies.[52] The tradition was begun in 1932 when Louis Meyer, after a long, hot drive to victory, wanted his favorite drink from childhood, buttermilk, in winner's circle.[53] As he was drinking the buttermilk, he was photographed.[54] In 1947, Wilbur Shaw presented a big silver cup of ice water to the winner, affectionately known as "Water from Wilbur." This continued through the 1955 race. In 1956, Hulman returned to the celebratory drink of milk.[55]

13

Celebrating the 50th Indy 500

In 1966, the Indianapolis Motor Speedway celebrated the 50th running of the Indianapolis 500. The month-long celebration began with the first day of qualifications. When the track was built in 1909, the first contest was a balloon race. Speedway founder Carl Fisher was one of the participants when six balloons sailed into the blue Indiana sky.

To commemorate the first balloon race at the track, on the opening morning of qualifications, the Speedway featured a two-balloon race involving Don Piccard, the son of the famous balloonist Jean Felix Piccard, and Paul Yost, the first man to balloon across the English Channel.[1] Unlike the balloon race in 1909 in which the contestants flew for hundreds of miles and the winners weren't known for several days, the reenactment was scheduled to last for just an hour.

During preparations for the balloon race, one of the balloons lost its tethering and started moving sideways. Its handlers were unable to control it and it smashed into a portable toilet facility with two women inside, tipping it over. In commemoration, the infield restroom facility in Turn 4 is adorned with a picture of an ascending balloon.[2]

Mario Andretti set a new track record with a four-lap qualifying speed of 165.899 miles per hour. When Chuck Rodee took to the track for his qualifying run, the joy of the Speedway crowd turned to horror and sadness when Rodee lost control of the car on the infield, shot across the track and hit the concrete wall backward. The force of the impact drove the starting shaft five inches into the concrete wall. The semi-conscious Rodee was taken to Methodist Hospital, where he died of a ruptured aorta a couple of hours later.[3]

The pre-race festivities also harkened back to the first running of the Indianapolis 500. In 1911, there was a massed band to entertain the spectators. In 1966, the Speedway had a band of 5,000 composed of 50 marching bands—one for each year in which the 500-mile race had been run. Included in the bands were the Gasoline Alley Pipers (a bagpipe ensemble), the American Legion National Band, three bands from Purdue University and numerous high school bands.[4]

The Peugeot that won the 1916 Indianapolis race led the pre-race parade. Also in the parade was a white Stoddard-Dayton driven by Tony Hulman. At the beginning of the 1911 race the car was driven by Carl Fisher, with James Allison in the front passenger seat.[5]

The 1966 race was very controversial. It started with a crash in the first turn on the first lap, which took 11 of the 33 cars out of the race.[6] Most of the drivers close to the action believed that Billy Foster, who had started on the fourth row, caused the wreck when he drove over the car of Gordon Johncock, who had started on the second row. Foster strongly defended himself, saying that he was hit from behind. He said, "All I know is that someone hit me on the right rear and I ended up going into the wall."[7]

Veteran driver Bill Cheesbourg, who failed to qualify for the race, who was sitting in the stands watching the race, said, "There was a lot of cheating on the start and some of the cheaters got caught." Veteran racer Dan Gurney pointedly said, "Everybody has a brake and an accelerator and should be able to drive down a straightaway without running into each other. In this case, I think enthusiasm took precedence over judgment. The cars were bunched but I don't think you can blame that. I think the drivers were at fault."[8]

The wreck resulted in the red flag being brought out so that the track could be cleared. Amazingly, the only injury was a cut finger suffered by A. J. Foyt when he climbed a fence.[9]

Apparently crossing the finish line in first position was rookie Graham Hill, with an average speed of 144.317 miles per hour. But Colin Campbell, car owner, and Andy Granatelli, sponsor, believed their car, driven by Jimmy Clark, had won a second straight race, despite being some 41.13 seconds behind Hill as they crossed the finish line. They maintained that Clark had lapped Hill's car on the 47th lap and had remained ahead through the remainder of the race. The controversy began to unfold on the 174th lap when Hill passed Clark. The question was whether Hill was passing Clark or was he simply unlapping himself.[10]

The Clark team felt so strongly that he had won the race that they immediately talked of filing a protest. They maintained that on lap 174, the official scoring had Stewart in first, Clark in second, and Hill in third. Stewart went out of the race with an oil pressure problem, and on the next lap Hill was reflected in first place and Clark in second. Colin Campbell said, "If they won't let us see them [the official tapes], then we'll protest the result. We feel the official timekeeper has given Graham (winner Hill) an extra lap. There is no way Hill could have gotten ahead of us." Since the race results are not posted until the following morning, they planned to be in Chief Steward Harlan Fengler's office at 8 a.m. to see the results the race.[11]

The next morning, Granatelli and Campbell reviewed the tape and concluded that Graham Hill had, in fact, won the race. A protest was not filed.

The messy start was another issue and became the topic of conversation. Ultimately, USAC reviewed the race and discussed potential changes which could have prevented the crash. The talk around the track centered upon three items. The first was whether or not the race start format should be changed from three abreast to either two abreast or single file. Some felt that there wasn't enough width on the track for starting three across, given the speeds. The second item was whether the pace lap should be driven only by a retired professional race driver. Chief mechanic George Salih wondered, "Why not have the pace car lead the parade lap and then let the pole car set the pace-lap speed? That's the way it's done at other tracks." Lastly, some attributed the problems at the start of the race to the mixing of race cars with multi-speed gear boxes with cars without this innovation. The issue was that multi-speed gear boxes have a different acceleration pattern than those without. One driver, however, wasn't in favor of having multi-speed gear boxes in any of the cars. "They ought to ban the things (multi-speed gear boxes). Even if everybody had them, it would just take one missed shift and we'd have the same situation all over again."[12]

At the victory banquet, Rodger Ward announced his retirement from racing. He said, "I always said that when it wasn't fun anymore, I would retire. Well yesterday, it just wasn't fun."[13]

On November 18, 1966, Hulman traveled to Indiana University for the opening of the new business school building. At the dedication, he received a Doctor of Laws, an honorary law degree awarded by Indiana University in recognition of specific or lifetime accomplishments in one or more areas. Hulman was recognized for his leadership of Hulman & Company during the Great Depression, a period in which many giants in the food industry failed. He had taken the family firm and turned it into a powerful national manufacturing and distribution company, which contributed to Indiana's economy during the Great Depression. He was also recognized for his purchase of the Indianapolis Motor Speedway and its transformation into one of the most known sporting events in the world.[14]

1967

Opening day for qualifying in 1967 saw Indianapolis blanketed with drizzling rain in the early morning. The track was to open at 9 a.m. However, due to rain, opening ceremonies were postponed until 10:30 a.m. The rules required one-half hour of practice before qualifications began so qualifications should have started at 11:05 a.m. When practice started, the green flag was out for a mere ten minutes when Ralph Ligouri's car stalled on the track, resulting in the yellow flag coming out until his car could be cleared. When the green flag came out again, Bobby Johns crashed into the wall, once again resulting in the yellow flag coming out after only a minute. Yet again, when the green flag came out, Mark Mosley crashed his car. The final crash during practice occurred with Ebb Rose.

Qualifications finally began at 12:45 p.m. Remarkably, 25 drivers qualified for the race on the shortened day, smashing the old record of 21 drivers qualifying in 1961. Taking the pole was Mario Andretti, with a four-lap speed of 168.982 miles per hour. He smashed the previous record, set in 1966, of 165.899 miles per hour. After taking the pole, Andretti said, "Just making the race is the greatest thing in a man's career."[15]

During practice, Parnelli Jones's car became controversial. It hit 163 miles per hour during practice and other drivers on the track complained of the turbine exhaust. Mario Andretti said, "It may be non-toxic fumes as they tell us, but let me tell you it can be felt in the car behind him. And with the heat coming out of that thing, my temperature gauges shot right up." Although the drivers knew it was too late to have the car ejected from the race, they gathered up a petition to present to USAC and hoped to have a special heat deflector added to the car. Chief Steward Fengler went to Andy Granatelli to see if a modification could be made to the car to address the drivers' concerns. Granatelli agreed to this request and said, "We've put a baffle back on the car. It's something we had used before and it doesn't affect the running at all. It does throw the exhaust up higher in the air."[16]

The 1967 race started on an overcast day. After eighteen laps, rain interrupted the race. Speedway officials hoped to restart the race but intermittent showers thwarted attempts to sufficiently dry the track. The race was postponed until 4:10 p.m. the following day. Thirty-two drivers took to the field with the restart of the race. Not participating for long was Lloyd Ruby, who dropped out of the race after two laps.[17] With the restart of the race, Hulman brought laughter from the larger-than-anticipated crowd when he said, "Gentlemen, restart your engines."[18]

The fastest car in the field was clearly the turbine driven by Parnelli Jones.

13. Celebrating the 50th Indy 500

The question was, did it have the staying power to go 500 miles? Jones led for 171 laps and had a fifty second lead over A. J. Foyt when suddenly, on lap 197, race fans on the backstretch noticed his car visibly slowing. Foyt, in second place, later commented, "The people really started yelling at me in the backstretch and waved me on so I knew something had to have happened to Parnelli. I finally caught up to him in the fourth turn and went by him as if he was barely moving."

Jones' gear box had faltered. Jones later said that there had not been an issue with the car until it lost power. He was able to cruise into the pits but the victory, which had seemed so sure on lap 196, was gone. Jones was ultimately awarded sixth place.[19]

Foyt, in second place when Jones's gear box faltered, was very surprised at the turn of events and would go on to win the race. After his victory, Foyt said, "I honestly thought I was out of it. Before the race was restarted, I figured the turbine would be out of it within 100 laps. When the darn thing was still going by then, I figured he had won and there was nothing I could do about it. I just tried not to let him lap me."[20]

But the racing excitement for the day wasn't over with the exit of Jones, and Foyt's victory wasn't assured. On his final lap, there was a crash on the main straightaway involving five cars. Foyt's focus after taking the lead was to drive carefully. As he exited turn four and saw the cars bouncing off of the walls and each other, he thought, "Oh, no." Foyt described the final seconds of his race:

> Somehow I had an instinct not to accelerate coming out of the fourth turn. I had been driving real careful and stayed back out of the traffic so I could keep out of trouble. Then I came out of the turn, looked ahead and there was the mess. The first thing I did was hit the brakes and then the next to look over my shoulder to see if anyone was close enough to ram me from behind. The only car I saw behind me was Art Pollard and he was slowing down so I came to almost a complete stop. I could have walked faster than I was moving when I came to the tangle. I shifted to low gear, went down close to the inside wall and then accelerated as I threaded my way through.[21]

Immediately after Foyt took the checkered flag, the race was red flagged. It was the first time just one car had completed 500 miles.[22] For his efforts, he took home $171,277 of the total record prize purse of $727,346.98.[23]

In 1967, Hulman traveled halfway across the globe to Japan for races at the Fuji Speedway. The track, built in 1963, was 3.728 miles long. Hulman had been invited by the race promoters to start this Indy-style race. Since Hulman always wrote out the starting phrase for the Indianapolis 500, imagine his nervousness at saying it in a foreign language. Hulman recalled, "I had to say, 'Gentlemen, start your engines' in Japanese! I must have done it right. They all did."[24]

1968

The 1965 Indianapolis 500 champion, Jimmy Clark, was killed in a Formula 1 race in Hockenheim, Germany, in April, 1968. He had been closely associated with cars built by Colin Campbell. At the Speedway in May 1968 for the first time, driving a Campbell car, was Mike Spence. Although a Speedway rookie, Spence was a veteran of Formula One racing, having driven in 37 contests. On May 7, he set the second fastest lap at the Speedway in practice, at 169.555 miles per hour. Toward the end of the practice session, he took a teammate's car out on the track. Losing control of the car in the first turn, Spence slid some 300 feet prior to crashing into the wall. His right front tire became airborne and smacked him in the head, killing him.[25]

An investigation into the crash revealed that the metals used in the STP Lotus turbines did not meet USAC requirements. Despite the fact they were not up to USAC standards, Chief Steward Fengler ruled that the remaining STP-Lotus Turbines were safe and permitted the cars to qualify and practice. In explaining this decision, Fengler said, "We are not trying to say that these parts are inferior or unsafe. In fact, from our investigation of the Spence accident, they appear to hold up very well."[26]

The field was not filled at the end of the qualification period and an extra qualifying day was held.[27] When the field of 33 cars took to the field, Joe Leonard, piloting an STP Lotus-Turbine, and Bobby Unser were in a duel. Leonard was leading by five seconds with eight laps remaining when his car lost power due to a broken fuel pump shaft.[28] At that point, Bobby Unser took the lead and went on to take took the checkered flag, with an average speed of 152.862 miles per hour.[29]

1969

Over the summer, Firestone, which had supplied tires for many years announced, that they were withdrawing from Indianapolis-type racing competition due to high costs. Ultimately, they decided to honor the last year of their three-year contract with Mario Andretti, and returned to the track for a final year. For the race, Goodyear was the dominant tire supplier, outfitting 25 of the 33 cars.[30]

Although none would win the race, the turbocharged cars had the potential to run away from the rest of the field. In an effort to keep speeds down, after the conclusion of the 1968 race, USAC reduced the annulus intake area from 15.99 inches to 11.99 inches. Andy Granatelli felt that with a reduced intake area the turbocharged cars would not be competitive, and indicated that he would not bring another turbocharged car to the Speedway. Evidently, other owners felt the same way, as only one turbocharged car was brought to the track in 1969. And Granatelli was correct, the car wasn't competitive—it failed to make the field being some four miles per hour slower that the slowest qualifier.[31]

Controversy erupted at the Speedway two days before the race. Earlier in May, Mario Andretti had crashed the car he expected to drive in the race when a hub broke during practice. In the fiery crash, Andretti suffered minor burns on his face and lips. His co-chief mechanics, Clint Brawner and Jim McGee, brought out a Hawk-Ford they had designed and built. After only two days of practice, Andretti qualified the car in the middle of the front row.[32]

After qualifying, to solve a heating problem and to help with fuel efficiency, the car was modified by adding a second radiator. Chief mechanic Clint Brawner had received approval from Chief Steward Fengler for the modification to the machine. This brought a protest from the pole sitter, A. J. Foyt, who had also requested permission from Fengler to add a radiator, only to have his request denied. Upon consulting with the USAC officials, Fengler reversed his position and told Andretti that the modification was not acceptable. In anger, Andretti threatened not to run in the race.[33]

Although he believed he had no chance of winning, when race day arrived Andretti was next to Foyt, his car minus the extra radiator. Unbeknownst to Andretti, chief mechanic Brawner had worked behind locked doors the night before the race, installing a radiator under the seat. Brawner tells the story of the extra radiator: "I put a radiator under the driver's seat. This didn't violate the rules. And no one—not even Mario—knew it was there." Andretti told Brawner it was the hottest race he'd ever had. Brawner continued, "He didn't know he was sitting on top of a radiator with 240-degree coolant running through it."[34]

Andretti convincingly won the race setting a new track record of 156.867 miles per hour—nearly four miles per hour over the record set in 1968. He was nearly three laps ahead of his closest competitor when he took the checkered flag.[35]

Hollywood returned to the Indianapolis Motor Speedway with the filming of *Winning*, starring Paul Newman and Joanna Woodward. In the film, Newman portrays a race car driver wanting to win the Indianapolis 500. The film's director wanted Hulman's voice saying the words which had become synonymous with the start of the race. After listening to the taped beginning of several Indianapolis 500s, the director felt the quality wasn't acceptable.

Hulman agreed to record the words for the film, and as a result, he had to join the Screen Actors Guild.[36]

Before the Indianapolis Colts, Indianapolis had a pro football team called the Capitols, or Caps, that played there from 1968 through 1971. Its games were played in the minor league baseball stadium, then known as Bush Stadium, but called Victory Field by many long-time Indianapolis residents. Bush Stadium was on 16th Street, east of the Speedway. Like the prior ownership groups of the Speedway, Hulman explored various ways to increase the Speedway property's utilization. One of Hulman's ideas was to build a football stadium for the Caps in the infield of the Speedway. Hulman recalled, "We gave it a good look. It seemed like quite a terrific investment before we could use it still for a race track and also a football field. But it could be done." The major hang-up was with the Speedway seating arrangements. There is no practical way to set up a football field, use the race seats, and still get the 56,000 seats a pro franchise would demand.[37]

1970

Indianapolis awoke to rainy skies the first day of qualifications for the 1970 race. Despite a limited window, twenty-three cars made attempts at earning a starting position. Taking the pole was Al Unser, by the barest of margins. His qualifying time was a mere 8/1000 second faster than second place Johnny Rutherford. That is about 2 ½ feet over a ten-mile qualifying run.[38]

One of the informal traditions of Speedway spectators was to bring a cooler filled with beer to the race, as Indiana prohibited the sale of all alcoholic products, including bee, on Sundays and some holidays. In 1970, the Indiana legislature lifted the ban on the sale of beer on Memorial Day. The Speedway was prepared for the consumer demand, with 96,000 bottles of beer for sale at the track. Although the Speedway was going to be selling beer, they did not ban bringing beer to the track in coolers.[39]

As the field assembled for the running of the race spectators were anticipating a fast pace, as this was the fastest field ever assembled. The race had a rain delay of an hour and three minutes. On the pace lap, Jim Malloy's car had a lower right radius rod fail when he was coming out of the first turn causing, the race to be halted. The cars returned to the starting line. After the cars got an additional two gallons of fuel, Hulman, in his 25th year as head of the Indianapolis Motor Speedway, again uttered the words "Gentlemen, Start your engines." With that, the machines roared to life and the race was on. The race was somewhat anticlimactic, as Al Unser dominated the race, leading for 191 laps. Slowing his pace was a crash involving five cars on his 172nd lap.[40]

1971

In 1970, Congress changed the celebration of Memorial Day from May 30 to the final Monday of May. Hulman's preference was to hold the race on Saturday so that if there was a rain delay, it could be run on Sunday, or on Monday if needed. Possibly contributing to the decision was past history reflecting that when the race was run on Saturday, attendance was higher than other days of the week.[41]

One of the issues on the drivers' minds when they arrived at the Speedway in 1971 was an up-coming race at the Langhorne Motor Speedway in Pennsylvania. This one-mile dirt track, opened in 1926, had developed a reputation as one of the most dangerous tracks in motor sports, claiming the lives, among others, of Mike Nazurek and Larry Crockett in 1955. Some drivers wanted to boycott Langhorne due to the dangerous conditions. But they knew that since this race counted in the points for USAC's National Championship some drivers would participate. To not participate could end up affecting the outcome of the year's racing championship.

Getting wind of the unhappiness about the Langhorne track was Leonard Laye, representative of the Professional Drivers Association, who was in Indianapolis attempting to drum up interest by the drivers in joining the union, which already represented NASCAR drivers.[42] Laye met with some of the drivers but was unable to generate interest in the union. A. J. Foyt said, "We do not have the same situation as NASCAR. We do not need the PDA." Rather, he favored a small group of drivers to convey the needs of the larger group to the track owners, similar to the system in place in Formula 1 racing. "I think we should have a short meeting say just before a race and discuss the things we feel need changing and then present them to USAC."[43]

The first day of qualifications was a very rainy day, but the track was sufficiently dry to permit the required thirty minutes of practice. A mere ten minutes before the closing of the track at 6:00 p.m. A. J. Foyt blew his engine in his qualifying attempt. Hulman wasn't obligated to refund tickets for this day of qualifying since an attempt had been made. Nevertheless, he made the decision to make the refunds.[44]

The worst storms since 1963 continued the next day. Heavy rains and hail struck the far east side of Indianapolis, and a tornado destroyed approximately eighty homes.[45] After the storms had cleared the Indianapolis area, qualifying resumed on Tuesday. Cosmetics heir and racing enthusiast Peter Revson took the pole position, with an average speed of 178.696 miles per hour.[46]

Creating additional consternation, the next day Fengler indicated that the speed to be run under the yellow was 80 miles per hour. The drivers wanted for the speed to be faster—somewhere between 100 and 120 miles per hour.[47]

After the expiration of the contract with Music Corporation of America for closed-circuit televising of the race, Hulman signed an agreement with American Broadcasting Company (ABC) to televise the race on a delayed basis, with the exception of the greater Indianapolis area, which would be blacked out.[48] Broadcast of the race in the Indianapolis market would be carried by several local radio stations. The American Broadcasting Company was already broadcasting other USAC races as well as NASCAR events. Underlying Hulman's decision was that the closed-circuit broadcasts never reached their anticipated revenues and ABC offered significantly more money. Estimated revenue for the multi-year contract was $1,000,000.

This was not without risk to the Speedway. The Ontario Speedway had opened in 1970 and had drawn 100,000 fans to its first race. Additionally, the Pocono Speedway, with its first race scheduled for July 1971, was built based upon a survey which indicated that the majority of travelers to the Indianapolis Motor Speedway were from the northeast. The market area for the Pocono Speedway was estimated at forty million people. With the opening of these two race tracks, which could dilute interest in the race, would the telecast of the race harm the gate in future years?[49]

The 1971 race could be described as a crash derby. It began at the end of the pace lap for the race. Eldon Palmer, an Indianapolis auto dealer, was driving the pace car. He pulled into the pit area as planned for the beginning of the race. During practice, he had used a small flag to signal where he should begin to brake. Unfortunately, on race day the flag wasn't there and by the time he realized it was gone, the car was too far down pit lane to come to a safe stop. It slammed sideways into a temporary stand holding photographers, injuring approximately sixty. In the car with Palmer were Hulman, astronaut John Glenn and ABC broadcaster Chris Schenkel.[50]

The crash at the beginning of the race wasn't the only crash for the day. There were three others. At the beginning of the race, Steve Krisiloff's engine developed problems and started spewing oil. Krisiloff's car spun in the oil, as did Mel Kenyon's. Kenyon wasn't injured when his car hit the wall, and he was standing up in the car to get out when Gordon Johncock lost control of his car. Johncock described the next few seconds: "All I could see was Mel trying to stand up in the car and the two firemen or whoever they were. I came swinging around and sliding into Mel's car. They must have seen me at the last second because the fireman disappeared and Mel crouched back into the cockpit. I thought sure I had him. If he hadn't squatted down, I'd have wiped him out because I ripped off the entire left side of my car and drove right over his head. He's got to be lucky to be alive."

In another crash, Mike Mosley's car ended up on top of Bobby Unser's car, resulting in both cars catching fire. Mosley suffered burns on his hands and face as well as a broken left leg and right elbow.

The third crash occurred when David Hobbs's engine failed on the straightaway and Rick Muther, in an attempt to slow down, spun and hit the front of Hobbs's car.

At the conclusion of the race, only twelve cars were running. Al Unser won the race on his birthday for a second consecutive year.[51] Unser's helmet was unique in that it had a radio that enabled him to communicate with his pit crew.[52]

1972

In what seemed to be a familiar pattern, the first day of qualifications in 1972 was rained out. On the second day twelve cars qualified for the race, and Bobby Unser took the pole with an average speed of 195.940 miles per hour.[53] During practice the following week, Jim Malloy was running in the high 180s when he lost control of his car. Malloy was trapped inside the fiery vehicle for ten minutes before the flames were extinguished and he was extracted. He was rushed to Methodist Hospital, where he succumbed to his injuries four days later.[54]

When the drivers returned to the track in 1972, the Speedway unveiled the "Electro Pacer," a new lighting system developed to eliminate the need for the pace car to return to the track during periods the race cars were running under yellow. It was also believed the lights would keep the drivers at safe speeds and prevent them from bunching. Harlan Fengler said, "We wanted to get them conscious of the lights first. Maybe by next week we can run some actual tests with the lights, either before the track opens or after it closes. We really don't know how we are going to handle the system yet but I'm sure it will work."[55]

About a week before the race, USAC officials believed that the drivers had had an opportunity to get accustomed to the Electro Pacer system. In an hour-and-a-half meeting, Fengler advised the drivers that after running under yellow light, the resumption of racing speed would be signaled by the green light returning rather than the green flag being waived at the start/finish line. He also indicated the pace car would not be leading the racers during yellow light periods but rather the drivers would need to depend upon the Electro Pacer system to maintain their order and speed. Another change would be that the black flagging of a car, historically only taking place at the start/finish line, would be also occur on the backstretch. This change was not well received even though it was in use at both the Ontario and Pocono speedways. The meeting became so contentious that several drivers stormed out.[56]

Mark Donohue won the race with an average speed of 165.463 miles per hour—nearly six miles per hour faster than the previous record. But his win was disputed by Jerry Grant, who finished in second place and was considering filing an appeal. In the lead on lap 186, Grant, whose car developed a tire issue, took an unanticipated pit stop. Going down pit row, Grant stopped at a teammate's pit rather than his own. Rumors circulated that in addition to the tire change he had taken on fuel, which he denied.[57] Upon review of the race, USAC officials determined that by stopping at his teammate's pit, Grant had taken an illegal pit stop and his position was dropped to twelfth.[58]

After the race, the Electro Pacer system received mixed reviews. The Speedway staff discovered they were quicker in cleaning up wrecks from the tracks, as the workers didn't have to worry as much about the cars. Harlan Fengler noted that there was less cheating during the yellow lights. "We weren't close to having to penalize anybody for going too fast. Some people gained a few seconds but we were able to control it." Most of the drivers' complaints were about the 80-mile-per-hour speed limit. Roger McCluskey believed that the spectators got more thrills from racing when the cars were bunched together.[59]

The head of USAC's technical committee, Frankie DelRoy, had become increasingly concerned about the speed on the race track. DelRoy had been affiliated with racing since the 1930s, when he was a riding mechanic. After the end of his racing days, he became a mechanic and was the chief mechanic for the 1941 co-winners Floyd Davis and Mauri Rose. (Rose had taken over for Davis partway through the race.) DelRoy planned to recommend a reduction in engine size and changes to the chassis to USAC, in order to reduce the speeds at the track.[60]

Hulman had received many complaints about having the race run on the Saturday before Memorial Day and decided to change the race date for 1973 to Memorial Day itself.[61]

14

Tough Times at the Speedway

The period beginning in 1973 through 1977 was very difficult. Hulman had successfully led the Speedway and auto racing to a resurgence. Events on and off the track would make this period one of the most difficult in Speedway history.

Hulman understood that the success of the Indianapolis Motor Speedway was intertwined with the viability of other racetracks. After twenty-five years of ownership of the Speedway, Hulman reflected, "I'm trying to be helpful to other tracks and promote that sport. I always felt that if racing was goinna be a big sport, we needed a lot of other nice facilities around. As long as I have got the responsibility of the Speedway, I think it's up to all of us to do the very best we can and go all out for its success."[1]

In April 1973, Hulman became involved with the Ontario Motor Speedway. Opened in 1970, the Ontario Motor Speedway was modeled after the Indianapolis Motor Speedway. In addition to a two-and-a-half-mile oval, the Ontario Motor Speedway featured a road course and a drag strip in order to host more days of racing. Attendance at the first race was approximately 180,000. With a cost of $35,000,000 and bonds of $25,500,000, the track failed to generate enough cash flow to service the debt. By November 1972 the track closed when it was unable to pay the semiannual interest payments. The signature event at the Ontario Motor Speedway was the California 500 race.

In an effort to keep the USAC Triple Crown schedule intact, an investor group headed by Hulman and Parnelli Jones signed a ten-year lease option on the Ontario Motor Speedway in April 1973.[2] Others investing in the Ontario

Speedway included auto dealer Mel Miletch, attorney Dudley Gray and public relations pro Jim Cook. Jones talked of the motivation behind the purchase. "We have considerable involvement in racing and we had promised our sponsors a full season of racing. There were rumors that Phoenix, Michigan and Trenton wouldn't be run and Ontario looked dead."

Discussions had been under way for some time. Initially, Hulman and Jones were uninterested, but the persistence by the Ontario Motor Speedway management team eventually paid off. Jones explained, "The people who were trying to keep Ontario open kept coming back to us. I didn't think there was any way we could get involved. But every time they talked to us, it looked better. Our group decided we could help ourselves and at the same time do something for racing by trying to keep Ontario running. We are going to take a good look at it for a year and if we can make a go of it the sport will gain."[3]

Jones, who was named the president of the Ontario Motor Speedway, said of the purchase, "This way we have a year to find out if the track can be operated successfully. We honestly don't know yet. We do know that it will take all the cooperation of the community, drivers, car owners, manufacturers, racing fans and sanctioning bodies to make it happen."[4]

Shortly after Hulman and Jones took control of the Ontario Motor Speedway, Roger Penske paid $2.9 million for the "right of redemption" for the Michigan International Speedway which was in bankruptcy, thus helping to keep the championship circuit viable.[5]

Subtly underlying the difficulties in 1973 was discontent in the Middle East over the United States' support of Israel. The friction with the Palestinians went back to 1947 when President Harry Truman recognized Israel within eleven minutes of its declaration of nationhood. Truman's recognition of Israel was to court the Jewish vote in America and his belief that Israel would stand with the United States against the Soviet Union. Increasing the anti–American sentiment was the sale of weapons to Israel for their protection from the Soviet Union and Palestinian states.[6]

Tensions continued to escalate. The oil-producing Palestinian states had formed an alliance, the Organization of Petroleum Exporting Countries (OPEC), in 1960. By 1973, OPEC limited the production of oil, causing oil prices to rise and gas rationing to occur in the United States. The oil crisis of 1973–1974 escalated when in the fall of 1973, Syria and Egypt attacked Israel (the Yom Kippur War). President Richard Nixon responded by approving the sale of Phantom jets to Israel. This led to the October 1973 embargo of oil to the United States by OPEC. By that point in time, the United States was importing 33 percent of domestic oil consumption. The embargo continued until Israel agreed to withdraw to the 1967 boundaries.[7]

14. Tough Times at the Speedway

Also creating difficulty was the January 1973 USAC decision to withdraw from the American Competition Committee for the United States (ACCUS), effective January 1, 1974, unless changes were made. ACCUS is the critical interface between the international sanctioning body, Federation Internationale Automobile (FIA), and various U.S. racing groups, including NASCAR, USAC, and Sports Car Club of America (SCCA). FIA is also responsible for issuing international competition driving licenses.

USAC, at one point the premier and richest racing league in the nation, had seen its position slip. Of the thirty-one Federation Internationale Automobile Grand National events held in the United States, NASCAR hosted seventeen, Sports Car Club of America hosted twelve while USAC hosted two. And SCCA was proposing an additional ten to twelve races in the Continental Series be open to any FIA-sanctioned driver, which would further weaken USAC's position. NASCAR had been successful in upgrading its races by hiring international drivers, including Jackie Oliver.

The leadership of USAC had become frustrated with FIA's wholesale listing of events placing them at a competitive disadvantage. Until 1970, one of the sanctioning groups could veto FIA listings. USAC wanted to limit the number of international listings so that other sanctioning groups could not use USAC drivers without a fair return.

If USAC withdrew from ACCUS, only USAC-registered drivers could participate in the Indianapolis 500 unless the other sanctioning bodies worked out an interchange agreement, which was prohibited by both FIA and ACCUS.[8]

At the Speedway, the focus of many racing teams by 1973 was trying to beat the 200-mile-per-hour speed limit. Although laps run during practice sessions aren't officially timed, they give an indication of the anticipated speed of various racers as well as bragging rights. On May 12, Art Pollard was running some practice laps at 192 miles per hour. Coming out of turn 1, Pollard lost control of the car, ending up on the grass. After his car regained traction, he hit the wall and his car exploded into flames. His car then flipped upside down and then right side up. Severely burned, he was rushed to Methodist Hospital. Having suffered from inhalation injuries, he died shortly after arriving at the hospital.

After cleaning the track of debris, qualifications started. Although the 200-mile-per-hour barrier wasn't breached, the estimated 175,000 spectators saw plenty of action. Twenty-four cars qualified, led by Johnny Rutherford with a qualifying speed of 198.413 miles per hour, establishing a new track record.[9]

There were those at the track including Andy Granatelli who felt the speeds were getting too fast. Granatelli remarked, "We must face the fact that our cars are going too fast for human control. We must slow them down and do it in the most simple, inexpensive manner." He proposed limiting the amount of fuel available during the race as well as the fuel capacity of the race car to slow the speed of the racers to approximately 160 miles per hour. For the race, he proposed having a maximum amount of fuel of 200 gallons as opposed to the then current limit of 350 gallons. He would also cut the fuel carried onboard the cars to 40 gallons from the existing 75 gallons. He explained his rationale: "The current limit of 350 gallons is preposterous. With a limit of no more than 200 gallons, mechanics would be forced to reduce horsepower by cutting down on the use of fuel. This could be done by the simple expedient of setting a screw in the waste gate system of the turbochargers, thereby reducing manifold pressure. The whole task would take about 15 minutes." Granatelli believed his suggestion would improve fuel efficiency from the existing 1.5 miles per gallon to 2.5 miles per gallon. He also thought a limit on speed would make the race more thrilling for the spectator. He said, "With the 160 mph speed limit, you would see cars running two and three abreast in the current one car groove at Indianapolis."[10]

The 1973 race was the most deadly since racing began at the Speedway in 1909. Under threatening skies and a forecast of winds and rain and after a four-hour weather delay, the field of thirty-three for the 1973 race started the pace lap. As the racers pulled off from pit row, the race cars roared down the main straightaway. Trying to gain an advantage, some racers in the middle of the pack were out of alignment.

Wally Dallenbach, who started in the middle of the seventh row, saw the action unfold. "I looked ahead and saw four cars abreast. It was a lousy start because a few guys had already passed me before I got to the starting line. When I saw four cars abreast, I noticed the blue car which must have been Salt. He turned sharp right and went into the wheels of a car that had been squeezed into the wall. He started flipping and I drove through a ball of fire and cranked the wheel left to miss him and spun out. Salt flipped right over me."

When Salt Walther lost control of his car as it entered the first turn, the impact of the car crashing into the barrier and turning cartwheels down the track caused the fuel tanks to break open. Spectators sitting close to the track in Grandstand A were sprayed with fuel and car parts. Thirteen spectators were injured in the crash, with three being taken to Methodist Hospital by the Indiana State Police helicopter, including two teenage girls in critical condition. Walther was also flown by State Police helicopter to Methodist where he was originally listed in critical condition. His injuries included a broken left wrist and burns primarily to his hands, left arm and face. The required fire-retardant suit protected him from more serious injuries.[11]

Because the field was tightly packed at the beginning of the race, twelve race cars were involved. Speedway officials immediately red-flagged the race.

Just as they were starting to get the race under way after clearing the track, the rains came and the restart of the race was postponed.

The second day of racing also had threatening skies. Despite the continuing threat of rain, race officials decided to start the race. While the pace car was on the backstretch, rains began to fall. Again, the race was red-flagged for the day.

On the third day of attempting to get the race under way, it was delayed in order to dry the track. Around 2:10 p.m. they were able to get the track sufficiently dry to begin the race.

The early pace was set by Swede Savage, a member of the STP Patrick team. After stopping for fuel and a new rear tire, he reentered the fray. On the fifty-eighth lap, coming out of the fourth turn, he lost control of his race car. The car hit the inside retaining wall almost head on, separating the tub of the racer from the remainder of the machine. The tub, with Savage inside, continued back across the track hitting the outside wall. The force of the crash ruptured the fuel cell of the racer causing a fireball. Savage was cut from the race car's tub and flown to Methodist Hospital. Although he was critically injured, he was conscious and talking despite having sustained significant injuries including burns to his hands and face, internal injuries, and a broken arm and both legs.[12]

In the pits, one of the STP crew members, Armando Teran, ran to aid Savage. He didn't see the emergency truck also rushing to the crash going the wrong way on the pit apron. The emergency truck struck Teran. He was rushed to Methodist Hospital where he died from his injuries.[13]

After a lengthy delay to clean the track, the race resumed. When rains returned to the Speedway late in the afternoon, the race was called after 332 miles. The race was a bittersweet victory for Gordon Johncock, another member of the STP Patrick racing team. This team had suffered the loss of a crew member as well as a race driver being seriously injured.[14] Savage would die of his injuries on July 2.[15]

Just as in 1909, the Speedway came under significant criticism for the accidents, and just as in 1909, when the original owners replaced the track surface of crushed rocks and oil with bricks, there were significant improvements planned to the Speedway's physical plant to make it safer for the drivers, officials and spectators.

1974

When the Speedway opened in May 1974, over $300,000 had been spent in modifications. The retaining wall had been raised to a uniform height of thirty inches. Previously, the retaining wall had multiple heights ranging from eighteen to thirty inches. The approach to the pits had been widened, and the inside wall of turn 4 had been repositioned further back. Additionally, the pits had been lengthened from thirty feet to forty feet for each car.

Another significant change was that a new tower had been built for the starter and chief steward. Traditionally, the starter had been on the track, and racers other than those in the first or second row complained they could not see the starter as their vision was obscured by the preceding cars. The chief steward in 1973, Howard Fengler, had to depend upon word of mouth to know what was going on around the track. With the new control tower, the chief steward would have better sight lines and also a communication system where he could be in direct contact with the observers around the track. The chief of the emergency response crew would also be located in the control tower. In prior races, there had been virtually no communication between the chief steward and the head of the crash team.[16]

Physical changes to the track weren't the only changes made as a result of the multiple incidents in the 1973 race. Chief Steward Fengler, who had served in that capacity since 1958, was replaced by Tom Binford, an Indianapolis businessman who owned Binford Lumber and D. A. Lubricants. He had significant experience in the auto racing world beginning with the sponsorship of race cars at the Indianapolis 500, including 1955 (Cal Niday), 1956 (Bob Sweikert) and 1957 (Johnny Thomson).[17] Binford had also served as president of USAC and later ACCUS. Binford explained his philosophy on auto racing: "My idea of officiating is to conduct practices, qualifications and the race as smoothly as possible. The purpose of officials and the sanctioning body is to protect the entrants with fair decisions which are for the benefit of all. It really is for their own good."

With gasoline continuing to be rationed due to the oil embargo, the Speedway shortened the time for practice and limited qualifications to sixteen hours over two days (four four-hour qualifying periods). Additionally, the amount of fuel which could be used during practice and carburetion day was limited to 300 gallons. An additional fifty gallons per entrant was available for qualifying tries. If all fifty gallons allocated for qualifying weren't used, it could be added to the allotment for carburetion day. So as not to unfairly punish those cars with rookie drivers, an additional twelve and a half gallons were allocated so that the drivers could take their rookie tests.[18]

The first mishap of the year occurred before the track was officially opened. The opening practice session was about to start, but the light indicating the opening of the track had not yet been changed from yellow to green. Anxious to be the first driver on the track, Mike Hiss and Tom Bigelow started driving their cars toward the track, causing Walt Myers, a seasoned track steward, to fall as he tried to get out of their way, breaking a hip and a wrist.[19]

In an effort to control the speeds at the Speedway, USAC required the use of a manifold relief valve, also known as a "pop-off valve," to regulate the amount of boost from the turbocharger. The valve was developed by Paul Baynes, an engineer at the Allison division of General Motors who also served on USAC's technical committee. The requirement was that the valve be set to eighty inches of mercury.[20]

Setting the pace on the opening day at the Speedway was Bobby Unser, establishing a new record for the first day of practice with a speed of 188.294.[21]

Because of the gas rationing, the Speedway also shortened the qualification period to two days, resulting in new qualifying procedures. On the first day of qualifications, the Speedway had two qualifying periods—the first from 11:00 a.m. until 2:30 p.m. and the second period began at 2:30 p.m.[22] The rule was that everyone in line at 11:00 a.m. would have a chance to make a qualifying run for the pole.[23] If there was a break in the line between the two periods, then the fastest car from the first qualifying period would occupy the pole. If there was no break in the line between the two periods, then the fastest car of the day would win the pole position.[24]

Qualifying day opened under cloudy skies with twenty-four racers in line at 11:00 a.m. waiting to make their qualifying run for the pole. At 12:25 p.m. the skies opened and showers stopped qualifying for three hours, forty minutes. Qualifying resumed briefly but was ended at 4:20 p.m. when rains again soaked the track. Only fourteen racers were able to take a qualifying run, leaving ten still to have a shot at the pole. The fastest for the day was A. J. Foyt with an average speed of 191.632 miles per hour. But he would have to wait until the remaining racers took their qualifying runs to see if he would sit on the pole.[25]

In between the two qualifying periods, the infield crowd in the first turn became rowdy. What had been a day of fun with drinking beer, occasional streakers and blanket tossing of spectators turned ugly when one person climbed the chain-link fence separating the infield from the track. When a policeman ordered the person to not climb the fence, the person responded by throwing a beer bottle, striking the officer. This turned into a melee when state troopers arrested the person responsible for throwing the beer bottle. The crowd responded by throwing beer bottles and shouting vulgarities at the officers. Eleven were injured and fourteen were arrested.[26]

Provisionally qualifying on the first row was Wally Dallenbach in a car with an oversized turbocharger. The turbocharger overrode the pop-off valve, and the car allegedly got more than the eighty inches of mercury in boost. Competitors howled to the press that Dallenbach's car had not followed the rules. Billy Vukovich, son of the famous driver who had been killed in the 1955 Indianapolis 500, fumed,

> I say they cheated. I'm running my tail off out there trying to go 183 mph and he (Dallenbach) isn't running any harder than I am and he's going five miles an hour faster. As far as I'm concerned, he doesn't have any business on the front row. His qualification should be thrown out, he should be fined $10,000 and be disqualified for breaking the rule.

Despite the turmoil and public complaints, the competitors failed to file a timely protest with USAC officials. In an interesting twist, Frank DelRoy, chair of USAC's Technical Committee, was aware of what the oversized turbocharger could do and that the pop-off valve could not properly monitor the engine boost. But since the rules did not address the size of the blower, track officials could not instigate an investigation. DelRoy explained, "If someone had filed a protest right after he finished the run, we could have impounded the car, run tests on it and established whether or not he was getting more than 80 inches of boost. But nobody did. Now it's too late. We can't prove now what they ran on Saturday."

George Bignotti, crew chief for Dallenbach's car, now had a problem. By using the oversized turbocharger, the car had provisionally qualified for the first row of the race. But to use the configuration in the race would increase fuel consumption during the race. As the amount of fuel which could be used in the race was limited, Bignotti approached USAC officials to allow him to use a smaller turbocharger in the race than used in qualifying. His request was denied as it would change the configuration used in qualifying.[27]

Bignotti continued to plead his case both in the newspaper and to USAC officials. In protest, he said, "I read in the paper that I freely acknowledge the blower overrode the pop off valve and that we got 106 more horsepower than with the smaller blower. I never said that to anyone—because we simply don't know. We didn't have any time to run any test on the blower. This is not an 'oversized' blower because there are no specifications about the blower." Bignotti continued, "This whole thing is sort of ridiculous. Everyone here knows that the pop off valve was supposed to make everything equal for everybody. But it doesn't; it definitely favors the Ford engine—yet nobody screams about that. I don't like to go to a racetrack knowing I'm going to get blown off by 8 to 10 miles an hour by another car, like Foyt's, because he has an advantage we don't have, so we have to find some way to compensate for it and we take a chance on something new and it works and all of a sudden we're bad guys."

Bignotti continued, "Nobody knows if the blower actually overrides the pop off valve like everybody is saying because there have been no tests made. I'm going to ask Tom Binford (the chief steward at the Speedway) to come over to our shop and we'll hook up the blower to an engine on the dyno and measure it and see what happens."[28] Despite the protests, the Speedway denied the request to run with a smaller turbocharger in the race. Bignotti had just a few days to figure out how to run the race with the larger turbocharger and still be within the fuel limitations.

On the second weekend of qualifying, rains again plagued the track. After the third period of qualifying, A. J. Foyt knew he was sitting on the pole. And by the close of the second and final day of qualifying, there was a full field. But this, too, was controversial.

There were still eleven cars which had not made a qualifying run. At the conclusion of the qualifying period, the impacted car owners and drivers asked Joe Cloutier for additional qualifying time. Cloutier's response was that the entry form did not require the Speedway to provide additional qualifying time if the field was filled. Additionally, he indicated that Johnny Rutherford had made a second qualifying run which "broke" the qualifying line. Cloutier indicated that Speedway management might reconsider if every qualified car owner signed an affidavit that they were willing for qualifications to be reopened and that the affidavits had to be presented by noon the following day.[29]

Longtime race car sponsor Lindsey Hopkins said, "I had a car driven by Mel Kenyon toward the end of the line on the second day of qualifications and it looked like the 6 p.m. deadline would prevent Kenyon's qualification attempt. I began to hear that the second qualification attempt by the 94 car would break the line and cause the session to end at 6 p.m." He asked Cloutier about the break in the line and was told to "read the fine print." Hopkins continued, "I thought for years that we (car owners and race officials in Speedway management) had a gentleman's agreement that we all get a chance to qualify."[30]

The likelihood of getting every qualified car owner to sign the affidavit was slim—there was no incentive for those at the back of the field to jeopardize their starting position in the field of thirty-three. The response from the Roy Woods Racing Team was to hire an attorney, Wright Hugus, to represent their interests. Hugus, who wasn't licensed to practice in Indiana, hired Indianapolis attorney Don Tabbert as co-counsel.

Representing six of the impacted teams, Hugus attempted to get Cloutier to reopen the qualifying period and proposed three extra spots be added to the field for the race. This suggestion was rejected by the Speedway. He then threatened, "Probably the first thing we could do is to go to court and ask for an injunction against the race and I can think of at least eight other legal actions we can take. But we don't want to do that. All we want is for every car to have at least one try at qualifications."[31]

Hulman said, "I feel terrible about this, nobody feels worse than I do. I would like to see everybody get a chance. I think this means we will go back to four days of qualifying next year." But Hulman was unwilling to allow additional qualifying. When asked about an additional qualifying period this year, Hulman replied, "Oh, no. We have a contract to fulfill. If we would allow this, we would open ourselves to all sorts of actions. The line was broken. The people who qualified before the deadline certainly deserve consideration."[32]

On May 20, Hugus announced the filing of an injunction to stop the race until all racing teams had a chance to qualify. In the suit filed on behalf of those racers denied a chance to qualify for the race, not only did Hugus and Tabbert request an injunction from the race being run, but they also requested $1 million in damages. The suit was heard by the Honorable Frank A. Symmes, Jr., Marion County Superior Court. Testifying on behalf of the Speedway were Hulman and Cloutier. Binford, testifying on behalf of USAC, said that when Johnny Parsons, Jr., made a second attempt at qualifying, the line was broken and the Speedway and USAC were not obligated to extend the qualification period.

Tabbert and Hugus also claimed a breach of contract. Tabbert had requested Hulman bring the entry forms for the five plaintiffs as well as financial records for the Speedway for the past four years. Not surprisingly, Hulman failed to produce the financial records in accordance with the long-standing policy of no financial or attendance disclosure. The Speedway attorney officially responded that the financial records were not germane to the case. While Hulman was testifying, Tabbert pointedly asked him about the cost of reopening the qualification period. Hulman's response was a noncommittal "Something in between someplace." The Speedway and USAC also requested a change in venue.[33]

Henry Ryder, representing USAC and the Speedway, filed a motion that the plaintiffs had not exhausted the appeal process with USAC and therefore did not have the right to file suit. Judge Symmes dismissed the case based upon a technicality. He specifically stated that he was not making any judgments on the merits of the case.[34]

With the legal case's dismissal, the plaintiffs filed an appeal with USAC for qualifications to be reopened. Representing USAC, Dick King, director of competition, said, "I regret that I must reject the appeal of the protest on May 18. USAC rules required that appeals must be filed by midnight the third day following the incident. You had until midnight May 21 to file. Instead, you decided to file legal action in state court. The president of USAC was prepared to immediately convene an appeals board to hear your arguments. However, I must reject your appeal because it was not filed on time."

Not surprisingly, Tabbert didn't agree with the ruling. He protested, "We feel the appeal time limit should have started when written notice was delivered from USAC to the entrants at 11 a.m. last Monday. The three-day limit would then have ended at midnight Thursday and King was served with an appeal notice by 8:45 p.m. Thursday."[35] Although the race would go on as scheduled, Tabbert subsequently refiled the $1 million damage case.[36]

After all of the drama leading up to the race, it was run on schedule. Hulman had changed the date of the Indianapolis 500 to the Sunday before Memorial Day, giving fans a travel day to the track and also providing a rain day.[37] Winning the 1974 race was Johnny Rutherford, who started in the twenty-fifth position, with an average speed of 158.589 miles per hour.[38]

Construction was beginning on the long-dreamed-about larger Indianapolis Motor Speedway Museum in 1975,[39] and the oil embargo had ended. A sense of normalcy was returning to the nation and the Indianapolis Motor Speedway.

1975

After the controversy over rain-shortened qualifications in 1974, the Speedway returned to four days of qualifying for 1975. On the first day, twenty-five racers made qualifying attempts and twenty-two earned a spot in the field. Sitting on the pole was A. J. Foyt, who tied Rex May's record of being on the pole four times. Foyt's average speed for the qualifying run was 193.976, significantly below the fastest qualification run which was made by Johnny Rutherford in 1973. It was also the first time that the front row was occupied by prior winners of the Indy 500—Foyt, Gordon Johncock and Bobby Unser.[40]

After two tumultuous years, the month of May passed with very little drama. Race day opened with hot temperatures and rains once again threatening. Temperatures on the track reached 150 degrees as the race progressed. The favorite to win the race, A. J. Foyt, was plagued by running out of gas as well as a blistered tire taking him out of contention.

Tom Sneva had a spectacular crash after tangling with Eldon Rasmussen's car on lap 125 in which Sneva's engine was ripped from the car as the car cartwheeled down the track in flames hitting the wall in turn 2. Sneva sustained second-degree burns to his hands, face, back, chest and legs when he was pinned under the car for several minutes.

Once again, the race was rain shortened. With sixty-five miles to go, the skies opened up with a deluge. Before race officials could red-flag the race, seven racers found themselves spinning on the suddenly wet track. Bobby Unser won his second Indianapolis 500 with an average speed of 149.213 miles per hour. He had led only eleven laps during the race.[41]

Once again, crashes at the end of the race led to criticism of Speedway officials. The Electro Pacer system did not have red lights to stop the race. Many felt that if red lights were part of the Electro Pacer system, the race would have stopped in a quicker fashion and the crashes might have been prevented.[42]

1976

Prior to the racetrack opening in 1976, Clarence Cagle's crew was busy not only with normal maintenance around the track but also repairing the track after a particularly rough winter. Cagle said, "The winter was not the easiest on the track. It was up and down and it cracked the asphalt. We're cutting away these places where the asphalt has parted and are replacing them with new material. Then there is the regular maintenance on the fences, walls and stands and we've repaved the north side and the back of the garage area." The Speedway had also upgraded the Electro-Pacer system to include red lights.[43]

As the racetrack opened for practice in 1976, finishing touches were also being made to the Indianapolis Motor Speedway Museum, which would open later in the month.

Hulman was an honoree at the Twin Tony Awards sponsored by the Indianapolis Chamber of Commerce. The other honoree was Butler University's Tony Hinkle, the longtime basketball coach. Earlier in the day, Hulman had attended an award event for the Hulman Classic sprint car race in Terre Haute and had flown into the Indianapolis airport. He unfortunately got lost on the trip from the airport to the award ceremonies and arrived about thirty seconds before the event concluded. In apologizing for his tardiness and accepting the award, Hulman said,

> I'm terribly sorry. The fact of the matter is I got lost between the airport and here. I thought I could [get] right down here but somehow I made a wrong turn—it must have taken me an hour to get here from the airport. I don't know what Tony (Hinkle) has said or hasn't said about receiving this award—but I'd like to second his words, if he made any. If not, it is a great honor for me to receive this.[44]

Making headlines was the appearance of Janet Guthrie as a rookie race driver at the historic track.[45] After having driven earlier in the year in Trenton, New Jersey, completing the race in fifteenth place, she was offered a ride at Indianapolis.[46] Due to issues with the car, she did not complete her rookie tests, and the car was withdrawn from the race.

Another rookie, Eddie Miller, wasn't as fortunate. According to witnesses, he was not in the groove when his car was coming out of the first turn. He lost control of the car, and it lost traction when it hit the dirt. The car jumped over the two fences separating the track from the spectators. The car ended upside down and Miller suffered a broken neck. Amazingly, he did not die or suffer from paralysis. In the crash, the car came within two feet of the tunnel through which cars enter the infield and within ten feet of spectators.[47]

Clarence Cagle and his maintenance crew responded to the crash overnight by building a catch fence from nine-gauge farmer's fencing between the first and second turns. This brought a protest from some drivers, the most vocal of whom was Gordon Johncock, who said, "It would have been better if they hadn't put anything there rather than what they have. That thing is more dangerous than nothing at all." Cagle responded, "I would have liked to put guard rail in but we had none available. I was on the telephone all afternoon trying to locate some. If we can locate some, we'll put it in. But I want to do the job right."

Johncock would rather have had a concrete barrier than the catch fence. His explanation was, "I'd rather see a concrete wall there than anything else. All I know is if a car were to get into the fence sideways and hit one of the posts, it would bend the car right around the driver. What they ought to do is take out the grass, blacktop it all the way and put in a cement wall." This suggestion wasn't well received by Cagle, who said, "Huh-uh. We had a cement wall there once and everybody complained about it and we dug it out. I like a double guard rail flush with the ground and up about 32 inches. If we can get hold of some, we'll put it in."[48]

The drivers and Cagle were in agreement that the solution wasn't the best one. Chief Steward Tom Binford also didn't think it was a good solution but believed it was a good temporary measure. Cagle continued his search for double guard rail. After qualifications closed, Cagle's crew ripped out the catch fence and installed double guard rail. Cagle said, "We found some and ordered it in. This is what I wanted to use in the first place—but it's not the easiest thing in the world to locate in a hurry." But the planned improvements to the track between turns 1 and 2 were not completed. Cagle explained, "The drainage ditch will be filled in and the guard rails will be thoroughly tested and certified. I didn't want to use just any kind of barrier—only something that had been certified and tested. The railing will be flush with the ground and extended about 32 inches high. This should keep any car from going underneath it."[49]

For the third time in four years, the race was shortened by rain. Johnny Rutherford won with an average speed of 148.425 miles per hour. The race was declared completed after 102 laps.[50]

1977

Clarence Cagle's crew had been busy making additional improvements to the Speedway for the opening of the 1977 race. The major improvement was repaving the track, including widening turns 2 and 3. The widening of the turns was in response to drivers' complaints. Another improvement was the addition of barbed wire on top of the concession stands and restrooms as some spectators would use the top of these facilities to view the action on the track.[51]

These would be the final improvements to the Speedway under the direction of Cagle. He had been at Hulman's side since the purchase of the Speedway in 1945. Initially, he was an assistant to Jack Fortner, the Speedway superintendent, during the initial work to get the Speedway open for the May 1946 race. When Fortner retired due to ill health, Cagle stepped into the role.

Cagle had been thinking about retiring for several years.

> I guess it was three or four years ago that I first thought about it. But I never got serious about it until 2 years ago. Finally, in February, 1976, I felt I should be honest with Mr. Hulman and I told him I would be leaving after the 1977 race.

At the time of his retirement, the only major structures which hadn't been replaced were Grandstand G in the southeast turn, most of the garages and the track hospital.[52] In his retirement announcement from the Speedway team after thirty-one years at the end of July 1977, he said, "I never said I wouldn't come back and help. I'd do anything to help Tony (Hulman). But I'm at a stage in life I don't want to work at it 12 months out of the year, and you can't run the place unless you're here 12 months out of the year."[53]

Two other familiar Indianapolis fixtures would be missing on race day. Longtime safety director Joe Quinn had died the previous winter.[54] Sid Collins, the familiar voice of the Indianapolis 500 broadcast heard by millions around the world, was discovered dead in his Indianapolis home. He had been despondent after having been diagnosed with Lou Gehrig's disease at the Mayo Clinic. An Indianapolis native, Collins had been a track announcer with the radio broadcast in 1948. When Indianapolis radio station WIBC started broadcasting the race from start to finish, Collins was named as the chief announcer. He was also the sports director for WIBC at the time of his death.[55]

When the track opened on May 7, 1977, the Speedway had eighty-five contestants, the second highest in the history of the Indianapolis 500.[56] Speculation was rampant of the impending fall of the 200-mile-per-hour barrier.

In tire tests prior to the opening of the track for practice, Gordon Johncock had unofficially gone over 200 miles per hour.[57] When the track opened, Janet Guthrie, the first woman to qualify for the race, set a pace of 185 miles

14. Tough Times at the Speedway

per hour in a practice session.[58] But Guthrie was not the first woman to drive on the Indianapolis Motor Speedway. Paula Murphy, who had set land speed records at the Bonneville Flats, tested tires for Goodyear at the Speedway in 1961.[59]

It was soon obvious the field was going to be very fast. The next day Gordon Johncock recorded an unofficial speed of 192.506 miles per hour.[60] Two days later, three former winners of the Indianapolis 500, Johnny Rutherford, Al Unser and Gordon Johncock, went over 196 miles per hour in practice. Of the twenty-four cars practicing on the Speedway on that day, seven went over 188 miles per hour.[61]

On May 11, the 200-mile-per-hour barrier was broken in a practice run by Mario Andretti at 200.311 miles per hour. Just minutes before the closing of the track for the day, he was joined by A. J. Foyt at 200.177 miles per hour.[62] When Johnny Rutherford turned a lap at the track of 200.624 miles per hour the next day, speculation in the garages centered on whether or not the regulator limiting the amount of boost from the turbocharger to eighty inches had contributed to the very fast speeds being driven at the Speedway. Most anticipated that qualifying speeds would be lower as the pop-off valve would be required.[63]

That question was answered on the first day of qualifying when Tom Sneva, a former schoolteacher, took the pole position with an average speed of 198.884 miles per hour.[64] Although the qualifying speed was less than 200 miles per hour, his first and second laps had exceeded this mark at 200.401 and 200.535 miles per hour. He had slid through one of the turns on the second lap, brushing the wall with his left front wheel. After almost meeting with disaster, he intentionally eased off the accelerator for the third and fourth laps with speeds of 197.628 and 197.032 miles per hour respectively.[65]

Many fans were stymied by A. J. Foyt's low qualifying speed of 193.485 miles per hour. After the qualifying run, a required inspection by USAC officials revealed that the pop-off valve had malfunctioned. Foyt was permitted to have the pop-off valve replaced and to make a second qualifying run, the first in Speedway history. On the second run, he got into the field with a speed of 194.363 miles per hour.[66]

On the final day of qualifying, Janet Guthrie got into the field along with seven other drivers.[67] Salt Walther, the son of a wealthy car owner, was bumped from the field. That night, the Walmotor team, owned by Walther's father and brother, bought the race car owned by Lee Elkins for $60,000 in which Bill Puterbaugh had qualified for the race with an average speed of 186.800 miles per hour. Puterbaugh told associates that he had been bumped from his car. This was the first time that someone had apparently "bought" their way into the race.

Under USAC rules, Walther's father had the ability to replace the driver. The requirement was that a replacement or a relief driver have either significant championship car experience or have been a participant in the Indianapolis 500 in one of the prior two races and that the replacement driver had practiced at the racetrack in 1977. Walther met both of these conditions.[68]

The seller of the car, Elkins, explained that if the Walthers had not purchased the car, he would have made it available to other teams. In his seventies and confined to a wheelchair, Elkins' motivation was money. He had been unable to find any commercial sponsors to help defray the costs of sponsoring a racing team. He said, "I hope and I pray that everything he's (Puterbaugh) gotten out of this makes him No. 1 and that he can get the commercialism where he has value. But right now you couldn't get a bogus 3 cent stamp for him in sponsorship. I can't afford this. I love Billy Puterbaugh, but I need the money."

Despite the largess by his family, Salt Walther turned down the ride. He explained, "I have more respect for myself than to buy my way into the field. I appreciate what my father and my brother, Jeff, and the Foreman Corporation (his secondary sponsor) tried to do for me. But it's not fair. I just wouldn't feel right."[69]

Indianapolis 500 driver Tom Sneva, the pole sitter for the 1977 race, was playing a round of golf on the Speedway golf course when he sliced the ball. At the same time, Hulman was driving his car, and in a shot that would be nearly impossible to replicate, the ball sailed through the car's open window. Hulman jokingly reminded Sneva that payday wasn't until Monday, waved and drove on.[70]

On Friday morning before the race, Hulman stood on the steps of the Indiana Soldiers and Sailors Monument in downtown Indianapolis and started a half marathon which would become a traditional part of the month-long 500 Festival. The race went from downtown Indianapolis to the Indianapolis Museum of Art before concluding at the Indianapolis Motor Speedway. Frank Shorter, a two-time Olympic winner, took the checkered flag being waved by Indianapolis 500 chief starter, Pat Vidan.[71]

Hulman faced a challenge with the beginning of the race. He was always nervous and wrote down what he would say to start the race, despite having uttered the familiar words since 1956. His challenge, of course, was the inclusion of Janet Guthrie in the field. As the crowd at the Speedway listened, Hulman said, "In company with the first woman ever to qualify Indianapolis, gentlemen, start your engines."[72]

Winning the 1977 race was A. J. Foyt, making him the first driver to win four races. The race had been a duel between Gordon Johncock and Foyt. Johncock had led for 125 laps when his engine quit on lap 186. Johncock had felt he was going to win the race. "I thought we had it in the bag. The last two laps I ran were the fastest we'd gone since early in the race and I don't think A. J. could have got by me." Foyt didn't think Johncock would win the race. He said, "I was savin' everything I had for one last bonzai and I don't think he [Johncock] could have stopped me. But I'm not saying that it wouldn't have been close."[73]

Among the people happy for Foyt at the Speedway was Hulman. As he waited for Foyt's car to roll into the Winner's Circle beneath the control tower, Hulman enthused, "Yes, this is my biggest thrill." For the first time, he gave the winning driver a kiss which landed on Foyt's helmet.[74] Hulman also enjoyed riding around the track with Foyt in the victory lap in the pace car.

Foyt's car had been specifically constructed for the Indianapolis 500 and had raced in both the 1976 and 1977 campaigns. After winning the race, Foyt donated the car to the Indianapolis Motor Speedway Museum with the proviso the car could continue to be used by Foyt for the remainder of the season as his backup car. In making the donation public, Foyt said, "That car no longer

Hulman and A. J. Foyt circling the Speedway in the pace car after Foyt won his fourth Indianapolis 500 in 1977 (Indianapolis Motor Speedway).

belongs to me. It belongs to the Indianapolis Motor Speedway. It was built especially for this race. It won at Pocono in 1975 but it was built for here. I drove it here last year and it was the same car today. It had the same engine in it that was in it a year ago. We didn't even take it out of the chassis until about four months ago."[75]

Hulman, who had owned the track for the past thirty-two years, had witnessed an evolution of the track and race cars. He was then seventy-six years old, long beyond when most people retire. And he had other business interests besides the Indianapolis Motor Speedway—the Coca-Cola Bottling Company of Indianapolis, Princeton Farms, extensive real estate holdings, the Hulman Foundation which owned among other things a media network consisting of both broadcast and print as well as significant gas company holdings. Wasn't he ready to relax, to turn it over to the next generation? This question was posed by his cousin, Don Smith. Fully energized by the Speedway, Hulman indicated he was looking forward to next year's race.

Six months later, Hulman would die at St. Vincent Hospital in Indianapolis where he had been rushed because of a ruptured aorta. The track continues under the stewardship of his family.

In a 1973 interview, Cloutier reflected on why the Indianapolis 500 was so successful under Hulman's leadership. "I think another reason for the success here, and everyone has come to believe it, is that we're not trying to bleed out as much profit as possible. We're not taking anything out of it. It's actually more of a civic operation. Sure we want to make money. If we didn't make money, we couldn't go on building grandstands and museums. It's a private enterprise and it's still operated as such, but we still have a lot of help from the community because they believe we operate the Speedway to serve the people."[76]

15

IMS Museum

As early as 1947, Hulman was thinking about establishing a museum focusing on racing cars and accessories, including those Indianapolis-manufactured nameplates—Marmon, National, Stutz and Duesenberg. At the 1947 Hundred Mile an Hour Club dinner honoring those drivers who completed an Indianapolis 500 race with an average speed greater than 100 miles per hour, Hulman disclosed his idea: "I have felt for some time that there should be some place where fans could see the historic cars and trophies of American auto racing history. There is also the need for a clubhouse at the track, and it might be combined with the museum in one building."[1]

Quietly, the museum began to take shape. Management believed that there was an interest as an estimated 250,000 dropped by annually just to see the track. Wilbur Shaw commented, "It has always been our desire to build a shrine to speed. There has never been a place where the importance of auto racing is recognized. Such a museum could add materially to the plant."

As part of the rejuvenation of the Speedway, Hulman decided that when they replaced Grandstand R a museum would be constructed as part of the replacement structure. As the oldest grandstand on the property, Grandstand R was next on the list for replacement when a section of another grandstand collapsed in 1949 during qualifications. Needing the seating for the race, the Speedway spent several thousand dollars refurbishing it for the race. As Hulman wanted the Speedway to be self-sustaining, the demolition and replacement of Grandstand R was put on hold, making the timing of a potential Speedway Museum uncertain.[2]

Hulman began collecting vintage automobiles and race cars around 1954. Karl Kizer, a veteran of the Speedway and riding mechanic with Earl Cooper in 1916, told of the quail-hunting trip shortly after Wilbur Shaw's death:

> We almost didn't go on that trip. But we planned it for so long, and he was always so enthusiastic about going, we decided to make it sort of a memorial to him. We talked about everything under the sun on that trip. But we always came back to the thing we couldn't get off our minds—Shaw's loss. He was such a great credit to the sport, and Hulman relied on him for everything where the Speedway was concerned. It was Shaw, who talked Hulman into buying the dilapidated old Speedway. If Shaw hadn't been successful ... well, we probably wouldn't have an Indianapolis 500 today.

Kizer broached an idea to Hulman. "You know how we could really memorialize Wilbur? We could build a museum on the Speedway grounds and dedicate it to Wilbur's memory." Hulman quizzed Kizer about the museum, "Who's going to take care of it?" Kizer replied, "I'll do what I can." Kizer reported Hulman agreed immediately.[3]

Hulman recalled the beginning of the collection: "About the time Wilbur Shaw died and we thought we wanted to preserve his auto. So we did get Wilbur's car and restore it and from then on we started."

Kizer, the owner of Century Tire in Indianapolis, became the driving force behind the museum and its curator. Kizer recalled how he purchased Shaw's "pay car," the Maserati in which Shaw won the 1939 and 1940 Indianapolis 500. "I came back to Indianapolis and went right to St. Paul and bought the Shaw car. I had to buy three and a half cars to get that one. I paid $3,750. Those are the cheapest cars we've ever bought."

Kizer also provided some cars from his personal collection. His collection began with a car built by Harry Miller and Harry Hartz which won the 1932 Indianapolis 500, driven by Fred Frame. In addition to the tire business, he also operated a machine shop which did a lot of work for various participants in the race. He was owed approximately $900 for a repair job by the owners of the car. In settlement of the debt, the car's owners offered to sell Kizer the car. Although he didn't want it, Kizer counteroffered $600 plus the car. When Kizer went to work for Tony Hulman, Hulman purchased Century Tire, and this car became part of the Speedway Museum's collection.[4]

The Speedway offices traditionally had been in downtown Indianapolis. When Hulman made the decision to relocate the offices to the track, the new administrative building contained space for the museum as part of the design. On July 25, 1955, with approximately 100 in attendance, Mari Hulman (Hulman's daughter), Boots Shaw (Wilbur Shaw's widow) and Bob Sweikert (1955 Indianapolis 500 winner) turned the first shovels of dirt for the new building.[5] By March 1956, the new administrative building was completed. The 7,200-

square-foot building cost $125,000 and included the ticket office, the accounting office and the museum.[6]

While the building was under construction, Kizer wanted to add two historic cars to the collection—the Marmon Wasp driven to victory in the inaugural Indianapolis 500 in 1911 and the National driven to victory in 1912 by Joe Dawson. Kizer was able to find both autos, and the owners were willing to sell them to the Speedway.[7]

When the Museum opened in April 1956, the displays were limited but included six racing cars. Included among the racing cars was Shaw's Maserati which won the Indianapolis 500 in 1939 and 1940, the Marmon Wasp which won the inaugural race, and the Miller-Hartz Special driven by Fred Frame to victory in 1932.[8] The Miller-Hartz Special raced at Indianapolis until 1947.[9] Unique racing cars on display included the Cummins Diesel Special which started the race from the pole position in 1952; the Junior Eight Special, the first front-drive race car which finished second in 1925; and the sixteen-cylinder, double-engine Sampson Special.[10] The Sampson Special's engine was built for Frank Lockhart's world speed record attempt at Daytona.[11] With a strong connection to the Speedway, Firestone Tire & Rubber also had a display showing the evolution of racing tires from 1911.

The museum also featured photographs of the thirty-three winners of the Indianapolis 500 and the Wheeler-Schebler Trophy.[12] The Wheeler-Schebler Company, manufacturer of carburetors, commissioned Tiffany's to create a seven-foot-tall silver vase at a cost of $10,000, to be presented to the winner of the 300-mile Wheeler-Schebler race at the first weekend of racing at the Speedway in 1909. Frank Wheeler, one of the founders of the Indianapolis Motor Speedway, was one of the owners of Wheeler-Schebler.[13]

By 1959, the Indianapolis Motor Speedway had 250,000 visitors annually to the museum, with May having an estimated 100,000 visitors. The collection had expanded to include an 1898 Canada quadracycle similar to the one purchased by Indianapolis Motor Speedway co-founder, Carl Fisher. Fisher had the first horseless carriage in Indianapolis. Also belonging to Fisher and a part of the collection was the 1903 Premier built specifically for the Vanderbilt Cup. This car was too heavy to qualify for the Vanderbilt Cup race despite having numerous holes drilled in the chassis in an attempt to lighten it.[14]

Over time, the collection of racing cars grew. Kizer talked about the excitement with each new acquisition: "I'll tell you, every time we found another car Tony [Hulman] and I were like kids at Christmas party. We couldn't wait to get our hands on our latest prize."[15]

In 1963 Hulman purchased a 14.9-acre property on the south side of 16th Street across from the Speedway for a new museum building. The plot was sold by the city at an auction. Although there were two other bidders present at the auction, Hulman was the only one to submit a bid of $100,000.[16] At the time, the Speedway Museum had on display seventeen race cars including a 1902 Panhard believed to be the first specially designed race car, the Duesenberg which Eddie Rickenbacker drove in 1914 and the Fuel Injection Special driven to victory by Bill Vukovich in 1953 and 1954.

Accessories on display included the first American crash helmet and the first rearview mirror fashioned by Ray Harroun for the Marmon Wasp.[17] The inspiration for the rearview mirror on the Wasp came when Harroun, a chauffeur to William Thorne, the president of Montgomery Ward, saw a cabbie driving a horse-drawn taxicab use a similar type of instrument in Chicago.[18] The driver had attached a mirror to a pole, which he used to check for bicycles coming from behind. Without room for a riding mechanic in the Wasp, Harroun faced expulsion from the race. He reasoned that if he could fashion a mirror for the car, he would not need a riding mechanic.[19]

By 1966, the museum was bursting at the seams with holdings of eighty-five racing cars, eleven of which won the Indianapolis 500. One of the racers in the collection is the car driven by Eddie Rickenbacker in the 1914 race. Kizer told the story of its discovery:

> Someone told my brother Howard that there was an old Indy car up near Farmland, Indiana. I thought it was another wild goose chase. But when we got up there, we found the largest four-cylinder engine Fred Duesenberg ever built, 360 cubic inches. You could've knocked me over with a feather. It turned out this was one of the original Mason cars from the 1911 and 1912 Indianapolis 500 races. Duesenberg entered it under his own name in '13 and '14, with Eddie Rickenbacker finishing 10th in it in '14. As far as we know, it's the only one left like it in the world. Finding it sure was a great surprise.[20]

They also had a collection of eighty-eight or eighty-nine vintage automobiles. The size of the collection permitted the displays at the museum to be rotated. Approximately half of the vintage automobiles were displayed at the Early Wheels Museum, also owned by Hulman, in Terre Haute.

Many of the race cars in the collection showed signs of wear, tear and age when acquired. Kizer told the tale of one such car. "We found Mauri Rose's Blue Crown Special, which he drove to victory in 1947 and 1948, in a Texas field. It had been trampled by cows. It was in terrible condition, but we managed to salvage it."[21] To do the restorations on the race cars, averaging two per year, the Speedway had two expert mechanics, Bill Spoerle and Barney Wimmer, on staff.[22]

The Chevrolet division of General Motors donated an experimental car, the Corvette SS, to the Speedway Museum. The Corvette, the first to make use of lightweight component materials, ran the twelve-hour Sebring in 1957.[23]

By 1971, the museum had added the first rear-engine race car, a 1937 Gulf-Miller. This car was one of three constructed. Not only was this car the first with a rear engine, but it also had disc brakes, an independent suspension and side-mounted fuel tanks. It set sixteen American and fourteen international speed records at the Bonneville Flats. The car was entered in the 1938 Indianapolis 500; however it did not qualify.

John Ley, part of the engineering team for the car, recalled its arrival at the Speedway in 1938. "When we got to the track, everyone was astonished to see the engine behind the driver's seat inclined at a 45-degree angle."

Although the car was ahead of its time, it never ran at Indianapolis. Ley explained,

> In 1939, one car crashed in practice and the other dropped out with a broken valve spring, but in 1940, we were ready. That year, the Miller was faster than anything at Indy. With four-wheel drive, we could run in any groove on the track but George Bailey, one of our drivers, was killed in the practice accident and we withdrew the other car. Then the American Automobile Association which sanctioned the Indianapolis 500, made us take the pontoon tanks off the car and it ruined the aerodynamics so it never ran right afterward.[24]

Needing more space and wanting to consolidate the collection, Hulman planned a larger museum. After several years of planning and two years of construction, the 96,960-square-foot building of cement and Wyoming quartz opened in 1975.[25] Kizer, the museum curator, said of the collection, "We go back to 1896 with the race cars. Most of them (other collectors) don't go anywhere near that far. And there is no place in the world that needs them more than here." Kizer continued, "If I knew where a good car was that we need we sure as the devil would be after it."[26] The museum cost $5,500,000 to build.[27]

For those visiting the Indianapolis Motor Speedway, one of the highlights is frequently a bus ride around the fabled two-and-a-half-mile oval. Hulman recollected how the tours by bus began. One cold, snowy winter day, he looked out of the Speedway windows to see two women determined to see the famous oval. Bundled to shield themselves against the cold windy day, they were trudging to take a look at the track. "They were dressed in black, the wind was whistling, six inches of snow on the ground, walking over to that grandstand. I thought, 'Good Lord. Those poor creatures. By golly, around here it seems like we could be considerate enough to have a heated bus or something so for a nominal fee we could take anybody around the track.' We ordered a little bus within a week or two after that."[28] The bus tours around the Speedway began in February 1960.[29]

16

F. W. Cook Brewing

Many associate beer with the influx of Germanic settlers during the mid-1800s, but beer came to America with the Jamestown Settlement in 1607. The beer was of the English variety—stout, porter and various ales.[1] The early settlers, concerned about the quality of water, used a variety of alcoholic beverages as their primary drink. Most beer was brewed in the home for home consumption.[2]

The immigration of German-speaking peoples to the United States introduced the lighter lager beer popular in Germany. Unlike the British beer, lager beer required constant chilling. The yeast, brought from Germany, fermented the beverage from the top.[3] Many Germanic people settled in the Midwest in towns such as Cincinnati, St. Louis, Milwaukee and Chicago. On a smaller scale, Evansville, Indiana, had a thriving German population.

The Old Brewery, established by Jacob Reis and Fred Kroener[4] in 1837 near the town of Lamasco, was southern Indiana's first brewery.[5] F. W. Cook Brewing, established in 1853 by Jacob Reis' son, Louis, and his stepson, Frederick W. Cook, was originally called Cook & Reis City Brewery even though the original facility was in a cornfield.[6] By 1860, Evansville had ten breweries.[7]

Cook was born in Washington, D.C., in 1832. While the family was relocating to Cincinnati, Ohio, that same year, his father died. His mother married Jacob Reis, and the family moved to Evansville, Indiana, in 1836. Like many young men of that era, Cook's education was very limited, with about eighteen months spread over six years. His first brewery experience was employment by Jacob Reis at a small brewery operation.[8]

The Cook & Reis City Brewery was initially capitalized with $330, with a $165 contribution from each of the partners. Louis Reis contributed his share while Cook's share was provided by his stepfather, Jacob Reis. Louis Reis was in charge of the brewery operations while Cook, who had attended the Anderson Collegiate Institute at New Albany, Indiana, was in charge of the business operations.[9]

In 1857, Reis sold his interest to his brother and was paid $3,500.[10] A year later, the brewery brewed the first lager beer in Indiana and added a malt house.[11] The partnership continued to operate until Jacob Reis died from injuries sustained in an accident in May 1872.[12] Cook continued to operate the brewery as a sole proprietorship.[13] At the time Cook took control of the business, it was producing 17,000 barrels of beer annually.[14]

With westward expansion, Evansville's location on the Ohio River led to it being a major stopping point. The town nearly doubled in population between 1860 and 1870. By 1870 Evansville had fifteen breweries and an estimated population of 21,000. Most breweries were short-lived, and by 1880, only the two oldest and strongest remained.[15]

In 1885, the brewery changed its ownership structure from a sole proprietorship to a corporation, and the name was changed to F. W. Cook Brewing Company. Ownership centered around the Cook family (Fred Sr. and his children, Fred Jr. and Henry E.) and senior management, including George Daussman (secretary and treasurer), Andrew Wollenburger (superintendent), Henry Foerlich (chief engineer), Phillip P. Puder (general agent) and Gus B. Mann.

The primary beer produced was a pilsner beer with the primary market being the Evansville area and the southern states. It is estimated that in 1889, the brewery produced 75,000 barrels of beer.[16] With the need for ice to cool the beer, following an industry trend, an ammonia compression machine was installed to make ice[17] and was essential for the growth of the brewery. By 1890, there were three breweries in Evansville, with Cook's production of 75,000 barrels significantly outpacing Fulton Avenue Brewery (50,000 barrels) and Hartmetz Brewery (25,000 barrels).[18]

Beginning in the 1870s, the beer industry in America began to consolidate. With a severe industrial downturn in Britain, British financiers looked abroad for investment opportunities. The first entrée into the American beer industry for the British was the consolidation of several New York breweries in 1888.[19] With the aging of the ownership and management of F. W. Cook, the owners sought to sell their interest. A British concern, F. W. Cook Brewing Company Ltd., was established to take over ownership of the brewery in January 1, 1892.[20]

One of the primary dangers at a brewery is fire, often is attributable to the heating of the mash during the brewing process. In December 1891, the brewery and offices were destroyed by fire. By March 1893, the new brewery had been constructed, with the capacity to produce 300,000 barrels of beer.[21]

One of the strategies used by British-owned breweries to drive their competitors out of business was severe price cutting. This tactic was used by F. W. Cook, resulting in the Fulton Avenue Brewery, Hartmetz & Sons and Evansville Brewing Company banding together to form the Evansville Brewing Association. In subsequent years, this brewery would become Sterling Brewers, F. W. Cook's primary competition in Evansville.[22]

By 1917, the brewery had been expanded to a capacity of 500,000 barrels of beer and had developed a national reputation for their "Goldblume" beer. It was the largest privately owned brewery in Evansville. The brewery also established a German room where people could drink not only Goldblume but other beers it produced.[23] But all was not rosy for the beer industry.

The anti-saloon league organized a march on Washington, D.C., with over 4,000 participants bearing a resolution for a constitutional amendment prohibiting the sale of alcoholic beverages. A vote in the U.S. Congress in December 1914 had 197 in favor of prohibition and 190 against. Since the amendment did not pass by a two-thirds majority, it did not go for a second vote.[24]

When the United States entered World War I, Congress passed the Lever Act on August 10, 1917. Section 15 of the act states, "No foods, fruits, food materials, or feeds shall be used in the production of distilled spirits for beverage purposes. Nor shall there be imported into the United States any distilled spirits." Under Food Commissioner Herbert Hoover, the distilleries were closed in 1917. The following year, there was a significant crop failure which led to the closing of the breweries.[25]

Prohibition sentiments were traditionally strong in the Hoosier state. In 1853, Indiana had gone dry, only to be repealed by the legislature in 1855.[26] With the increasing national movement toward Prohibition, Indiana's legislature passed a statewide prohibition which became effective on April 2, 1918, resulting in the state going dry before the rest of the country.[27]

In September 1918, Congress passed a national Prohibition amendment which became effective in November 1918. On January 19, 1919, a constitutional amendment was passed banning the sale of any alcohol beverages.[28]

Those breweries which survived Prohibition did so by producing other items. Many breweries chose to produce "near beer." F. W. Cook Brewing clung on by producing ice during Prohibition. The Great Depression contributed significantly to the passage of the Volstead Act in 1933, permitting the manufacture of 3.2 percent beer in those states which did not have state dry laws.[29] Much of the testimony before Congress prior to the passing of the Volstead

Act focused on the impact of the thousands of jobs to be gained related to the production and sale of beer.[30]

It was an expensive proposition for a company to reenter the brewery business. The soft drink industry had changed during the Great Depression from primarily being consumed at soda fountains to home consumption in bottles. The bottling machinery used by the breweries prior to 1920 was obsolete and had to be replaced. Additionally, the growth of the automobile industry resulted in breweries needing to buy a fleet of delivery trucks.[31]

Thirty-one breweries began production during 1933. Within a year, the number of breweries had risen to 754,[32] including F. W. Cook. Although many breweries were returning to production, they faced an uphill climb. During Prohibition, the soft drink industry had expanded and for many people became the drink of choice. Additionally, during Prohibition, many people lost the habit of going to a tavern to drink beer. With the end of Prohibition and the acceptance of bottled beer, many consumers began drinking beer at home. When they did go to a tavern, the choice was to have a bottled beer rather than a draft beer, which had dominated prior to Prohibition.[33]

World War II also presented challenges to the breweries in terms of the labor supply and a shortage of materials. Initially, the shortage was of crowns for the bottles. By mid–1942, the industry was concerned that the War Production Board might prohibit the sale of bottled beer. Ultimately, the packaging of beer in cans was prohibited except for that sent to the military.[34] Despite the challenges the industry experienced during World War II, beer consumption increased from 53 million barrels in 1942 to 80 million barrels in 1945.[35]

Following World War II, the British owners of F. W. Cook announced an expansion program. By November 1949, a cornerstone had been laid by Charles Schwab, the chairman of F. W. Cook, and John Neubling, an employee of the company for fifty-five years. The project with an estimated cost of $2 million would double capacity.[36]

The company also decided to package beer in cans for the first time.[37] This followed an industry trend which started in 1935 when the American Can Company and Krueger Brewing Company of Newark, New Jersey, introduced canned beer. Consumers liked canned beer as it was lighter to carry and did not have to be returned to the store for the return of a deposit. Additionally, consumers felt reassured by the sanitary benefits of canned beer since the cans had not been previously used.[38] By June 1948, the company had installed seven new electric engines, replacing three old gas-powered engines. It was also announced that the firm would tear down the old one-story office building and replace it with a new five-story brewhouse and office.[39]

By February 1949, it appeared the financial investors in the brewery were readying it for a buyer. For many years, the president of the company representing the British and New York owners was Charles Schwab. Over the next several months, a series of announcements were made strengthening local management.

The first announcement in February 1949 was the hiring of L. C. Holm as controller. He had extensive experience in the brewery business, having been the controller and later an assistant to the president of G. Heileman Brewing Company of LaCross, Wisconsin. Two months later, the firm hired O. L. Forster as general sales manager. Forster had fifteen years of experience in the industry beginning with F. W. Cook and later with Miller Brewing Company as a district sales manager.[40]

The next month, F. W. Cook created a new position, general manager, to provide active management control of the brewery. Edmund F. Ortmeyer, an Evansville attorney, a member of the board of directors and the corporate attorney, was chosen to fill this position.[41] Also in May 1949, the company changed its articles of incorporation to allow for 100,000 shares of no par value from 4,000 shares of $25,000 par value.[42] By September 1949, Charles Schwab announced that Ortmeyer would assume the duties of president of the firm while he, who had served in this capacity since 1932, would become chairman of the board.[43]

With a brewing capacity of 400,000 barrels, F. W. Cook Brewing was among the fifty-two largest breweries in America.[44] After the repeal of Prohibition there had been a trend from small regional breweries to large national breweries.

In the years following the end of World War II, Hulman had explored on several occasions the possibilities of purchasing the brewery. In January 1950, Hulman purchased controlling interest (52 percent) of F. W. Cook Brewing. After the purchase was consummated, the corporate officers were announced. Hulman was elected president; Joseph Cloutier, treasurer; Ortmeyer, vice president; and L. C. Holm, secretary. Hulman indicated he would take an active role in the management of the brewery.[45] Hulman said of the company, "In the course of 97 years, Cook's Brewery has become a great institution." He pledged to continue the modernization program. At the time of the purchase, about 70 percent of the brewery's products were distributed in the southeastern United States.[46]

Hulman purchased the brewery as a turnaround project. He believed the problem was sales driven and the solution would be to reorient the marketing and sales effort. Although initially successful at increasing the sales level, about six months after the purchase they began to hear that the beer tended to foam. So, the problem with sales was really attributable to the characteristics of the beer. It took three brewmasters and several years to figure out the cause of the foaming and to make the corrections.[47]

After correcting the foaming issues with the beer, the union contract was expiring. At the time, there were only two breweries in Evansville and the union contract was simultaneously negotiated for both Sterling and F. W. Cook. The union wanted an increase in wages. Hulman, who had lost all of his investment into the brewery due to the foaming problem, needed to make a decision about whether or not to keep pouring money into the company with the hope that it would become profitable.[48]

Cloutier discussed the economics of the situation:

> We had a brewery in Terre Haute at that time—Terre Haute Brewing Company—which was going great guns. But to me it was very clear that the brewing business was going the way of the automobile business, the steel business and a lot of other businesses. You were either going to be a big frog or you weren't going to be in the pond. You can't be way down the line. And that's where a regional brewery is.

As negotiations continued, Cloutier believed that Sterling wanted to get rid of F. W. Cook. Sterling had agreed to the union demands, which Sterling knew Cook wouldn't do. If Cook agreed to the union demands, they would need to rebuild the sales effort, but there was no guarantee the company would survive the consolidation of the industry.[49]

Unable to reach an amicable agreement, the union called for a strike in June 1955 with about 180 members of the Beer Bottlers Local 133 and Brewery Workers Local 84 walking out. Unwilling to meet the demands of the union, Hulman shuttered the business in September 1955. An official of the brewery disclosed to the *Evansville Courier* that the financial position of the firm had been "on unsound financial grounds since 1949 and if it had been owned locally, it would have been closed long ago."[50] Another press release of the closing said, "In an effort to permit the operation to continue until it became possible to determine the potential of the increase, an offer of a wage increase was made to the union. The employees were not willing to accept a continuation of the contract based on the increase offered, and the company did not feel justified in making further demands upon the stockholders."[51]

F. W. Cook's Brewing, an Evansville tradition since 1853, was among the seventeen large breweries which were sold to another concern and the four which closed between 1942 and 1958.[52]

The firm's signature product, Goldblume, continued to be made by other manufacturers including the crosstown rival, Sterling, until 1972.[53] The machinery was sold through a salvage equipment company.[54] Eventually the brewhouse and offices were demolished for the construction of a civic center and city jail.[55]

17

Coca-Cola Bottler

In 1965, Hulman had the opportunity to acquire a quintessential American brand—Coca-Cola. The Indianapolis bottler, James Yuncker, owner of the franchise since its origination, had died in December 1964. His estate was selling this valuable franchise. For Hulman, it represented an opportunity to diversify his business holdings with one with a stable cash flow.

When John Pemberton, an Atlanta pharmacist, formulated the drink in 1886, Coca-Cola was one of many counter drinks in the country. Unfortunately for Pemberton, he wasn't successful in marketing the drink. In need of money, he sold the formulation to Asa Candler.

From the beginning, Candler left the sale of his product to jobbers and drug stores. He would sell the syrup, which is key in making the product, at an average cost in 1895 of $1.29 per gallon to the jobbers. Candler's profits were thirty cents per gallon of syrup. When used at the retail level, the gallon of syrup would produce 128 fountain drinks priced at a nickel apiece, for a total of $6.40 in drinks.[1] Although there were other costs assumed by the jobbers and drug stores, this was a very profitable product.

In a move that would cost the Coca-Cola Company millions of dollars in the future, Candler decided to provide two Chattanooga attorneys, Benjamin F. Thomas and Joseph B. Whitehead, the rights to bottle the product on a nationwide basis with the exception of six New England locations. The sale was with the proviso that they maintain the quality of the product.[2] Candler allowed Thomas and Whitehead to draw up the contract which required the sole use of Coca-Cola syrup and banned the sale of the product to soda fountains. Candler would maintain the rights to the sale of the syrup to drugstores.[3]

Although Thomas and Whitehead opened a bottling plant in Chattanooga, they did not have the financial resources to expand the operations. Since the contract with Candler required they "supply the demand in all territory embraced in this agreement,"[4] they needed to establish bottling operations throughout the United States. Their resolution was to franchise the territories and they would become the "parent" bottlers. They also agreed to split the territories. Whitehead would take the South while Thomas would take the North, Midwest and West Coast. In order to provide a bottler for Atlanta, Whitehead took on a partner, J. T. Lupton, for his territories.[5]

One of the issues facing the newly formed bottlers was the quality of bottles and in particular the caps for them. At the time, the Hutchinson bottle cap was very similar to that traditionally used for champagne bottles—an internal seal held down by wire. To uncap the bottle, the consumer would need first to remove the wire loop.[6] Unfortunately, this type of cap was ineffective at maintaining the carbonation in the bottle. As a result, franchising went very slowly.

William Painter, a Baltimore mechanical engineer, created the crimped bottle cap which improved the quality of the product and ultimately led to rapid growth.[7] Although effective, this cap required new bottles and bottling equipment, an expense most bottlers didn't want to absorb. The adoption of the cap took a while to gain traction,[8] but by 1903, there were thirty-two franchises nationally. Growth exploded over the next several years, and by 1909 there were 397 bottlers throughout the United States.[9]

In Indianapolis, James Yuncker started Yuncker Bottling Works in 1906 at 710 E. Michigan Street. Within a year, Yuncker moved his bottling plant to Massachusetts Avenue. In 1915, Yuncker bought the rights to the Indianapolis Coca-Cola Bottling Company. He continued to operate this as a separate facility until 1929 when he merged Yuncker Bottling Works and Indianapolis Coca-Cola Bottling. The bottling company's franchise allowed for a territory of fifty miles.[10]

Despite start-up costs which could be as high as $100,000 for the cost of bottling equipment and building, a franchise could be very lucrative. Just as with the drug store soda fountains, the margins for the bottlers were very attractive. With the demand for the product growing rapidly, many bottlers became very wealthy. The downside of the rapid growth was that many franchisees were unable to fill the demand. With transportation of the product by horse-drawn delivery dray, another challenge for the bottlers was the size of the territories, which could be substantial. As a solution, many franchisees sold some of their rights to sub-bottlers. These smaller franchises could meet local demand in the smaller towns throughout the United States.[11]

Yuncker expanded his operations to include the purchase of bottling rights for South Bend, Logansport and Gary. Subsequently, he sold some of the rights to sub-bottlers in the Indiana towns of Anderson, Attica, Bloomington, Columbus, Crawfordsville, Elwood, Frankfort, Greencastle, Goshen, Kokomo, Lafayette, La Porte, Marion, Michigan City, Muncie, Monon, New Castle, Peru, Plymouth, Rushville and Shelbyville. In return, the sub-bottlers paid Yuncker a royalty on the syrup.[12]

From the early days, one of the keys to Coca-Cola's success has been its marketing. Coca-Cola utilized a variety of marketing tools including signs painted on buildings, and premiums such as trays, calendars, posters and baseball cards. At its heyday, Coca-Cola signs covered about 5 million square feet of buildings.[13]

What would help the branding of Coca-Cola would be a uniform bottle. One of the challenges during the early bottling phase was that all soft drinks had the same sort of bottle—nondescript and eight ounces. There were multiple problems with this, including that different sodas would be in the same barrel at a retailer and the label identifying the brand would frequently fall off in the ice-water filled barrel.

Veasey Rainwater, chief executive officer for the southern bottlers, understood the value of a bottle design that would be distinguishable from the others.[14] In the early 1900s, the company asked several of its bottle manufacturers to design a bottle.

One of the bottle suppliers for Coca-Cola Company was Root Glass Company of Terre Haute, Indiana. Root Glass Company traced its history back to 1901 when it was founded by Chapman J. Root to manufacture both beer and carbonated beverage bottles.[15] When Terre Haute was hit by a devastating tornado on March 23, 1913, destroying hundreds of homes and businesses, Root Glass Company was among the businesses flattened. The company was quickly able to rebuild its manufacturing facilities.[16]

While the Root Glass Company's building was being rebuilt, Earl R. Dean, a Root Glass Company employee, designed a new bottle based upon the coca bean pod. Although not one of the ingredients for Coca-Cola, the fluted pod was the inspiration for the design of the now-familiar bottle.[17] Another feature of the bottle is that it held six and a half ounces of liquid rather than the eight ounces held by other soda bottles. Chapman J. Root negotiated a royalty of five cents per gross of bottles produced. This deal ultimately made Root the richest man in Indiana.[18] The bottle was tested in several bottling operations in 1913. Acceptance of the bottle took a while because it represented an additional expense to the bottler. As more bottlers adapted the uniform bottle, the bottle became easily identifiable with the brand.

James Yuncker, the owner of the Indianapolis franchise, commissioned Indianapolis architects Preston, Rubush & Hunter to design a new bottling plant for him in the late 1920s. The architectural firm was well known in Indianapolis, having designed some of the more important buildings around town including the Indiana Theatre, the Circle Theater, and the Columbia Club.

The contractor, William J. Junclaus Company, had challenges in constructing the new facility as it was located on the same site as the building constructed in 1907. They had to accommodate the continued operations at the bottling plant. Across the street from the bottling facility was a garage also used by the bottling company. During the initial phase of the construction, the offices were moved into the garage on a temporary basis. After a portion of the new building was completed, the bottling operations moved into that section. The old building was then demolished and the new building was completed.

The building, constructed in 1931, is art deco in style, with the exterior covered in terra cotta. It has 165 feet fronting on Massachusetts Avenue and is 260 feet deep.[19] The main entrance to the building included a two-story foyer with a circular staircase and a brass medallion ceiling. When it was expanded in the 1940s, it was the largest Coca-Cola bottling plant in the world.[20]

In 1954, the Coca-Cola bottling plant in Indianapolis could produce 67,000 six-and-a-half-ounce bottles of Coca-Cola every hour with four bottling lines filling 260 bottles a minute. Approximately 50 percent of the bottles sold were from vending machines.[21] In January 1956, after the Coca-Cola Company had test marketed both a twelve-ounce and a twenty-six-ounce bottle, they introduced a twelve-ounce bottle. This was the first change in the hooped-skirt bottle since it was introduced in 1915. In 1956, Yuncker explained the rationale for introducing the new bottle: "More than 50 percent of soft drinks today [is] consumed at home. For home consumption, the public has shown it wants soft drinks in a variety of bottle sizes for convenience." To handle the new twelve-ounce bottle, Yuncker converted an existing six-and-a-half-ounce bottling line. The company still had four six-and-a-half-ounce bottling lines.[22]

Coca-Cola was also exploring the possibility of using tin cans. Tests revealed the need for a liner, and Coca-Cola was unable to find a liner that would not alter the taste of the product. Although thwarted in their effort to develop a can, Coca-Cola was able to perfect the delivery of Coke in a paper cup. They had previously tried paper cups prior to World War I; however, they were unable to successfully deliver the syrup and carbonated water mixture with consistency as there were mechanical issues with the machinery used. Paper cups filled with Coca-Cola were introduced to the Indianapolis market in January 1955.[23]

Yuncker died in December 1964. In early January 1965, the franchise was sold to Hulman for a reported $2 million. As had been the case with other acquisitions, Hulman quickly announced an upgrading of equipment. In a familiar formula, Hulman became the president, and Cloutier the vice president. The day-to-day operations would be overseen by David Cassidy who was named the manager of the Coca-Cola bottling plant.[24] At the time of its acquisition by Hulman, the Indianapolis bottling plant turned out 13.5 million bottles of Coca-Cola annually.[25] In addition to the Indianapolis bottling facility, there were thirteen sub-plants around the state of Indiana.[26]

Cassidy, a familiar and trusted part of the extended Hulman family, joined the Speedway staff in 1960. In 1961, he became the concessions manager, and in 1963 he became the manager for the Speedway Motel.[27]

The 1960s were a time of change for Coca-Cola and for the franchises. What had been a one-product company was now bottling various types of product, which required multiple bottling lines. One product introduced as a competitor for 7-Up was Fanta, originally developed in Nazi Germany. In 1961, Sprite was introduced, followed in 1962 with Coca-Cola's first diet drink, TaB. By 1964, TaB had 10 percent of its market.[28] More new products were introduced to the market, with Mr. Pibb in 1972 and Fresca in 1996. Mello Yello joined the Coca-Cola family in 1979.[29]

Not only was the product line expanding but convenience was becoming increasingly important to the consumer, particularly women who were joining the workforce in greater numbers and had less time for shopping. The Coke bottle, the long-familiar trademark of the company, had to be returned to the bottler. The bottler then had to wash the bottles prior to refilling them. As a response, the product began to be delivered in forms other than the familiar six-and-a-half-ounce bottle. The company responded with multiple-size bottles (ten, twelve and twenty-four ounce) in 1955, steel cans in 1960, nonreturnable bottles in 1968 and the polyethylene terephthalate two-liter bottle in 1979.[30]

Although the Indianapolis bottling facility was the largest in the world in 1940, the continued increase in demand, the expansion of the products offered and the increase in the bottling options made this plant outdated. In 1969, the Coca-Cola Bottling Company of Indianapolis moved to a new plant located in Speedway, Indiana. The 234,000-square-foot building was located on a twenty-acre plot. The estimated cost for the new building was $3.5 million.[31] When the new bottling plant was opened, it had the capacity of filling 600 bottles per minute. As a comparison, the early bottling lines were capable of filling seven bottles a minute.[32] Hulman sold the old bottling plant to the Indianapolis Public Schools.

In the early days of Coca-Cola bottlers, the initial strategy was to have

The new Coca-Cola bottling plant in Speedway, Indiana, in 1965 (Indianapolis Motor Speedway).

bottling facilities approximately fifty miles apart so their customers could be serviced by a horse-drawn dray. With the advent of good roads and the use of gasoline- or diesel-fueled trucks by the 1930s, the multitude of bottlers became an inefficient delivery system for Coca-Cola. By the 1970s, of the 800 bottlers in the United States, approximately two-thirds were in towns with a population of less than 50,000. Coca-Cola responded by establishing a Bottler Consolidation Department to help facilitate the sale and acquisition of franchises.[33] By this point in time, it was much more efficient for bottlers to have one centralized plant and to ship out the product.

An additional challenge facing Coca-Cola by 1970 was supplying grocery stores. Large grocery chains, such as A&P and Kroger, did not want to negotiate with individual bottlers. When the national Coca-Cola salesmen negotiated a deal with the chain grocery stores, it was without the input of the individual bottlers who would supply the product, leading to tension between Coca-Cola and its individual bottlers.[34]

In 1971, the world changed for Coca-Cola Company and its bottlers. The Federal Trade Commission accused the company as well as Pepsi-Cola and six other soft drink manufacturers of Sherman Antitrust infractions, arguing that the franchises were in fact monopolies limiting competition since territories were exclusive. For Coca-Cola, this represented an opportunity to renegotiate the syrup agreement with their franchises. With the bottlers threatened by the antitrust action, Coca-Cola felt they might be amendable to a change in this long-standing agreement. This agreement historically had not been beneficial to Coca-Cola. Eventually, Coca-Cola and the bottlers agreed to a sliding scale for the syrup purchases.[35]

The antitrust action had a significant impact upon the bottlers, including Hulman's organization. The Federal Trade Commission action was not resolved until 1980 when Congress exempted soft drink bottlers from this action[36] with the passage of the Soft Drink Interbrand Competition Act. Although by the late 1970s the number of bottlers had decreased to approximately 550, with the passage of this act, significant distributor consolidation began.[37]

An audit of the Indianapolis bottling company books by external accountants in 1976 revealed discrepancies in equipment. As one who built relationships based upon trust and loyalty, Hulman must have been saddened when an investigation by the Speedway, Indiana police, over a two-and-a-half-month period uncovered a theft ring operating for the prior six years. Transportation manager Edward Vance, an employee since 1951, and route salesmen Robert Marratta and Marshall McCellom were arrested. Police uncovered equipment owned by the bottler on a farm owned by Vance. Additional investigation uncovered the sale of bottles, cans and syrup to an Indianapolis restaurant chain and service stations for less than the standard pricing.[38]

In late April 1981, the Indianapolis bottling company was sold by Hulman's estate to the Spectrum Group for a reported $30 million. The sale included the bottling plant at Indianapolis and distribution centers at Anderson, Lafayette, Fort Wayne, and Marion.[39] At the time of sale, 49 percent of the company was owned by the Hulman estate, with the remainder being owned by the Hulman Foundation and Rose-Hulman Institute.[40]

Within a couple of weeks, the Spectrum Group sold the majority of the company to Marvin Herb. He had been an executive vice president of Borden Inc., owner of the Indianapolis Pepsi-Cola franchise. Herb would relocate from Houston, Texas, where he headed Borden's consumer products division, to Indianapolis.

At the time of the sale, Pepsi-Cola was outselling Coca-Cola in the very competitive Central Indiana market. Herb said, "I'm trying now to figure out why that is and how to reverse it." To help the company achieve dominance in the cola wars in central Indiana, Herb hired Robert C. Cole as the new plant manager and Anthony Stroinski as marketing manager. Both had been key executives with Pepsi-Cola in Indianapolis.[41] Herb would later become a significant franchisee with Coca-Cola with the purchase of the operation in Chicago.

18

Hulman, Orville Redenbacher and Popcorn

Sometimes business interests expand not through either internal growth, the acquisition of companies or innovation but rather through marriage. That happened when Anton Hulman, Sr., married Grace Smith. The Hulman family became involved with Grace Smith's father's coal-mining interests.

In the 1880s, Indiana experienced a surge of economic expansion driven by the discovery of natural gas in the northeastern part of the state, powering the growth of industry. Unfortunately, the amount of natural gas wasn't substantial and soon ran dry. However, the Wabash Valley area of southwestern Indiana, near Terre Haute, had sizable coal reserves. After the crash of the short-lived natural gas phenomenon in Indiana, coal became essential in powering Hoosier industries.

In 1902, Robert J. Smith, Hulman's maternal grandfather and a Terre Haute businessman, founded the Deep Vein Coal Company in Terre Haute. He expanded the coal operation by starting the King's Mine Station, a deep vein mining operation south of Princeton, Indiana, in 1924.[1]

Wanting to expand the mining operation again, Smith, who had been joined by Tony Hulman, explored purchasing the coal rights. Instead they decided to purchase 12,000 acres of Indiana farmland which included the mineral rights. The resulting farming operation, originally called McDonner Farms,[2] became the largest farm in Indiana, operating under the trade style of Princeton Farms,[3] with ownership by the Smith and Hulman families.

The mining operation spread over 10,000 acres of land in southwest Indiana and Illinois. The topography of this part of Indiana is flat to gently rolling, ideal for a farming operation. Since the majority of the mining operations involved deep vein mines, the Smiths established a farming operation. In 1940, Robert Smith and his son, Hy, talked to the Vigo County Agricultural agent, Orville Redenbacher, about taking over the management of Princeton Farms.

Named for Orville Wright, Redenbacher was born on a farm near Brazil, Indiana, in 1907. By age twelve, Redenbacher was growing his own popcorn and selling it on the cob in fifty-pound bags.[4] While studying vocational agriculture in high school, Redenbacher participated in 4-H, led by Horace Abbott, who became a mentor. Although he had received an appointment to the U.S. Military Academy at West Point, Redenbacher chose to go to Purdue University to pursue a degree in agriculture.[5] With Dr. Arthur Brunson and Dr. George Christie on the staff, Purdue was the premier research institute for popcorn.[6]

After graduating from Purdue University, Redenbacher taught vocational agriculture and established a 4-H Club in Fontanet, Indiana. The Clay County, Indiana, county agricultural agent, Horace Abbott, asked Redenbacher to join him in Vigo County to be the 4-H Club agent. When Abbott became the Marion County agricultural agent in 1932, Redenbacher assumed the role in Vigo County. While the agricultural agent in Vigo County, Redenbacher had five-minute farm news and crop reports broadcast on WBOW in Terre Haute.[7]

In January 1940, the Smiths hired Redenbacher to manage the farm for $4,500 annually plus 10 percent of the farm's profits. While at Princeton Farms, Redenbacher was one of the first Indiana farmers to plant hybrid dent seed corn used to feed livestock. In his second year at Princeton Farms, Redenbacher planted hybrid popcorn developed by Purdue University scientists,[8] which he also expanded to the Princeton Farms location in Homestead, Florida.[9] Initially, this corn was grown as seed corn sold to popcorn processors throughout the United States and Canada.[10] Princeton Farms' largest seed buyer was J. A. McCarty Seed Company of Evansville, Indiana, one of the largest popcorn processors in the United States.[11]

In the 1930s, the primary market for popcorn was movie theaters, with popcorn processors selling their finest corn in bulk to the movie theaters. Lower-quality popcorn was sold to consumers, as in those days consumers were very price sensitive—the cheaper the better. In a world driven by low price, consumers were satisfied with lower quality for home popping. In 1944 and 1945, under Redenbacher's leadership, Princeton Farms began selling popcorn in one-pound, two-pound and five-pound cans or polyester bags.[12]

In 1944, Princeton Farms began selling popcorn for supermarket consumption. Princeton Farms' strategy was different from most popcorn producers in that they focused on home consumption. They were at the beginning of the surge of popcorn sales for home consumption. Going against conventional wisdom, Princeton Farms used their best corn for the home market focusing on quality retail markets. Undoubtedly helpful in getting the product into the stores was its sister company, Hulman & Company.

While at Princeton Farms, Redenbacher produced a viable popcorn hybrid different from the Purdue University hybrid in 1946. Princeton Farms was successful in producing a superior product because of harvesting and drying it by the ear rather than by the combine, which separates the kernel from the ear.[13]

Years later in a television interview on *PM Magazine*, Redenbacher recalled his interest in developing a better popcorn seed: "I collected all the different brands that I could, tin cans or cardboard treated with paraffin, to protect them, so you couldn't see the corn. So one night we opened up eleven different brands and popped them. And some of them were almost junk. And that's when I decided that someone ought to have a better brand of popcorn on the market."[14]

When Redenbacher left Princeton Farms on December 31, 1951, the size of the farming operation had increased to 18,000 acres.[15] Charles Bowman, manager of the Purdue University Alumni Seed Improvement Association, had an opportunity to purchase the George F. Chester & Son Seed Company in Valparaiso, Indiana. Bowman had been a trusted adviser to Redenbacher when he was managing Princeton Farms.[16] Bowman asked Redenbacher to join him in this venture and to assume management of the company.[17] Under Redenbacher and Bowman, the company became the largest producer of hybrid popcorn seed corn and soybeans in northwest Indiana.[18]

In 1959, George F. Chester & Son Seed Company hired Carl Hartman to work on improving the hybrid popcorn seed. Over several years, Hartman experimented with eighty-three different varieties of corn. By 1965, Hartman's experiments had produced a popcorn which was superior to the others on the market. Not only was the popcorn light and fluffy, but its popping ratio (popped corn vs. unpopped corn) was also significantly better than other commercial varieties. They marketed the seed under the name of Redbow, a combination of Redenbacher's and Bowman's names.[19] Although superior to other popcorn seed in terms of fluffiness and percentage of kernels popped, Redbow did not have much acceptance by the major popcorn processors as it was higher priced than the majority of corn. Redbow's higher cost was attributed to the lower yield per acre and a higher cost of raising.[20] By 1970, Redenbacher and Bowman decided to stop selling Redbow to popcorn processors and to market their own brand, which became Orville Redenbacher premium popcorn.[21]

By 1965, Princeton Farms was the largest independent producer in Indiana.[22] The operation included the production, processing and distribution of the popcorn.[23] Most of the popcorn produced at Princeton Farms was sold in the Midwest, but they also sold bulk popcorn in 100-pound bags, fifty-pound moisture-proof bags and fifty-pound cases for theater and vending operations throughout the United States.

In addition to the farming and mining operations, Princeton Farms also had a commercial cattle-feeding program with approximately 1,000 head per year. This means of using the by-products of the farming operation with the waste materials from the processing of crops being fed to the cattle is similar to Hulman's grandfather feeding pigs and cattle from the refuse from McGregor Distillery. Although Princeton Farms' primary crop was popcorn, they had approximately 1,000 acres which produced other crops such as barley, rye, oats and corn.

19

Diversification

Over the years, Hulman utilized the excess profits to diversify the family's holdings. There was a commonality to the purchases: they were all cash-flow-based businesses.

Real Estate

Herman Hulman began the family tradition of owning real estate when he purchased the office building for H. Hulman & Company in 1867 and the development of the H. Hulman & Company complex in Terre Haute in 1893. Anton Sr. continued the tradition with the purchase of the warehouses in Evansville and Matoon, Illinois. Tony Hulman also invested in real estate to support various needs of the company. Unlike his father and grandfather, he also bought commercial real estate as an investment.

The first piece of commercial real estate purchased was the Hulman Building in Evansville, Indiana, a ten-story office building built by Central Union Bank in 1929–1930. Central Union Bank was a combination of Morris Plan of Evansville and Mercantile-Commercial Bank. The art deco building's lower two and top two floors were faced with Indiana limestone while the middle floors were of deep red brick. The bank leased the top eight floors to third parties.

Unfortunately, the building was not fully occupied due to the Great Depression, and when the bank failed in the mid–1930s, the property went on the auction block.[1] Hulman remembered the purchase of the Hulman building: "I went to Evansville not necessarily thinking I'd buy those buildings. They were auctioning off the buildings at a street corner sale. I started bidding and the first thing I knew I had bought them."[2]

One of Hulman's investing precepts appears to have been to have them close enough to Terre Haute so that he could understand the market. Investments took place not only in Terre Haute and Evansville but also in Dayton, Ohio, and Louisville, Kentucky. A variety of companies were used to purchase the real estate, including the Hulman Foundation, Terre Haute Realty, Hulman Realty Corporation of Dayton, Hulman & Company as well as individually.[3]

In Louisville Hulman purchased the fifteen-story Washington building built in 1907. When constructed, the Washington building was the tallest in Louisville and was representative of the commercial building styles of the Victorian age.[4] Designed by architect Alfred W. Joseph, the three lower and two upper stories were in white granite while the middle floors were bricked, giving the building a distinctive style. At the top of the building were gargoyles of lion heads looking down at the city streets.[5] The named tenant in the building was the Lincoln Savings Association.[6] The building was demolished in 1967. Hulman also purchased the ten-story Realty Building in Louisville.

In 1945, Hulman purchased the Mutual Home Savings Association building in Dayton, Ohio. Built in 1931, it was the tallest building in Dayton until 1969. After acquiring the building, the name was changed to the Hulman building. It is an art deco building with twenty-three stories constructed of brick and limestone. Today, it is known as the Liberty Tower.[7]

Capitalizing on the construction of Interstate 70 which effectively replaced the Old National Road (U.S. Route 40), in the mid–1950s Hulman was an investor in the development of the Meadows Shopping Center through Terre Haute Realty. Located just south of I-70, it was the first shopping center in Terre Haute. As with other shopping center developments, it had the unintended consequence of drawing business away from downtown. Hulman later was behind the construction of the Plaza North Shopping Center in the 1960s.

In 1959, Hulman bought two significant historical Terre Haute properties—the Opera House built in 1897 and the Terre Haute House, the city's landmark hotel. Shortly after purchasing the Grand Opera House, Hulman decided to close it due to fire safety concerns.

The Terre Haute House, called "Tony's Hotel" by many city residents,[8] traced its roots back to the early founding of Terre Haute when Chauncey Rose built the Prairie House. In 1928, the family of Crawford Fairbanks built a ten-story Terre Haute House. With the development of Interstate 70 and the construction of a Holiday Inn near the interstate, the hotel's occupancy plummeted and it became unprofitable by the mid–1960s. By 1970, the Terre Haute House was closed due to lack of traffic.[9] After standing empty for thirty-five years despite efforts within the Terre Haute community to revitalize this landmark structure, the building was razed and a new hotel was built.[10]

In 1977, Schulte High School closed. The Hulman family was involved in the redevelopment of the property as Corporate Square, a 50,661-square-foot office building.[11]

Over time, building upon the family farms he inherited, the Hulman & Company properties and the shopping centers, Hulman became the largest landowner in Vigo County.[12]

Media

Hulman became very involved in the purchase of media properties. His first media property was the purchase of 82 percent of the stock of WTHI, Terre Haute's first radio station begun in 1948.[13] Hulman was the driving force in the founding of WTHI-TV, Terre Haute's first television station. At the time, the only television available in Terre Haute was from stations in Indianapolis and Bloomington.[14] WTHI-TV was started in July 1954 as a CBS affiliate.[15] The Hulman family sold WTHI-TV and its related radio stations, WTHI-AM and WTHI-FM, to Emmis Broadcasting in 1998.[16]

In the 1950s, Hulman also bought the local newspapers, the *Terre Haute Tribune* and the *Terre Haute Star*.

Utilities

Hulman's entry into utilities started in the 1950s when he was approached by Ralph Beatty, a resident of Columbus, Ohio. Beatty was forming a group to purchase the Richmond Gas Company from Associated Gas. Later, Hulman was able to purchase a block of Indiana Gas and Chemical Company stock which owned the Terre Haute Gas Company.[17] The Hulman family sold their interest in Terre Haute Gas Company and Richmond Gas Company to Indiana Energy in 1998. At that time, the company supplied natural gas to approximately 47,000 customers.[18] At the time of sale, the Hulman family owned approximately 13 percent of Indiana Energy stock.[19]

He also purchased a significant block of stock in Southern Indiana Gas & Electric Company which serviced southwestern Indiana including Evansville. In 1999, SIGECO and Indiana Gas Company merged to form Vectren, headquartered in Evansville.[20]

Finance

Hulman invested in two financial institutions in Terre Haute. He served on the board of directors of the city's largest bank, Terre Haute First National Bank. This bank was formed by the merger in 1932 of two Terre Haute banks,[21] Second State Bank and the Bank of Southern Indiana. His grandfather, Herman Hulman, had served as a director of McKeen National Bank, founded by his friend, William McKeen, and the U.S. Trust Company.[22] Both banks were successor corporations to Second State Bank and the Bank of Southern Indiana. Leonard Marshall, who was one of Hulman's trusted advisers, was the bank's chairman from 1938 until 1968.[23]

20

Giving to Education

Terre Haute, a town of 70,000, has three institutions of higher learning: Rose-Hulman Institute of Technology, a private school with a focus on engineering; Indiana State University, a public supported school; and Ivy Tech, an Indiana community college.

Hulman had a passion for education. With a tradition of charitable giving handed down through the generations from father to son, Hulman gave generously to the Terre Haute community, with a special emphasis on the Rose-Hulman Institute of Technology and Indiana State University.

The Hulman family's relationship with the Rose-Hulman Institute of Technology goes back to its early days. Its name pays homage to the two people who were very influential in the school's history, Chauncey Rose in the 1870s and Hulman a hundred years later.

Chauncey Rose was born on December 24, 1794, in Wethersfield Meadows, Connecticut. His grandfather, John Rose, had immigrated to the United States from Scotland in the early 1700s. Rose was one of seven boys and one girl born to John and Mary Warner Rose.

At age twenty-three, he left his home to make his fortune. Utilizing $2,000 from his brother, George, he traveled to Mount Sterling, Kentucky, where some friends had settled. Rose described his journey: "In the fall of 1817, I traversed the States of Indiana, Illinois, Missouri, Kentucky, Tennessee and Alabama, looking for a location at which to reside and engage in business. I spent several days at Terre Haute; it had been laid out the previous year. The following winter I spent in Kentucky. Favorably impressed with the location and the people in and about Terre Haute, I returned and became a resident in April 1818. There were but two cabins in Terre Haute, and the nearest boarding-place was at Fort Harrison where I boarded, as did the county officers, at a house kept by Mrs. Stewart."[1]

Rose's first business was a partnership with Captain Brooks and Moses Robbins at Fort Harrison. They started a mill, a distillery and a general store. In honor of one of its early settlers, Fort Harrison was later renamed Roseville.[2] In 1819, Rose moved to nearby Parke County where he was involved in a milling operation.[3]

After inheriting $8,000 from his brother George's estate, Rose again relocated in 1825 to the small town of Terre Haute where he and Chauncey Warren established a mercantile business. The inheritance also enabled Rose to invest in land near Terre Haute.[4]

In the 1830s, Rose expanded his landholdings with the purchase of 320 acres for $3,400. In 1837, Rose built a two-story federal-style hotel called the Prairie House. The location of the hotel several blocks east of the center of town resulted in little business, leading some to call the hotel "Rose's Folly."[5] This venture was not profitable due to the distance from the business district, and in 1841 Rose closed it.[6]

Although Rose's education was limited to the common schools in Wethersfield Meadows,[7] it was adequate for him to become an astute businessman. He discovered that his brother's will had bequeaths in excess of $1 million. If settled under the laws of the state of New York, it would not provide the funds to honor his brother's intentions. Rose decided to contest the will. Over the next six years, he was involved in the litigation of the will, paying all of the litigation expenses himself. When the will was settled, it was valued in excess of $1.6 million. Rose provided over $1.5 million in bequeaths to a variety of charitable institutions.[8]

Rose, a significant landholder in the early days of Terre Haute, recognized that the future of his adopted town depended on the transportation of goods. He was the driving force behind the establishment of the first railroad to reach Terre Haute. During the construction of the Richmond & Terre Haute Railroad, Rose became frustrated at the lack of trained engineers willing to come to the area and work on the railroad.

One of the underlying issues was the fact that most education in Indiana focused on agriculture. By the early 1870s, Terre Haute had one school, the Indiana State Normal School, operating which focused on educating future teachers.

Understanding that Indiana also had a need for trained engineers, Rose started planning for a school to address this need. Rose commissioned two friends and business associates, Charles R. Peddle and William A. Jones, to travel to the east to study engineering schools. Based upon their travels, they recommended that the school be patterned after the Worcester Free Institute (later Worcester Polytechnic Institute).[9]

Assembling a group of nine friends and business associates, Rose established the Terre Haute School of Industrial Science in October 1874. In December 1874, Rose gave the school ten acres of land at Locust and 13th Street and $186,000 in securities, providing seed money for the school. The board of managers, with Rose as president, contracted with McCormick & Sweeney, a Columbus, Indiana, firm, to build a four-story brick building containing forty-six rooms.[10] The cornerstone for the building was laid on September 11, 1875, and the school was renamed Rose Polytechnic Institute, saluting the school's primary benefactor.

Rose did not live to see the school he envisioned come to fruition. Upon his death in August 1877, his estate provided an additional bequest to the school of $100,000, bringing his total gifts to over $500,000. The board of managers delayed the opening of the school until the school's endowment could provide $25,000 per year in income.[11]

By 1882, the board of managers of Rose Polytechnic Institute decided it was time to open the school. After a search for the first president of the school, Dr. Charles O. Thompson, the president of Worcester Free Institute of Industrial Science, was hired. His compensation package was $4,000 per year and a year of European travel to study engineering schools. Thompson also negotiated $10,000 to compensate him for the loss in consulting income he would suffer by moving to Terre Haute. The $10,000 was not taken from the school coffers but was raised from three members of the board of managers—Firmin Nippert, owner of Terre Haute Nail Company, donated $5,000; Josephus Collett, president of the Evansville, Terre Haute & Chicago Railroad, donated $1,335; and Demas Demming, local banker and financier, donated $1,000. Two other community leaders, Herman Hulman and William Riley McKeen, owner of the McKeen Bank, each donated $1,332.50.[12]

About the same time as Chauncey Rose was dreaming of his engineering school, the state of Indiana wanted to improve education for the state's residents. The Indiana legislature established Indiana State Normal School with a focus on educating teachers for the primary and secondary grades. The bill passed on December 20, 1865, and granted $50,000 in seed money. Rather than directing which Indiana city would become the home to Indiana State Normal School, the legislature mandated the school be established in whichever locality "would offer the greatest advantages" and with the proviso that the city would provide $50,000 toward the school's establishment. The citizens

20. Giving to Education

of Terre Haute petitioned the city council for funding for the school. No other city in Indiana took similar steps, and Terre Haute was granted the school charter.

The City of Terre Haute purchased a plot located on 6th Street between Eagle and Mulberry for the school's location. Additional progress was made in 1867 when the Indiana state legislature appropriated an additional $50,000 for the construction of the school. This appropriation was subject to Terre Haute agreeing "to forever maintain and keep up one-half of necessary repairs incident to keeping in proper order the building or buildings of the same."

With funding in hand, the building's cornerstone was laid. The building's design was an elegant four-story structure of French Renaissance style. The building was nearing completion in 1869 when funding ran out. The building's second and third floors were completed while the basement and fourth floor were roughed in. There was no money to provide lighting fixtures, and heat was provided by small stoves in the classrooms.[13]

Indiana State Normal College opened on a bitterly cold January day. The initial student body consisted of twenty-one students, of whom nineteen were from Terre Haute or Vigo County. Tuition was free to the students; however, they had to commit to being a teacher in the Indiana common (public) schools for a period equal to twice their time at Indiana State Normal College. Women could be admitted at sixteen while men had to be eighteen.[14]

A few years after the school had opened for classes, a fire ignited in the attic on April 9, 1888. All 600 people in the building were able to safely exit; however, the building was destroyed.[15] The aftermath was described in these words: "All that was left was smoking, broken walls of the building, six-hundred earnest students, about thirty faculty members and the intangible real spirit of the Indiana State Normal School." On a temporary basis, classes were moved to Centenary Methodist Church, with some classes being held in private homes or other churches. On a more permanent basis, the classes were subsequently moved to the second floor of the city high school. Valuing the contributions to the community of this school, on April 17, the citizens petitioned the Terre Haute city council for $25,000. The Indiana legislature appropriated $100,000 for the rebuilding of the building ($60,000), boiler house ($13,000), and library, scientific equipment and other incidentals ($27,000). By the fall, the new structure had been built on the footprint of the original school.[16]

By the early 1900s, Rose Polytechnic, located at 10th and Chestnut streets, was outgrowing its physical plant. In 1908, the board of managers began discussing the need for an expanded campus. They initially bought one property only to discover that there were no adjacent tracts available. They then bought a forty-acre tract on Fort Harrison Road only to discover that the city of Terre Haute wanted the property for a park. By 1913, the board of trustees located another promising location—a 123-acre tract east of Terre Haute owned by Herman Hulman and Anton Hulman, Sr. This tract was purchased from the Hulmans in 1914. In 1917, the Hulman heirs returned the purchase price to Rose Polytechnic.[17] The school hired Herbert Foltz, an Indianapolis architect and Rose Polytechnic alumni of the class of 1884, to design the school's six buildings. Financing of the buildings was provided by a fundraising campaign totaling $500,000, of which $300,000 would be for the buildings and the remaining $200,000 for the endowment.[18] The cornerstone for the new buildings was laid in 1922.[19]

Herman Hulman and Walter Ely were elected to the Board of Managers of Rose Polytechnic in 1919. Hulman subsequently resigned in 1920 due to a hearing problem.[20]

Anton (Tony) Hulman, Jr., returned to Terre Haute after graduating from Yale University in 1924 to join Hulman & Company. With his experience of playing on the Yale University football team, he became the football coach for Rose Polytechnic's freshman football team in 1924. He also assisted football coach Hezlep Clark with the varsity football team. The 1926 Rose Polytechnic yearbook, *The Modulus*, saluted Hulman's contribution to the football team:

> The generosity of Tony Hulman, in offering his services to Rose Poly, has allowed Coach Clark to give his entire time to the varsity squad. In taking the yearlings under his wing in the past two years, Tony Hulman has developed two victorious teams. Besides winning the majority of the games allowed them with other college freshman squads, Tony's men have provided valuable opposition to the varsity squad in practice.[21]

Hulman also contributed to the athletic program at Indiana State by providing forty-seven acres for an athletic field in 1945. Indiana State's athletic tradition goes back to baseball, and then in 1894, football and basketball were added. The school joined the Indiana Intercollegiate Athletic Association in 1895 and sported track-and-field teams. Until the gift by Hulman for the athletic field, the Terre Haute Municipal Stadium was used for outdoor athletic events beginning in 1920. The state of Indiana appropriated $50,000 for development of the athletic field. Although a field house was planned for the property, Indiana State sold the property to the city of Terre Haute in 1955 in order to raise some money. The city of Terre Haute used the property for the building of a grade school.[22]

In 1944, Hulman was elected to the Board of Managers of Rose Polytechnic.[23] In 1965, the Hulman Foundation provided a gift of $250,000 to Rose Polytechnic.[24] The contributions of the Hulman family either directly or through the Hulman Foundation were honored by the school in 1966 when the student union was named the Hulman Memorial Student Union in memory of Tony Hulman's parents, Anton and Grace Hulman. A plaque on the building says,

> Grace and Anton Hulman
> Memorial Union
> This center for student activity was erected
> as a memorial to Grace and Anton Hulman, Sr. Mr.
> Hulman and his brother, Herman, donated the present
> 123-acre campus in memory of their father and mother.
> This memorial union was made possible by the generosity
> of the Hulman Foundation.
> June 11, 1966[25]

In 1965, Indiana State acquired the Terre Haute landmark, the Demming Hotel, to house male upperclassmen. It was renamed the Hulman Center in honor of the Hulman family's contributions to the school.[26]

The generosity of Hulman continued in 1970 when on December 31 the assets in the Hulman Foundation were transferred to Rose Polytechnic.[27] The foundation was started in the 1930s with an initial contribution of $5,000. By the time of the donation to Rose Polytechnic, the value of the foundation had increased to multimillions. Hulman said of the donation, "I've loved Rose all my life, in fact, I've grown up under the influence of Rose. I've spent most of my life trying to develop the foundation so it would do some good and I feel it can accomplish a lot at this institution."[28]

The president of Rose Polytechnic, John A. Logan, before an assembly of students, professors and friends of the college said, "Value of this generous gift at least equaled, if it did not exceed, the total value of the physical assets of the college and the endowment."[29] Logan also paid homage to the contributions of the Hulman family to the school over multiple generations: "Mr. Hulman has continued the interest of his father and uncle, and serves as a life member of our board of managers. Most recently the Hulman family has been instrumental in the construction of our student union building named in memory of Mr. Hulman's mother and father."[30] In light of the Hulmans' donation, the board of managers voted to rename the school the Rose-Hulman Institute of Technology, thus paying homage to the two men who had significantly contributed to the school.[31]

In 1973, Hulman was named chairman of the Rose-Hulman Centennial Drive with a goal of raising $5 million. He made a $1 million leadership contribution to the effort.[32]

In December 1973, Indiana State opened a new basketball arena named the Hulman Civic University Center. A gift valued at $2.5 million in land and cash had significantly aided in the construction of the facility. The citizens of Terre Haute donated $1,250,000 toward the arena, and the university sold $6 million in bonds which would be repaid through student fees.[33]

Following his death, the Hulman family donated the St. Anthony's Hospital property, which had been erected in honor of his grandmother to Ivy Tech for a health care training facility. There was a clause in the real estate deed for the property requiring that if the property were not used as a hospital, it would revert to the Hulman family. In 1974, the Sisters of St. Francis leased the hospital to the Hospital Corporation of America which changed the name to Terre Haute Regional Hospital. In 1979, the Hospital Corporation of America built a new regional hospital abandoning the original location. After the property was given to Ivy Tech, the cost of retrofitting the hospital made it impractical. The building was destroyed, and a senior housing complex, Anthony Square, was erected.[34]

21

Giving Back

Hulman grew up in a home which emphasized giving back to the community. During World War I, his father chaired the local bond campaign. His grandfather had been one of the leaders in funding for his church, established a hospital and paid off debt for the cemetery in which his family was buried.

The 1940s was when Hulman became a civic leader.[1] Terre Haute was the primary beneficiary of Hulman's generosity and time.

Terre Haute had an airport, Cox Field, named for Paul Cox, one of Hulman's friends who died in an airplane crash in 1932. Cox Field, started in 1929, had two unpaved landing strips. In 1942, the federal government rejected the application to have transcontinental flights from Cox Field.[2] Responding to Terre Haute's need for an airport to handle larger planes, Hulman gave Terre Haute $100,000 toward the purchase of property for a municipal airport in 1943. Federal funds were used for airport improvements.[3] The airport, Hulman Field, was named for Hulman's father, Anton Hulman, Sr.[4] Hulman was also responsible for bringing a modern sewage disposal plant to Terre Haute.[5]

Hulman, envisioning a place for the recreation and enjoyment of his employees, purchased the 360-acre Forest Park property from trustees of the former Terre Haute Trust Company in 1938 after a fire had destroyed the historic grist mill.[6] After clearing the brush and making improvements to the property, including a $60,000 clubhouse, it was opened to the employees of Hulman & Company on Easter Day, 1941, with an egg hunt.[7]

In March 1965, the lodge at Forest Park was destroyed by fire. When a watchman discovered the fire around 7:30 a.m., it was too late to save the structure with an estimated value of $150,000 despite the firemen fighting the flames for two hours. The fire was possibly started by a discarded cigarette from a party the previous night.[8] Hulman subsequently donated the property to Vigo County in 1967.[9]

Terre Haute had enjoyed professional baseball as a farm team for the Philadelphia Phillies. Organized in 1883, the Terre Haute Phillies experienced declining attendance in the 1950s. Hulman joined with other civic leaders including Vern McMillan and Paul Frisz in an attempt to save the team. They were able to negotiate a tentative agreement with the Detroit Tigers. The continued decline in attendance led to the severing of the potential relationship. The last professional baseball game of the Terre Haute Phillies was on July 4, 1956.[10]

Following in his father's footsteps, Hulman headed the war bond campaign for Vigo County during World War II. In this capacity, he began his public speaking career with which he was never comfortable.[11]

From 1941 until 1950, Hulman was the president of the Terre Haute Chamber of Commerce.[12]

Hulman had shown his interest in maintaining historical places with the purchase of the Indianapolis Motor Speedway and F. W. Cook Brewery. In 1957, he and Mrs. Hulman purchased the Sage-Robinson-Nagel house which was donated to the Terre Haute Historical Society. The house, circa 1867, is a two-story structure in the Italianate style. Among the collection is one of the original Coca-Cola hobble-skirt bottles designed by Root Bottling Company.[13]

In 1973, Hulman gave 230 acres of land and $265,000 in cash to the city of Terre Haute to help build a city golf course. Matching funds were obtained from the federal government in the amount of $465,000 to build the eighteen-hole course. In addition to the golf course, facilities included an eighteen-acre lake and tennis courts.[14] The golf course, named the Hulman Links at Lost Creek, was designed by David Gill of St. Charles, Illinois.[15]

Hulman also gave generously of his treasure and time to the state of Indiana. As chairman of Indiana's Flood Control and Water Resources Commission, founded in 1946, Hulman was very familiar with issues of flooding in Indiana.[16] One of the early projects of the commission involved flood mitigation of the Eel and White rivers in the western part of the state. In 1952, the Army Corps of Engineers erected a 900-foot dam across Mill Creek to protect 43,000 acres of prime Indiana farmland, the first flood control reservoir in Indiana.[17] Related to the flood mitigation project, the state hoped to create a state park. In 1949, Hulman donated $50,000 to match funds provided by the state of Indiana to build a state park at Cloverdale. The state acquired 8,075 acres of land, and Hulman's donation provided the funding for cabin and picnic areas for the park to be known as Cagle's Mill Lake.[18] The lake spans 1,400 acres.[19]

Hulman remained chairman of the Flood Control and Water Resources Commission until December 1962, when he was named chairman of the State Conservation Commission.[20] Indiana governor Henry F. Schricker praised Hulman's charitable efforts, calling him an "outstanding citizen of Indiana who has taken a keen interest in worthy projects of this kind in the public interest, often a personal sacrifice."[21]

Hulman also was a member of the board of the Indiana State Penal Farm. The farm, part of the Indiana prison system, was used for those convicted of minor offenses.

Hulman's work on the Flood Control Commission gained attention on a national level. In 1957, Hulman was named to the Public Health Service Water Control Advisory Board.[22]

22

Dreams of Riding the Rails

In 1965, Hulman purchased the opulent private railroad car formerly known as the Florida East Coast #90. This "private varnish" (the name for private railroad cars in the trade) had a personal connection for Hulman. In the days before airplanes, he had accompanied his father on business trips to Florida, sometimes joining Standard Oil co-founder, Florida East Coast Railway and Florida real estate developer Henry Flagler on one of Flagler's private varnishes.

Flagler was born in Hopewell, New York, on January 2, 1830.[1] As a young teenager, Flagler left his family home to go to Ohio where his half brother, Dan Harkness, had settled. He quickly showed an ability as a salesman and in 1845 became a partner in a general store.[2] At age twenty-three, he married Mary Harkness, Dan Harkness' first cousin.[3]

In August 1859, drilling for oil was successful in western Pennsylvania, setting off a rush to make further strikes in the area.[4] Although Flagler lived in Bellevue, Ohio, this occurrence would change his life and make him a fortune. As a merchant based in Bellevue, he was called upon by John Rockefeller, a partner in the firm of Clark & Rockefeller, commission merchants from nearby Cleveland, Ohio.[5]

In February 1863, Flagler sold his business interests in Ohio and went to Michigan in search of riches. The source of his wealth was to have been the production of salt, a hot commodity during the Civil War. Unfortunately, as with many booms, there was stiff competition, and when the war ended, salt prices collapsed. Flagler lost all of his investment and was in debt.[6] He returned

22. Dreams of Riding the Rails 189

to Cleveland, Ohio, and began selling barrels to Rockefeller to be used for transporting oil.[7]

Living in the same neighborhood, Flagler and Rockefeller soon began talking business while walking to and from their offices. Meanwhile, the oil business was booming and both Flagler and Rockefeller closely followed the developments. In 1867, Rockefeller opened a sales office in New York to export oil to Europe. To finance the operation, he approached Stephen Harkness, Dan Harkness' half brother. Stephen Harkness agreed, with the stipulation that Flagler have complete control of the business. With money in hand, the partnership of Rockefeller, Andrews and Flagler began refining oil.

Although the partnership initially was one of many in the Cleveland area refining oil, Flagler made two business decisions catapulting the firm to dominance. The first was to build an additional refining operation. The second was to negotiate a rebate with the railroads for transportation of the product to the East Coast.[8] This gave the firm a cost advantage enabling them to undercut the prices of other refiners and ultimately dominate the market. By 1869, the Rockefeller, Andrews and Flagler refineries were the largest in the world.[9]

As the partnership expanded, they were easily able to raise additional funds to support the growth. The vexing problem was that a partnership or sole proprietorship as the primary owner of a business was not a good mechanism for a large business. Flagler decided to incorporate the business, a relatively new concept. This eliminated the personal liability of the partners and made raising capital easy. On January 10, 1870, the partnership was incorporated as Standard Oil with Flagler drawing up the incorporation papers.[10] By 1884, Standard Oil controlled the national transportation of oil.[11]

Flager's wife, Mary, was always fragile and had considerable respiratory issues. When Flagler's primary office shifted to New York, she relocated to New York in the winter of 1876–1877. The cold winters took a toll on Mrs. Flagler. After being advised that warmer weather would be beneficial for his wife,[12] Flagler decided to take Mary to Florida during the winter months. Riding a train, the primary mode of long-distance transportation, to Savannah, Georgia, the Flaglers then took a steamboat to Jacksonville. Not finding accommodations to his liking, he took his family to St. Augustine, which he also found to be unacceptable. Shortly thereafter, Flagler returned to New York, family in tow.[13] By 1881, Mary's health had deteriorated and Flagler hired a full-time companion, Ida Alice Shourds. Mary died on May 18, 1881. Almost immediately, Shourds became an object of Flagler's attention and they were married in June 1883.[14]

In December 1883, Henry and Alice took an extended trip to Florida, and Flagler found the situation much changed. In the intervening years, the

San Marcos Hotel, a six-story building, had been built in St. Augustine. While staying at the San Marcos, Flagler was soon studying the construction of the hotel. By the time the Florida vacation ended in March 1884, Flagler had decided to build a grand hotel, the Ponce de Leon, which opened January 10, 1888. The Flaglers made a suite at the Ponce de Leon their winter headquarters.[15]

Over the next twenty years, Flagler would push southward along the east coast of Florida, establishing resorts at Palm Beach and Miami. To transport people to the resorts, he began acquiring multiple short railroad lines in Florida, By upgrading the tracks to a single gauge rather than the multiple gauges that previously existed, passengers could ride from Jacksonville to points south without having to transfer from one train to another.

Before automobiles and airplanes, trains were the primary mode of long-distance travel in America. In 1834, a group of well-to-do businessmen arranged with the Boston & Providence Railroad for a designated coach in which to ride to and from their Boston offices for fifteen dollars a day—a princely sum.[16] This was the beginning of what would become a private railroad car. President-Elect William Henry Harrison had a "distinct car" for his travel to his inauguration on the Baltimore & Ohio Railroad.[17]

In the economic boom following the Civil War, railroads quickly expanded across America. In 1867, the nation had 39,000 miles of track. By 1907, there were 229,000 miles of track.[18] The private varnish became the domain of the very rich. In the 1880s and 1890s, private varnishes reflected the elegance of the Victorian age. The cars on which the upper class traveled were adorned with heavy fabrics, beveled glass and elaborate inlaid woods. The cost of the interior decor normally approximated one half of the total cost of the car.[19]

The first to own a private railroad car was Commodore Cornelius Vanderbilt, president of the New York Central Railroad.[20] Between 1880 and 1929, the private railroad car dominated the mode of travel for the rich just as private jets do today.[21]

There were multiple builders of railroad cars, the largest of which was Pullman Palace Car Company, founded in 1867. The Florida East Coast #90, however, was built by Jackson & Sharp Company in Wilmington, Delaware. The firm was founded by Job H. Jackson and Jacob Sharp. Jackson (1833–1901) was born in Chester County, Pennsylvania. After quitting school at an early age, he entered the trades, becoming a tinsmith and mechanic.[22] The older of the partners, Sharp was born in Hunterdon County, New Jersey. He gained experience as a carpenter and bridge builder before joining the car-building firm of Harlan and Huntingsworth located in Wilmington, Delaware.[23] In 1865, Jackson and Sharp joined forces to start the company bearing their names. Jackson ran the office while Sharp was responsible for the shop.

22. Dreams of Riding the Rails

A mere five years after founding, Sharp retired. Jackson funded the buyout of his partner by forming a stock company. Jackson was the driving force which built Jackson & Sharp into one of the premier railroad car construction companies in America.

The company, known for its high-quality palace cars and yachts, built the *Denver*, the first narrow-gauge passenger car for the Denver & Rio Grande Railway, in 1871. For the 1876 Centennial Anniversary of American Independence in Philadelphia, the Jackson & Sharp exhibit included the private varnish *Dom Pedro* built for Dom Pedro, the emperor of Brazil. When he attended the exhibition, Pedro was the first foreign royalty to visit the United States while in office.[24] Jackson & Sharp also constructed a palatial railroad car for King Oscar II of Sweden.[25]

Although the Pullman Company produced the majority of private railcars, Jackson & Sharp gained a reputation for producing among the most beautiful. The best of the era was the *Manhattan*, built for New York real estate mogul and railroad entrepreneur Austin Corbin. The interior was decorated with Mexican mahogany, dark brass hardware and soft tapestry coordinated with the sage-colored rug, and featured a bathtub hidden under the couches. The windows featured French plate and leaded colored glass.[26]

Flagler placed an order for a private railroad car with Jackson & Sharp to be built in the Empire style. Constructed in 1899, this car is seventy-one feet, six inches long, with the platform extending another seven feet, two inches.[27] During Flagler's lifetime, it was one of his private railroad cars. Unlike the palace cars of the 1880s and 1890s, the car's interior was not in the heavy dark wood normally found on private varnishes but rather reflected the Sunshine State to which it traveled. The interior was decorated in light hues with bright curtains, and the furnishings were of sandalwood rather than mahogany. The exterior of the railroad car matched the color design of the Florida East Coast Railway—sunflower yellow with chocolate brown trim.[28]

The Florida East Coast #90 reflected the wealth of Henry Flagler. The car had a Tiffany roof and gold filigree applied over blond African mahogany. Additionally, the car had a parlor/dining room, a master bedroom, guest bedroom, gallery and butler's pantry, and lavatory and shower.[29] When Flagler went to the opening of the Florida East Coast link to Key West, the Florida East Coast #90 was among the cars which formed the special train transporting dignitaries for the occasion.

In 1950, the Florida East Coast Railway sold the Florida East Coast #90 to Ike Duffey, president of the Central Indiana Railroad. Duffey repainted the exterior to dark green, and the car was renamed *Duchess* after Duffey's dog.

When discovered on a siding in Anderson, Indiana, the car didn't look like it did during its heyday. Reuben Darby, owner of the Custom Railroad Car Company Inc. which restored it, described the discovery:

> While I was in Chicago on a business trip I heard about a car on an old siding in Indiana in a tiny town. I really wasn't interested but after debating with myself, decided to take a look. I wasn't impressed by the outside. I climbed up and found the roof in a terrible shape. But when I went inside I couldn't believe my eyes. Around me was the original décor of the gay 90's with all of the intricately hand carved paneling intact. I knew I had seen the car somewhere before. Then I remembered seeing five photographs taken in the 1890's of Henry Flagler's car. I couldn't believe I had found it.[30]

Darby's primary business was a lumberyard in Hagerstown, Maryland. The railroad car restoration business was founded by Darby when he received a $20,000 cashier's check from a man interested in Darby restoring a railroad car. One of his foremen had previously paneled a railroad car. Shortly after that, word spread about the work, and he received a phone call from the man. Darby recalled the conversation: "I hear you people are the experts to locate and repair private cars." His reaction to the phone call was, "Brother, this was news to me. I didn't know one end of a railroad car from another." He continued with the tale, "Then a cashier's check for $20,000 arrived ... no strings, no contract, no nothing. I didn't even know where to get a coach, but there I was with 20 grand."

With cash in hand, Darby started the business in 1960. He found an old Baltimore & Ohio dining car and leased three hundred feet of siding in Hagerstown.[31]

The interior renovations to the Florida East Coast #90 included the delicate job of stripping the paint from the Tiffany ceiling's filigree and meticulously restoring the coach to its original condition. The interior of the coach was restored with primarily two shades of green with highlights of gold leaf. The parlor and dining room had the original furniture. The dining room had the original dining room table, and the living room's seating consists of three wicker chairs. The exterior was returned to the East Coast Railroad colors of sunflower yellow with brown trim.

This private varnish was bought by Tony and Mary Hulman. Upon taking delivery of the railcar, Mary Hulman said, "It would be nice to attach it to a train and take a trip. It's been a long time since we've done that."[32] To travel with the car, the Hulmans would contract directly with a railroad which would include it either at the beginning or the end of its train.[33] Sadly, the Hulmans never found the time to take this car on a rail trip.

The Florida East Coast #90 is on loan to the Indiana Transportation Museum in Noblesville, Indiana.

23

Controversy

In 1900 Terre Haute was full of optimism. With a population of 36,000, it had a stable industry base. With three foundries in town, Terre Haute fancied itself as the "Pittsburgh of the West."[1] Its robust economy centered around a strong coal-mining industry, four railroad maintenance facilities, a strong liquor industry with two of the three largest distilleries and the nation's seventh-largest brewer, and three bottle manufacturers.

The town also thought it was progressive. It had an opera house. When the original opera house was destroyed by fire in 1896, a new one opened in 1897. With 160 miles of crushed gravel roads, it proclaimed its streets were "the finest in the state."[2]

But there was an underside to the town. By the early 1900s, Terre Haute had been branded "Sin City," which alluded to the vice and political corruption that was a part of the structure of the town.

A coalition of city leaders and businesses joined hands to expose the link between city hall, crime and special interests. With a strong history of fraudulent elections, the coalition of civic and business leaders petitioned for the federal monitoring of elections. In the early 1900s, three Terre Haute mayors faced charges of misconduct: Edwin Bidamin, impeached in 1906; Louis Gerhardt, arraigned for contempt of court in 1911; and Donn Roberts, convicted of election fraud in 1915.[3]

In the 1920s, the town's reputation for prostitution had spread as far as Chicago, 165 miles away. The brothels and houses of ill repute were located in a six-block area lining the Wabash River.[4]

As the twentieth century progressed, things began to unravel for the town. Historically, the coal industry surrounding Terre Haute was labor-intensive deep vein mining. The Guffy Act, which set minimum wages and hours for coal miners as well as establishing the minimum and maximum price for coal, led to greater mechanization of the industry.[5] Additionally, the use of electricity and oil for power and heat led to the long-term decline of the coal industry.[6] Over time, the industry switched to strip-mining which requires significantly fewer workers.

Prohibition was devastating to the liquor industry in Terre Haute. The two large distilleries were sold, and Terre Haute Brewing, the nation's seventh-largest brewery, manufactured near beer. The two distilleries and Terre Haute Brewing were replaced by illegal distilleries, speakeasies and roadhouses. Organized crime invaded the town.[7]

It also negatively affected the bottle industry, a major supplier to the liquor manufacturers. Prior to Prohibition, the town had three bottle manufacturers, but only Root Bottling thrived due to its manufacturing of bottles for Coca-Cola.

Terre Haute also saw the heyday of the railroad maintenance shops end with the change from steam locomotives to diesel locomotives. In the days of steam locomotives, the engines needed maintenance or refueling of water and coal every 100 or so miles. Although the development of the diesel railroad engine was in the 1910s, it took several years before the technology began to have the efficiency of the steam locomotive. By the mid–1920s the railroads were able to haul freight longer distances without the frequent need for maintenance or fuel. They closed their maintenance facilities in Terre Haute.

The town was also a hotbed of union organization going back to 1877 when a nationwide railroad strike resulted in U.S. Army infantry troops being used to restore order. In 1935, there was a prolonged and violent strike at Columbian Enameling & Stamping. In a series of moves, tensions in the town escalated after Columbian Enameling management declared a lockout of the plant. Some workers broke into the office, destroying equipment. Management responded by hiring strikebreakers. This resulted in a general strike being declared in the town—the first general strike east of the Rocky Mountains. Indiana governor Paul McNutt responded by declaring martial law and sending the Indiana National Guard to the town. This action resulted in Terre Haute's labor problems gaining national attention.[8] This along with other strikes earned the town a reputation as a "bad town" for labor.

After World War II, the election of Vernon McMillan as mayor brought positive changes to the town. A 1947 *Kiplinger's Personal Finance* article lauded the turnaround of the Terre Haute economy, which had been in decline since

23. Controversy

1919. It also praised the leadership of Hulman and McMillan who had enticed industry to Terre Haute. Hulman, chairman of the Chamber of Commerce from 1944 until 1950, is credited with crafting a plan to bring new industries into Terre Haute. After two existing businesses, Commercial Solvents Corporation and Great Lakes Steel, expanded their presence in Terre Haute, numerous other companies, including Visking Corporation, Chesty Foods and Recipe Foods, established facilities in Terre Haute.

Underlying this resurgence was the development of the Terre Haute airport which could handle commercial traffic where the existing airport could not. Hulman made a leadership gift in this effort. Hulman was also credited with turning around the local gas company which he purchased in 1945.

A good part of the resurgence was attributed by the *Kiplinger* article to the cleanup of the vice which had long plagued Terre Haute. Additionally, labor relations in Terre Haute had improved significantly. In an era where strikes were frequent, Terre Haute had not experienced significant issues during World War II. Finally, the town had improved the citizens' overall health with a new sanitation system which was spearheaded by Hulman.

The article also indicated that Hulman's employees were among the best paid in the wholesale grocery business. Union representatives described Hulman as "a man you can reason with."[9]

Although the *Kiplinger Personal Finance* article was very positive about the changes in Terre Haute, prostitution and gambling remained embedded in the town. In 1957, federal authorities raided a gambling house in Terre Haute which had been doing an estimated $1.5 million in business a month.[10] This gambling business appears to have had connections at the very top of Terre Haute's government. The town's then three-term mayor, Ralph Tucker, had been actively supported by Leo Light. Light and Joe Traum, an ex-convict and Terre Haute's top gambler, were partners in the Manor House restaurant. The gambling operation was located next door to the restaurant and was leased by Traum to Leo Shaffer's sports gambling syndicate.[11]

In the 1950s and 1960s, Terre Haute was pointed out as an example of a town with social issues, including the number of bars and prostitutes. In the 1950s, a *Fortune* magazine article attributed Terre Haute's social issues directly to Hulman. "Hulman & Co. has a vast reputation as a doer of good works in the community but as an employer it falls flat on its face." *Fortune* indicated that the underlying problem was Hulman & Company's low wages, which the company was able to maintain by keeping other businesses out.[12]

Was the underlying problem of low wages in Terre Haute caused by Hulman & Company? Since 1919 the town, with the exception of one year during World War II, had suffered from chronic unemployment. Desperate for work, men would go to the mayor's office and the county commissioner's hoping to find day labor.[13]

Joe Cloutier, Hulman's closest associate and adviser, vigorously disagreed with the idea that Hulman did not want additional business in Terre Haute. He recalled an earlier conversation with a Terre Haute resident when the issue was raised:

> We still had the foundation operation which owned the *Tribune-Star*, and since we were kind of the Godfathers of the foundation, we were interested in the newspaper. We had the television station. We've got this business here; and we had about 200 acres right out here that we had put into the city for development, which very few developers do. Most of them build out in the country because it can be done so much cheaper. But we put it in the city. This man said the same thing. He knew why things didn't go better, because Tony Hulman, Hulman & Company and our whole outfit was not interested in getting new industry. And I agreed with him. I said, "You're entirely right. We've got a television station over here—the only way they operate is by selling advertising, and the only people that want to buy advertising is people who have something to sell to people. We've got a newspaper that's much the same thing—they've got to have people to sell the newspaper to as they can sell advertising. We've got 200 acres of ground out there that we'd like to build houses on. We've got some warehouses over here that are crammed full of food that nobody uses but people. I'm sure you're right, that we don't want any more people in Terre Haute."[14]

Cloutier also indicated that the Hulman organization remained active in wanting business to come to Terre Haute. In 1963, Cloutier, Terre Haute mayor Ralph Tucker, the director of the local Chamber of Commerce John K. Lamb, and an auto dealer who was on the Chrysler dealer advisory board went to Chrysler Corporation to promote Terre Haute for the location of a new automotive plant. The focal question on the minds of the folks at Chrysler was if Terre Haute had any area planning. They did not. That seems to have ended Terre Haute's chances for a Chrysler auto plant.[15]

In 1961, Hulman was the largest landholder in Vigo County, which included not only his residence; his residential retreat, Lingen Lodge; and the family farms but also Terre Haute's largest hotel, the long-distance bus terminal, and interests in the town's largest shopping center and a residential development, Hulman Meadows. The article also indicates that he was the largest landholder in downtown Terre Haute.

Like many towns and cities, the development of shopping centers which followed the development of suburban residential areas caused Terre Haute's downtown to decline. By 1961, the downtown was in shambles. Wabash Avenue, the town's primary east–west corridor, was described by John Lamb, the Chamber of Commerce's executive director: "We challenge anyone to walk down Wabash Avenue from Third to Ninth streets, taking an inventory of the ancient, dilapidated buildings; antiquated store fronts; vacant upper floors; unpainted, unwashed, unclean exterior walls; garish, dirty streets; overhanging signs and traffic jams, without realizing something needs to be done—and quickly. Downtown Terre Haute hasn't had a face lift or even a face washing in decades."[16]

Some in Terre Haute blamed the abandonment of downtown on Hulman. Cloutier responded with a tale:

> Some years ago a local shoe merchant whose father and himself had been renting their property for many, many years, decided to buy the property that they had their shoe store in. He immediately got concerned as to whether he had paid too much for it and he got concerned about what was going to happen downtown now that he had his own money invested in it. And he had a friend in New York—a big real estate firm—asked him to stop in here and take a look at Terre Haute and see what he could determine. The real estate man came to Cloutier's office and said "You have control of the downtown area. I understand nothing can be done without the Hulman interest."

Cloutier responded to the man's charge,

> We don't control it, but I can tell you what's going to happen. You've got people with the property down there that are living off of depreciation. The rents are clear out of proportion to what the buildings are worth. It's a prime location. There's not anything going to happen to it until it gets worse, and it's going to get much worse. You've got widows whose husbands have bought that piece of property as their life legacy to their wife to keep them for the rest of their lives. The only way you can buy that property is to give enough money that they can re-invest it and get the money they're getting out of it, and that's too much for the property. Until the rents go down to where you can afford to buy the property at the proper land values and then tear the buildings down, it's not going to get any better."[17]

A 1961 *Saturday Evening Post* article exposed the rampant vice in Terre Haute— the gambling houses, the bookies and the prostitution. Hulman, who owned the two newspapers, the only television station, the gas company, a trucking company, and the town's largest bank, as well as being the town's largest landowner, was targeted by complaints that he called the shots in the town. The *Saturday Evening Post* said that Terre Haute's citizens were apathetic and indifferent to their town and some had the attitude of "let Tony do it."[18]

Hulman, who had been a leader in bringing improvements to Terre Haute in the 1940s, pulled back after an anti–Hulman campaign changed things at the Chamber of Commerce. Historically, the level of contributions determined how many votes that person had for the Chamber offices. Because Hulman gave more than anyone else, he had more votes. Not only did he serve for six years as the president, but others in his organization served for eight additional terms. Under John Lamb's leadership, the election methodology was changed to one vote per person, with the end result of Ray Hahn being elected president over Hulman. This was seen by all, including Hulman, as being directed toward him. After having given of himself to various efforts around town, he was hurt by this action.[19]

Hulman did not see Terre Haute as being particularly sinful. He commented, "I don't feel it's any different than any other community in this part of the country." This sentiment was also expressed by Terre Haute resident Joe Petty, an employee of the Terre Haute employment office. "The ones who've always lived here think every other place is the same way. They sort of like it the way it is."

John Lamb, executive director of the Chamber of Commerce in 1961, said of the problems faced by Terre Haute, "It's a matter of civic conscience, which we do not have. People just don't care."[20] Vern McMillan, Terre Haute's mayor who worked closely with Hulman on reforms in the 1940s, said, "It's a lack of leadership."[21]

In 1961, *Saturday Evening Post* reporter Peter Wyden asked Hulman about Terre Haute's future in addressing the issues the town faced. Hulman responded, "I feel the city will eventually make progress. When, I don't know. And again, I may be mistaken."[22]

24

The End

Because of the Indianapolis 500, Hulman, the shy, quiet businessman, had become known on an international basis. He was beloved by many and was considered not only the savior of the Indianapolis 500 but also of auto racing.

In late October 1977, Hulman had not been feeling well for several days and was admitted to Union Hospital in Terre Haute for tests. His cousin, Don Smith, who talked with him while he was in the hospital, related, "He had complained of some pain but was making plans to go duck hunting in a few days along the Illinois River with some friends." He and Smith were also planning to fly to Houston, Texas, on October 28 where he was to be honored. Afterward, he would continue on to the Phoenix race.[1]

On October 27 the doctors recommended he transfer to St. Vincent's Hospital in Indianapolis. The diagnosis was an aneurysm, and upon arrival in Indianapolis, Hulman was immediately taken into surgery. During surgery, his heart stopped at 9:45 p.m.[2]

The citizens of his beloved hometown, Terre Haute, had lost a civic leader. The citizens of Indianapolis, where he had spent much time over the past thirty-two years, lost a good friend and somebody who elevated the city of Indianapolis to a national basis because of the running of the Indianapolis 500.

The funeral was held on a rainy day at St. Benedict's Catholic Church[3] which his grandfather had been instrumental in establishing. It was attended by a wide variety of people. Among race drivers attending were Peter DePaolo, winner of the 1925 Indianapolis 500; Sam Hanks, winner of the 1957 Indianapolis 500; Jim Rathmann, winner of the 1960 Indianapolis 500; and Johnny Rutherford, three-time winner of the Indianapolis 500 (1974, 1976 and 1980). Also from the driver ranks was A. J. Foyt, Jr., with whom Hulman rode in the pace car in a victory lap around the Speedway after Foyt won his fourth Indianapolis 500 just six months earlier.

Others in the racing and sporting community included John Mecom, Jr., a former racing car owner and owner of the New Orleans Saints; Lindsey Hopkins, a car owner; and Dr. Joseph D. Mattoli, owner of the Pocono International Raceway, home of the Pocono 500. Representing USAC were Dick King and Ray Marquette.[4]

A lifelong Democrat, Hulman had served Indiana in many capacities. He was widely recognized as having been significant in the election of Birch E. Bayh, Jr., to the United States Senate. Other well-known politicians attending the funeral included former Indiana governor Edgar D. Whitcomb and Indiana secretary of state, Larry Conrad.

Leading the business community was Hulman's right-hand man, Joseph Cloutier; retired Indianapolis Motor Speedway grounds superintendent, Clarence Cagle; and Fran Derr, director of ticket sales for the Speedway.

Those who attended the funeral heard Father Hubert Koblinski, pastor of St. Benedict's, eulogize Hulman, saying, "But the greatest eulogy will be in hearts of living men and women who remember his generosity. Tony will be remembered simply as a good and decent man who saw needs and tried to meet them, saw wrongs and tried to right them, saw suffering and tried to heal."[5] Koblinski continued, "Much will be written, much will be said about his accomplishments. Yet the voices I hear ... will remind us about the wisdom, generosity and goodness of this man. I hear the voice of the little people; they're speaking not about the big things Tony accomplished in his life, but they are telling me of his kindness, concern, regard for his fellow man—and all of it anonymously. The greatest eulogy we could have given him is a living monument in the hearts of grateful people who remember his goodness. This man loved his fellow man and he served his fellow man."[6]

He was laid to rest next to his parents in the Calvary Cemetery[7] on a hill on the east side of his beloved Terre Haute, overlooking fields which during the summer would be filled with corn.

Hulman once described his philosophy of life: "Basically I'm for living and let live. I wanted to accomplish as much as I could, but without being pushy at all and without hurting anyone along the way."

His accomplishments were many. Throughout his business career, he owned multiple companies operating in multiple industries, including Hulman & Company, Coca-Cola Bottling Company of Indianapolis, and F. W. Cook

Brewing. He served on the board of directors of Indiana National Bank, Terre Haute First National Bank, Chicago & Eastern Illinois Railroad, and Alton Box Board Company.[8]

In September 1977, he was inducted into the auto racing Hall of Fame. Posthumously, he was inducted into the Motorsports Hall of Fame in the United States in 1991. The Motorsports Hall of Fame induction says, "Born into wealth, Anton (Tony) Hulman, Jr., embellished his personal resources with courage, foresight and a personal passion for automobile racing to become the savior of America's foremost motorsports facility and its greatest one-day sports spectacular, the Indianapolis 500."[9]

Chapter Notes

Introduction

1. "Tony Hulman, Mr. 500, Dies," *Indianapolis Star*, October 28, 1977, p. 1.
2. Shaplen, "The Hoosier Pied Piper, Part II," *Sports Illustrated*, June 2, 1958, p. 60.
3. Cavinder, "Tony Hulman: Hoosier in Profile," *Star Magazine*, May 28, 1972, p. 6.
4. Ibid.
5. Snodgrass, "Hulman's 500 Richest, Best-Run Race," *Indianapolis Star*, May 24, 1975, p. 32.
6. Cavinder, "Tony Hulman: Hoosier in Profile," *Star Magazine*, May 28, 1972, p. 6.
7. "Ultimate Responsibility Is Hulman's but 'Family' Decides Many Things," *Indianapolis Star*, July 12, 1973, p. 1.
8. "'Pop' Will Be There as Usual," *Indianapolis Star*, May 26, 1948, p. 26 supplement.
9. Fuson, "Few Hoosiers Ever See the Real Anton Hulman," *Indianapolis News*, February 6, 1961, p. 14.
10. "TH Means Tony Hulman of Terre Haute," *Indiana Business and Industry*, October 1966, p. 21.
11. "Ultimate Responsibility Is Hulman's but 'Family' decides Many Things," *Indianapolis Star*, July 12, 1973, p. 1.
12. "Anton Hulman Jr.: The Story of a Shy Tycoon," *Indianapolis Times*, May 25, 1962, p. 8.

Chapter 1

1. Bloemker, *500 Miles to Go*, 24.
2. Lewis, *Eddie Rickenbacker*, 80.
3. Sonnenberg and Schoenberger, *Allison: Power of Excellence*, 57.
4. Leyes and Fleming, *The History of North American Small Gas Turbine Aircraft Engines*, 520.
5. Ibid., 521.
6. Goldwaithe Oral History, 4.
7. Bloemker, *500 Miles to Go*, 175.
8. "Speedway Was at Peace during War Years," *Indianapolis Star*, May 27, 1995, p. s7.
9. Patton, "Hoosier Buys Speedway," *Indianapolis Star*, November 15, 1945, p. 1.
10. Shaw, *Gentlemen, Start Your Engines*, 274.
11. "Cochran Puts Wheels in Motion to Save Speedway from Ruin," *Indianapolis Star*, May 9, 1993, p. K-4.
12. Ibid., K-5.
13. Shaplen, "The Hoosier Pied Piper, Part I," *Sports Illustrated*, May 26, 1958, p. 61.
14. Dorson, *The Indy 500: An American Institution under Fire*, 35, 36.
15. Shaplen, "The Hoosier Pied Piper, Part I," *Sports Illustrated*, June 2, 1958, p. 61.
16. "Cochran Puts Wheels in Motion to Save Speedway from Ruin," *Indianapolis Star*, May 9, 1993, p. K-5.
17. Patton, "Hoosier Buys Speedway," *Indianapolis Star*, November 15, 1945, p. 1, 16.
18. "New Speedway Owner Plans Face-Lifting Job at Track," *Indianapolis News*, November 15, 1945, p. 1.
19. Patton, "Hoosier Buys Speedway," *Indianapolis Star*, November 15, 1945, p. 1, 16.
20. Ibid.

21. Dorson, *The Indy 500: An American Institution*, 34.
22. Cloutier Oral History, 25.
23. Patten, "Hoosier Buys Speedway," *Indianapolis Star*, November 15, 1945, p. 1, 16.
24. "The Speedway Changes Hands," *Indianapolis News*, November 15, 1945, p. 10.
25. "Hoosier at Speedway 'Wheel,'" *Indianapolis Star*, November 16, 1945, p. 14.
26. Daniels, Moore, Eggert and Cadou, *75 Years of the Indianapolis 500*, 1945.
27. "Cochran Puts Wheels in Motion to Save the Speedway from Ruin," *Indianapolis Star*, May 9, 1993, p. K-4.
28. Ibid.
29. "The Changing Face of the Speedway," *Indianapolis Star*, May 9, 1993, p. K-8.
30. Mittman, "Longtime IMS Superintendent Cagle Dies at 88," July 7, 2003, www.indianapolismotorspeedway.com.
31. Ibid.
32. Collins, "Memories Galore: Ol Indy and Me Go Back a Long Way," *Indianapolis Star*, May 25, 1991, p. D-4.
33. Kramer, *Indianapolis Motor Speedway 100 Years of Racing*, p. 133.
34. Ibid., 129.
35. Ibid., 137.

Chapter 2

1. Markle and Collins, *The House of Hulman*, 2.
2. Ibid., 1.
3. Ibid., 10.
4. Ibid., 12, 13.
5. Taylor, *Peopling Indiana*, 163.
6. Ibid., 147.
7. Ibid., 15.
8. Ibid., 16.
9. Goebel, *William Henry Harrison*, 54.
10. McCormick, *Terre Haute, Queen City*, 21.
11. McCormick, *Terre Haute, Queen City*, 24.
12. Markle and Collins, *The House of Hulman*, 24.
13. Bloxsome, *Rose: The First 100 Years*, 9.
14. Markle and Collins, *The House of Hulman*, 27.
15. McCormick, *Terre Haute, Queen City*, 36.
16. Bloxsome, *Rose: The First 100 Years*, 16.
17. Markle and Collins, *The House of Hulman*, 31.
18. Ibid., 34.
19. Ibid., 22.
20. Ibid., 34.
21. Ibid., 37.
22. Ibid., 38.
23. Ibid., 44.
24. Ibid., 45.
25. Ibid., 46, 47.
26. "Monthly Record of New Events," *Harpers' New Monthly Magazine*, vol. 17, 1858, p. 829.

Chapter 3

1. Markle and Collins, *The House of Hulman*, 49.
2. Ibid., 51.
3. Taylor, *Peopling Indiana*, 161.
4. Markle and Collins, *The House of Hulman*, 60.
5. Ibid., 55, 56.
6. Ibid., 57.
7. St. Benedict's Church, *Centennial of the Parish of St. Benedict*, 15.
8. Furer, *The Germans in America*, 42.
9. St. Benedict's Church, *Centennial of the Parish of St. Benedict*, 16.
10. Markle and Collins, *The House of Hulman*, 63.
11. Taylor, *Peopling Indiana*, 165.
12. St. Benedict's Church, *Centennial of the Parish of St. Benedict*, 17.
13. Blanchard, *A History of the Catholic Church in Indiana*, 449.
14. Markle and Collins, *The House of Hulman*, 68.
15. Ibid., 65.
16. Ibid., 64.
17. Ibid., 44, 54.
18. Ibid., 82.
19. Ibid., 66.
20. McCormick, *Terre Haute, Queen City*, 56.
21. Markle and Collins, *The House of Hulman*, 53, 54.
22. Ibid., 56.
23. Ibid., 54, 55.
24. Ibid., 66.
25. Ibid., 103.
26. Ibid., 105, 106.
27. Ibid., 109.
28. Ibid., 67.
29. Ibid., 75.
30. Ibid., 91.
31. Ibid., 111, 112.
32. Ibid., 90.
33. Ibid., 120.
34. St. Anthony's Hospital, *Diamond Jubilee*, 12.
35. Ibid., 13.
36. Markle and Collins, *The House of Hulman*, 123, 124.
37. Ibid., 143, 144.
38. McCormick, *Terre Haute, Queen City*, 64.
39. Markle and Collins, *The House of Hulman*, 143, 144.
40. Ibid., 145.
41. Ibid., 145, 146.
42. Ibid., 128.
43. Ibid., 146.
44. Ibid., 133, 135.

45. Ibid., 137, 138.
46. Ibid., 141.
47. Ibid., 188, 189.
48. "The Hulman," September 29, 1893, Scrapbook, 97A, Vigo County Library Special Collection, p. 11.
49. Markle and Collins, *The House of Hulman*, 148, 149.
50. Dollase, "Can You Still Call Her a Girl When She's Eighty-Seven Years Old?" *Indiana Preservationist*, vol. 1, January/February 1993, p. 10, 11.
51. Markle and Collins, *The House of Hulman*, 151.
52. Ibid., 152.
53. "The Hulman," September 29, 1893, Scrapbook, 97A, Vigo County Library Special Collection, p. 11.
54. Markle and Collins, *The House of Hulman*, 153.
55. "The Hulman," September 29, 1893, Scrapbook, 97A, Vigo County Library Special Collection, p. 11.
56. Markle and Collins, *The House of Hulman*, 153.
57. Taylor, *Indiana: A New Historical Guide*, 278.
58. "The Hulman," September 29, 1893, Scrapbook, 97A, Vigo County Library Special Collection, p. 11.
59. Markle and Collins, *The House of Hulman*, 163, 164.
60. Ibid., 165.
61. Ibid., 166, 168.
62. Dollase, "Can You Still Call Her a Girl When She's Eighty-Seven Years Old?" *Indiana Preservationist*, vol. 1, January/February 1993, p. 10, 11.
63. Markle and Collins, *The House of Hulman*, 185, 186.
64. Ibid., 173.
65. St. Benedict's Church, *Centennial of the Parish of St. Benedict*, 18.
66. Ibid., 16.
67. Ibid., 18.
68. Blanchard, *History of the Catholic Church In Indiana*, 450.
69. Ibid., 451.
70. Markle and Collins, *The House of Hulman*, 180.
71. Ibid., 181, 182.
72. Ibid., 191.
73. Ibid., 192.
74. Taylor, *Indiana: A New Historical Guide*, 278.

Chapter 4

1. Markle and Collins, *The House of Hulman*, 192.
2. Ibid., 193.
3. Deutsch, *Building a Housewife's Paradise*, 13.
4. Ibid., 18, 19.
5. Levinson, *The Great A&P*, 49.
6. Ibid., 51.
7. Ibid., 59.
8. Ibid., 64.
9. Markle and Collins, *The House of Hulman*, 207.
10. Ibid., 210.
11. Ibid., 218.
12. Ibid., 219.
13. Ibid., 225.
14. Levinson, *The Great A&P*, 64, 65.
15. Ibid., 71.
16. Markle and Collins, *The House of Hulman*, 229.
17. Ibid., 230.
18. Zahorchak, *The History of St. Joseph's and Calvary Cemeteries*, 4.
19. Ibid., 11.
20. Ibid., 15.
21. Ibid., 14.
22. Clark and Simon, *The Labor Movement in America*, 99.
23. Markle and Collins, *The House of Hulman*, 232.
24. Ibid., 233.
25. Ibid., 231.
26. Ibid., 228.
27. Ibid., 231.
28. Ibid., 233.
29. Ibid., 233.
30. Ibid., 236, 237.
31. Levinson, *The Great A&P*, 74.
32. Markle and Collins *The House of Hulman*, 234.
33. Levinson, *The Great A&P*, 74.
34. Ibid., 77.
35. Clark and Simon, *The Labor Movement in America*, 98.
36. Markle and Collins, *The House of Hulman*, 235.
37. Ibid., 236.
38. Ibid., 236, 237.
39. Ibid., 240.
40. Ibid., 241.
41. Ibid., 238.
42. Ibid., 242, 229.
43. Levinson, *The Great A&P*, 85.
44. Markle and Collins, *The House of Hulman*, 242.
45. Ibid., 246.
46. Ibid., 246.
47. www.iga.com.
48. Markle and Collins, *The House of Hulman*, 246.
49. Levinson, *The Great A&P*, 130.
50. Deutsch, *Building a Housewife's Paradise*, 62.

51. Markle and Collins, *The House of Hulman*, 251.
52. Levinson, *The Great A&P*, 84.
53. Meserole and Sevin, *Effective Grocery Wholesaling*, 121, 125.
54. Markle and Collins, *The House of Hulman*, 252.
55. Wiley, "The Hulman-Fendrich Wedding: Folk Present Still Talking of Beautiful Ceremony," *Terre Haute Tribune*, October 6, 1926, p. 8.
56. "Hulman Dynasty 1850–1997," *Tribune-Star*, May 26, 1997, special section.
57. Wiley, "The Hulman-Fendrich Wedding: Folk Present Still Talking of Beautiful Ceremony," *Terre Haute Tribune*, October 6, 1926, p. 8.
58. "Hulman Dynasty 1850–1997," *Tribune-Star*, May 26, 1997, special section.
59. Cavinder, "Tony Hulman, Hoosier in Profile," *Star Magazine*, May 28, 1972, p. 6.
60. Shaplen, "The Hoosier Pied Piper, Part II," *Sports Illustrated*, June 2, 1958, p. 63.
61. Markle and Collins, *The House of Hulman*, 264.
62. Levinson, *The Great A&P*, 122.
63. Ibid., 100.
64. Levinson, *The Great A&P*, 106.
65. Ibid., 82.
66. Ibid., 129.
67. Markle and Collins, *The House of Hulman*, 270.

Chapter 5

1. American Chemical Society website, www.acswebcontent.acs.org/landmarks/bakingpowder/development.html.
2. Levinson, *The Great A&P*, 39.
3. Ibid., 40.
4. Markle and Collins, *The House of Hulman*, 67.
5. Dollase, "Can You Still Call Her a Girl When She's Eighty-Seven Years Old?" *Indiana Preservationist*, vol. 1, January/February 1993, p. 10, 11.
6. Markle and Collins, *The House of Hulman*, 81.
7. Dollase, "Can You Still Call Her a Girl When She's Eighty-Seven Years Old?" *Indiana Preservationist*, vol. 1, January/February 1993, p. 10, 11.
8. Markle and Collins, *The House of Hulman*, 198.
9. Ibid. 199–200.
10. Cloutier Oral History, 2.
11. Markle and Collins, *The House of Hulman*, 254.
12. Cavinder, "Tony Hulman, Hoosier in Profile," *Star Magazine*, May 28, 1972, p. 6.
13. Ibid.
14. Cloutier Oral History, 28.
15. "The Hulmans Coming to America (Tony's Touch Impacts Terre Haute and Beyond)," *Terre Haute Tribune-Star*, May 26, 1997, special section.
16. Markle and Collins, *The House of Hulman*, 272, 273.
17. Dollase, "Can You Still Call Her a Girl When She's Eighty-Seven Years Old?" *Indiana Preservationist*, vol. 1, January/February 1993, p. 10, 11.
18. Cloutier Oral History, 29.
19. Levinson, *The Great A&P*, 140.
20. Ibid., 148.
21. Ibid., 149.
22. Ibid., 148.
23. Ibid., 165.
24. Roznowski, *An American Hometown*, 168.
25. Cloutier Oral History, 34, 35.
26. Ibid., 29.
27. Wilkinson, "Hulmans Give Foundation's Huge Assets to Rose Poly," *Indianapolis Star*, January 7, 1971, p. 24.
28. Markle and Collins, *The House of Hulman*, 338.
29. Ibid., 291.
30. Cloutier Oral History, 37.
31. Markle and Collins, *The House of Hulman*, 273.
32. Cloutier Oral History, 12.
33. Ibid., 13.
34. Ibid., 34.
35. Cavinder, "Tony Hulman, Hoosier in Profile," *Star Magazine*, May 28, 1972, p. 6.
36. "Anton Hulman Jr.: The Story of a Shy Tycoon," *Indianapolis Times*, May 25, 1962, p. 8.
37. Cloutier Oral History, p. 24.
38. Markle and Collins, *The House of Hulman*, 317.
39. Cavinder, "Tony Hulman, Hoosier in Profile," *Star Magazine*, May 28, 1972, p. 6.
40. Fuson, "Few Hoosiers Ever See the Real Anton Hulman," *Indianapolis News*, February 6, 1961, p. 14.
41. Meserole, *Effective Grocery Wholesaling*, 9, 120.
42. Dollase, "Can You Still Call Her a Girl When She's Eighty-Seven Years Old?" *Indiana Preservationist*, vol. 1, January/February 1993, p. 10, 11.

Chapter 6

1. *Terre Haute Tribune-Star* and McCormick, *Century: 100 Years in the Wabash Valley*, 1.
2. Ibid., 15.
3. Power, "Tony Hulman—It Can't Be," *Indianapolis News*, October 31, 1977, p. 21.
4. Shaplen, "The Hoosier Pied Piper, Part II," *Sports Illustrated*, June 2, 1958, p. 63.

5. Ibid.
6. "Inside Indianapolis," *Indianapolis Times*, January 19, 1946, p. 7.
7. Snodgrass, "Hulman's 500 Richest, Best-Run Race," *Indianapolis Star*, May 24, 1975, p. 32.
8. "The Hulmans Coming to America (Tony's Touch Impacts Terre Haute and Beyond)," *Terre Haute Tribune-Star*, May 26, 1997, special section.
9. Yale University Records, Torch Society, 4.
10. Shaplen, "The Hoosier Pied Piper, Part II," *Sports Illustrated*, June 2, 1958, p. 63.
11. Patton, "Hoosier Buys Speedway," *Indianapolis Star*, November 15, 1945, p. 1.
12. Snodgrass, "Hulman's 500 Richest, Best-Run Race," *Indianapolis Star*, May 24, 1975, p. 32.
13. Cohane, *The Yale Football Story*, 220.
14. Ibid., 225.
15. Shaplen, "The Hoosier Pied Piper, Part II," *Sports Illustrated*, June 2, 1958, p. 63.
16. "Inside Indianapolis," *Indianapolis Times*, January 19, 1946, p. 7; and Mills, "Tony Hulman Is Mr. Speedway," *Indianapolis Times*, May 28, 1959, p. 3.
17. Shaplen, "The Hoosier Pied Piper, Part II," *Sports Illustrated*, June 2, 1958, p. 63.
18. Ibid.
19. Ibid.
20. "Hulman Dynasty 1850–1997," *Terre Haute Tribune-Star*, May 26, 1997, special section.
21. "Inside Indianapolis," *Indianapolis Times*, January 19, 1946, p. 7.

Chapter 7

1. Taylor, *Indy: Seventy-Five Years*, 101, 102.
2. Ibid., 101, 102.
3. Ibid., 103.
4. "Speedway Entry List Boosted to 50 Cars," *Indianapolis Star*, May 2, 1946, p. 22.
5. Wilkins, "Best Driver in the World Visits Speedway, Thinks It's Wonderful," *Indianapolis Star*, May 24, 1946, p. 15.
6. "Qualifying Trials to Start May 18 for 500-Mile Race," *Indianapolis Star*, May 5, 1946, sect. 3, p. 41.
7. "Trials to Open Today for 500-Mile Classic," *Indianapolis Star*, May 18, 1946, p. 1.
8. Patton, "Thousands See Speedway Preview," *Indianapolis Star*, May 19, 1946, sect. 1, p. 1.
9. Patton, "150,000 Jam Roadways; 60,000 at Speedway," *Indianapolis Star*, May 20, 1946, p. 1.
10. Patton, "Hepburn Shatters Trial Record with Blazing 133.944 MPH Run," *Indianapolis Star*, May 27, 1946, p. 1.
11. Patton, "Rudi Caracciola, European Race Champion, Badly Hurt in Crash into Speedway Wall," *Indianapolis Star*, May 29, 1946, p. 1.
12. Davidson and Shaffer, *Autocourse*, 104.
13. Popely, *Indianapolis 500 Chronicle*, 79.
14. Cavinder, "Tony Hulman, Hoosier in Profile," *Star Magazine*, May 28, 1972, p. 6.
15. Fuson, "Tony Hulman—Savior of the 500 Speedway Track," *Indianapolis News*, October 28, 1977, p. 1.
16. Wilkins, "33 Racers Poised for Starting Bomb, Throngs Jam City," *Indianapolis Star*, May 30, 1946, p. 1.
17. "Trains Operate to Speedway by Special Permit," *Indianapolis Star*, May 30, 1946, p. 1.
18. "Speedway Jam Is Greatest in City's History," *Indianapolis Star*, May 31, 1946, p. 3.
19. O'Reilly, "Hulman Has More Big Plans For Speedway," *Indianapolis News*, May 2, 1957, p. 43.
20. Shaplen, "The Hoosier Pied Piper, Part I," *Sports Illustrated*, May 26, 1958, p. 76.
21. Songwriters Hall of Fame Website, www.songwritershalloffame.org.
22. "183 Inch Type Is Likely to Prove Leader," *Indianapolis Star*, June 1, 1918, sect. 3, p. 25.
23. Davidson and Shaffer, *Autocourse*, 104.
24. Popely, *Indianapolis 500 Chronicle*, 115.
25. Daniels, Moore, Eggert and Cadou, *75 Years of the Indianapolis 500*, "1946."
26. Cavinder, "Tony Hulman, Hoosier in Profile," *Star Magazine*, May 28, 1972, p. 6.
27. Taylor, *Indy: Seventy-Five Years*, 144.
28. Patton, "Robson Wins as Eight Finish," *Indianapolis Star*, May 31, 1946, p. 1.
29. Keating, "Speedway Resurrection," *Indianapolis Star*, October 31, 1977, p. 21.
30. Cavinder, "Tony Hulman, Hoosier in Profile," *Star Magazine*, May 28, 1972, p. 6.
31. Kramer, *Indianapolis Motor Speedway: 100 Years of Racing*, 139.
32. Keating, "Speedway Resurrection," *Indianapolis Star*, October 31, 1977, p. 21.
33. Popely, *Indianapolis 500 Chronicle*, 80.
34. Taylor, *Indy: Seventy-Five Years*, 107.
35. Ibid.
36. Mittman, "1947 500 Had Similar Drivers' Split," *Indianapolis Star*, May 24, 1996, S-22.
37. Bloemker, *500 Miles to Go*, 213, 216.
38. Shaw, *Gentlemen, Start Your Engines*, 288.
39. Davidson and Shaffer, *Autocourse*, 108.
40. Kramer, *Indianapolis Motor Speedway 100 Years*, 148.
41. Harrison, "AAA Refuses to Reopen Race Entries to Let In ASPAR Cars," *Indianapolis Star*, May 8, 1947, p. 27.
42. Ibid.
43. Harrison, "Race Trials Start Today," *Indianapolis Star*, May 17, 1947, p. 1.
44. Harrison, "Horn Wins Pole Position," *Indianapolis Star*, May 18, 1947, p. 1.
45. Bloemker, *500 Miles to Go*, 291.
46. Harrison, "Way Cleared for ASPAR," *Indianapolis Star*, May 23, 1947, p. 1.

47. Mittman, "1947 500 Had Similar Drivers' Split," *Indianapolis Star*, May 24, 1996, S-22.
48. Shaw, *Gentlemen, Start Your Engines*, 291.
49. Ibid., 290.
50. Ibid., 291.
51. Shaw, *Gentlemen, Start Your Engines*, 292.
52. Davidson and Shaffer, *Autocourse*, 109.
53. Harrison, "Two More Qualify, in Special Trials; Waiver OK Needed," *Indianapolis Star*, May 30, 1947, p. 1.
54. Davidson and Shaffer, *Autocourse*, 117.
55. "Rose Wins 500 Mile Race" *Indianapolis Star*, May 31, 1947, p. 1.
56. Shaw, *Gentlemen, Start Your Engines*, 292.
57. "Six Wheeled Race-Car Dispels that 'Nothing New' Theory," *Indianapolis Star*, May 12, 1948, p. 29.
58. Harrison, "6 Wheeler Qualifies; Race Field Now 23," *Indianapolis Star*, May 22, 1948, p. 1.
59. Harrison, "Novi Veteran Smacks into North Turn Wall," *Indianapolis Star*, May 17, 1948, p. 1.
60. "Tony Hulman, Speedway Owner, Planning Constantly for Improvement of Track," *Indianapolis Times*, May 29, 1950, p. 2 supplement.
61. Popely, *Indianapolis 500 Chronicle*, 86.
62. Stranahan, "Rose Wins Third '500' Mile Race," *Indianapolis Star*, June 1, 1948, p. 1.
63. "Tuna a Sucker for Hoosier-Cured Sowbelly," *Indianapolis Times*, September 8, 1948, p. 1.
64. "Rookie Driver Critically Injured in Smashup," *Indianapolis Star*, May 3, 1949, p. 33.
65. Stranahan, "Horn Hurt Critically during Test," *Indianapolis Star*, May 3, 1949, p. 1.
66. "Rookie Driver Critically Injured in Smashup," *Indianapolis Star*, May 3, 1949, p. 33.
67. Stranahan, "Nalon Gets Sizzling Pole Slot with Sizzling 132.939," *Indianapolis Star*, May 15, 1949, p. 1.
68. Hunt, "One in Serious Condition after 20 Foot Plunge," *Indianapolis Star*, May 15, 1949, p. 1.
69. Cotton, "Grandstand Crash Sudden, Terrifying," *Indianapolis Star*, May 15, 1949, sect. 4, p. 1.
70. "Nalon's Novi Fastest of 14 Qualifiers; Mays 2d, McGrath, 3d," *Indianapolis Star*, May 15, 1949, sect. 7, p. 1.
71. "33 Race Fans Injured," *Indianapolis Star*, May 15, 1948, sect. 4, p. 1.
72. "Television Broadcasts First Speedway Views," *Indianapolis Star*, May 29, 1949, p. 1.
73. Ibid.
74. Stranahan, "'500 Cars Hitting 180 on Stretches; Some Could Reach 200 on Salt Flats," *Indianapolis Star*, May 24, 1950, p. 31; and Stranahan, "Hollywood Gives Track, City a Boost," *Indianapolis Star*, May 30, 1950, p. 1.

75. "Race Sabotage Probed," *Indianapolis Star*, May 29, 1949, p. 1.
76. "Speedway Begins Probe as Abrasive Is Found in Engine of Ted Horn's Car," *Indianapolis Star*, May 28, 1949, p. 17.
77. "Race Sabotage Probed," *Indianapolis Star*, May 29, 1949, p. 1.
78. "Speedway on Guard for Any 'Sabotage,'" *Indianapolis Star*, May 30, 1948, p. 1.
79. "Hulman Helps U.S. Team Win Tuna Fishing Title," *Indianapolis Times*, September 11, 1949, p. 1; and "Tony Hulman Lands a Beauty in International Tuna Tournament," *Indianapolis Times*, September 21, 1949, p. 15.
80. Snodgrass, "Hulman's 500 Richest, Best-Run Race," *Indianapolis Star*, May 24, 1975, p. 32.
81. "The Hulmans Coming to America (Tony's Touch Impacts Terre Haute and Beyond)," *Terre Haute Tribune-Star*, May 26, 1997, special section.
82. Popely, *Indianapolis 500 Chronicle*, 93.
83. Stranahan, "Speedway Marks Topple," *Indianapolis Star*, May 14, 1950, p. 1.
84. Ibid., 23.
85. Stranahan, "Parsons 1st, Holland 2d," *Indianapolis Star*, May 31, 1950, p. 1.

Chapter 8

1. "New Grandstand Rises," *Indianapolis Star*, May 30, 1951, p. 26.
2. Stranahan, "Speedway Dealt Two Bad Blows," *Indianapolis Star*, May 2, 1951, p. 1.
3. Ibid., 4.
4. "Increased Speed Claimed for New Contoured Shoes," *Indianapolis Star*, May 30, 1951, p. 33.
5. Stranahan, "Best Lap 137.049; Wins Pole," *Indianapolis Star*, May 12, 1951, p. 1.
6. "AAA Rule Keeps Holland from Try at More Laurels," *Indianapolis Star*, May 30, 1951, p. 44.
7. Hynes, "WIBC to Radio Speedway Race," *Indianapolis Star*, May 30, 1951, p. 36.
8. Stranahan, "Lee Wallard Wins '500,'" *Indianapolis Star*, May 31, 1951, p. 1.
9. Popely, *Indianapolis 500 Chronicle*, 97.
10. Stranahan, "Lee Wallard Wins '500,'" *Indianapolis Star*, May 31, 1951, p. 1.
11. Popely, *Indianapolis 500 Chronicle*, 105.
12. "Shortage of Gas in City Acute," *Indianapolis Star*, May 9, 1952, p. 1.
13. "Rationing No Threat, Speedway Chief Claims," *Indianapolis Star*, May 6, 1952, p. 1.
14. "Zionsville Union Okays Pay Offer," *Indianapolis Star*, May 8, 1952, p. 1.
15. "T-H Act May End Oil Strike," *Indianapolis Star*, May 13, 1952, p. 1.
16. "Accept U.S. Ceiling on Wage Boost," *Indianapolis Star*, May 15, 1952, p. 1.

17. Stranahan, "Speedway's 'Big Push' On; Extra Practice Hour Ok'd," *Indianapolis Star*, May 14, 1952, p. 20.
18. "Speedway Is Test Tube for Cummins Engine," *Indianapolis Star*, May 30, 1952, p. 48.
19. Stranahan, "Agabashian Hits 139.104 mph," *Indianapolis Star*, May 18, 1952, p. 1.
20. Stranahan, "More 500 Cars Qualify," *Indianapolis Star*, May 25, 1952, p. 1.
21. "Vukovich, Miller Establish New Records," *Indianapolis Star*, May 25, 1952, sect. 4, p. 24.
22. Stranahan, "Ruttman Wins in '500' Duel," *Indianapolis Star*, May 31, 1952, p. 1.
23. Stranahan, "Ferrari to Try for 500 Field," *Indianapolis Star*, May 7, 1953, p. 41.
24. Shaplen, "The Hoosier Pied Piper, Part II," *Sports Illustrated*, June 2, 1958, p. 63.
25. Taylor, *Indy: Seventy-Five Years*, 134.
26. "Connor Turns 153 MPH Lap in Tolan Car," *Indianapolis Star*, May 3, 1953, sect. 4, p. 1.
27. Anderson, "Speedway Grows Safety Conscious," *Indianapolis Star*, May 10, 1953, sect. 4, p. 3.
28. Stranahan, "16 Year Veteran's Novi Strikes Wall; Trials Open Today," *Indianapolis Star*, May 16, 1953, p. 1.
29. "Chet Miller's Tragic Accident Raised Toll to 53," *Indianapolis Star*, May 30, 1953, p. 6 supplement.
30. Stranahan, "Vukovich Paces 7 Qualifiers," *Indianapolis Star*, May 18, 1953, p. 1.
31. Lamm, "Heavy Footers Set for 500," *Indianapolis Star*, May 30, 1953, p. 1.
32. Lamm, "Vukovich Wins Hottest Race, Scarborough Dies," *Indianapolis Star*, May 31, 1953, p. 1.
33. Lamm, "Vukovich Captures 500," *Indianapolis Star*, May 31, 1953, sect. 4, p. 1.
34. Davidson and Shaffer, *Autocourse*, 127.
35. Wolfe, "Unprecedented Team Will Cover Action," *Indianapolis Star*, May 30, 1953, p. 19 supplement.
36. "Train Shuttle to 500 Mapped in Bus Strike," *Indianapolis Star*, May 5, 1954, p. 1.
37. Cadou, "Calls 'Em," *Indianapolis Star*, May 4, 1954, p. 28.
38. Cadou, "Calls 'Em," *Indianapolis Star*, May 14, 1954, p. 32.
39. Cadou, "McGrath's 141 Takes Pole as Speedway Record Falls," *Indianapolis Star*, May 16, 1954, p. 1.
40. "Scorching 141 Leads Field," *Indianapolis Star*, May 16, 1954, sect. 4, p. 1.
41. Anderson, "Crankshaft Ills in 10 Cars Bared," *Indianapolis Star*, May 26, 1954, p. 1.
42. Cadou, "Vukovich Wins Record 500," *Indianapolis Star*, June 1, 1954, p. 1.
43. Cadou, "Calls 'Em," *Indianapolis Star*, May 14, 1954, p. 32.
44. "Vuky Proved to All He Could Win from Anywhere in Field," *Indianapolis Star*, May 30, 1955, p. 3.
45. Cadou, "Vukovich Wins Record 500," *Indianapolis Star*, June 1, 1954, p. 1.
46. "Hulman Named Director of Indiana National," *Indianapolis News*, October 13, 1954, p. 53.
47. "Wilbur Shaw, 2 Others Died in Air Crash Near Decatur," *Indianapolis Star*, October 31, 1954, p. 1.

Chapter 9

1. Bloemker, *500 Miles to Go*, 38.
2. Fisher, *The Pacesetter*, 51.
3. Bloemker, *500 Miles to Go*, 60.
4. Scott, *Indy: Racing before the 500*, 47, 49.
5. Bloemker, *500 Miles to Go*, 63.
6. Scott, *Indy Racing before the 500*, 65, 66, 70.
7. Fisher, *The Pacesetter*, 52.
8. Bloemker, *500 Miles to Go*, 67.
9. Fisher, *The Pacesetter*, 52, 53.
10. Scott, *Indy Racing before the 500*, 73.
11. Bloemker, *500 Miles to Go*, 126.
12. Clymer, *Floyd Clymer's Indianapolis 500 Race History*, 97.
13. Davidson and Shaffer, *Autocourse*, 52.
14. Clymer, *Floyd Clymer's Indianapolis 500 Race History*, 179.
15. Lewis, *Eddie Rickenbacker*, 295.
16. Clymer, *Floyd Clymer's Indianapolis 500 Race History*, 200.
17. Bloemker, *500 Miles to Go*, 178.
18. Ibid., 185.
19. Ibid., 187.
20. Ibid., 209, 210.
21. Shaw, *Gentlemen, Start Your Engines*, 287.
22. Davidson, *The Formation of USAC*, foreword to *United States Auto Club*, iii.
23. Yates, *Against Death and Time*, 15.
24. Ibid., 7.
25. Ibid., 15.
26. Ibid., 16.
27. Ibid., 23.
28. Ibid., 2.
29. Ibid., 23.
30. Ibid., 18, 19.
31. Ibid., 26.
32. Ibid., 28.
33. Ibid., 30.
34. Ibid., 31.
35. Ibid., 35.
36. Davidson, *The Formation of USAC*, foreword to *United States Auto Club* iii.
37. Yates, *Against Death and Time*, 80.
38. "Nazaruk, Picked to Drive in '500,' Dies in Eastern Sprint Car Crash," *Indianapolis Star*, May 2, 1955, p. 1.
39. Yates, *Against Death and Time*, 72.

40. Ibid., 73.
41. Ibid., 79.
42. Cadou, "Vuky Serves Notice, Turns Lap at 141.2 mph," *Indianapolis Star*, May 13, 1955, p. 34.
43. Cadou, "Hoyt Wins Pole at 140.045," *Indianapolis Star*, May 15, 1955, p. 1.
44. Yates, *Against Death and Time*, 94.
45. Cadou, "Hoyt Wins Pole at 140.045," *Indianapolis Star*, May 15, 1955, p. 1.
46. Yates, *Against Death and Time*, 95.
47. Cadou, "McGrath Shatters Record," *Indianapolis Star*, May 16, 1955, p. 1.
48. Beal, "Ayulo Hits Wall at 139 mph," *Indianapolis Star*, May 17, 1955, p. 1.
49. Yates, *Against Death and Time*, 97.
50. "Ayulo Dies of Speedway Crash Hurts," *Indianapolis Star*, May 18, 1955, p. 1.
51. "He Died Trying," *Indianapolis Star* (editorial), May 18, 1955, p. 20.
52. Yates, *Against Death and Time*, 98.
53. Ibid., 98.
54. Ibid., 107.
55. Beal, "Ward's Skid Out of Southeast Turn Caused Crash That Killed Vukovich," *Indianapolis Star*, May 31, 1955, p. 1.
56. Yates, *Against Death and Time*, 114.
57. Beal, "Ward's Skid Out of Southeast Turn Caused Crash That Killed Vukovich," *Indianapolis Star*, May 31, 1955, p. 1.
58. Yates, *Against Death and Time*, 108, 109.
59. Ibid., 114.
60. Cadou, "Calls 'Em," *Indianapolis Star*, May 31, 1955, p. 18.
61. Yates, *Against Death and Time*, 116.
62. Popely, *Indianapolis 500 Chronicle*, 125.
63. Yates, *Against Death and Time*, 124.
64. Ibid., 140.
65. Ibid., 126.
66. Ibid., 139.
67. "71 Killed in Race Car Blast," *Indianapolis Star*, June 12, 1955, p. 1 (from International News Service).
68. Cadou, "Calls 'Em," *Indianapolis Star*, June 19, 1955, sect. 2, p. 2.
69. Ibid.
70. "Seek Solution to Race Deaths," *Indianapolis Star*, July 10, 1955, sect. 2, p. 4.
71. "Hoyt Hurt Badly in Western Race," *Indianapolis Star*, July 11, 1955, p. 1.
72. "Driver Jerry Hoyt Dies of Race Crash Injury," *Indianapolis Star*, July 12, 1955, p. 13.
73. Cadou, "Calls 'Em," *Indianapolis Star*, July 13, 1955, p. 25.
74. Cadou, "Calls 'Em," *Indianapolis Star*, July 14, 1955, p. 34.
75. Cadou, "Calls 'Em," *Indianapolis Star*, July 30, 1955, p. 15.
76. Davidson, *The Formation of USAC*, foreword to *United States Auto Club*, iv.
77. Cadou, "500 Will Run—Hulman; SCCA Sponsorship Seen," *Indianapolis Star*, August 4, 1955, p. 1.
78. "AAA Quits Racing as Criticism Mounts," *Indianapolis News*, August 3, 1955, p. 1.
79. Ibid.
80. Cadou, "500 Will Run—Hulman; SCCA Sponsorship Seen," *Indianapolis Star*, August 4, 1955, p. 1.
81. "Racing Seeks New Sanction Body to Replace Existing AAA," *Indianapolis News*, August 4, 1955, p. 39.
82. Cadou, "500 Will Run—Hulman; SCCA Sponsorship Seen," *Indianapolis Star*, August 4, 1955, 1.
83. Cadou, "Calls 'Em," *Indianapolis Star*, August 4, 1955, p. 32.
84. Ibid.
85. Davidson, *The Formation of USAC*, foreword to *United States Auto Club*, iv.
86. Cadou, "Calls 'Em," *Indianapolis Star*, August 6, 1955, p. 15.
87. Cadou, "Calls 'Em," *Indianapolis Star*, August 11, 1955, p. 32.
88. Davidson, *The Formation of USAC*, foreword to *United States Auto Club*, iv.
89. Ibid.
90. Ibid.
91. Waldon, "Col. Herrington Sees Changing 500," *Indianapolis Star*, May 15, 1965, p. 8.
92. Davidson and Shaffer, *Autocourse*, 104.
93. Angelopoulous, "New Organization Gives Auto Racing Folks Assurance," *Indianapolis News*, August 11, 1955, p. 44.

Chapter 10

1. "Speedway Boasts 'New Look' Offices, Museum," *Indianapolis Star*, May 30, 1956, p. 12.
2. Eggert, "2 Cars Crack Lap Record," *Indianapolis Star*, May 14, 1956, p. 1.
3. Eggert, "New '500' Rules in Making?" *Indianapolis Star*, May 1, 1956, p. 22.
4. Cadou, "Flaherty Wins Pole at 145.5," *Indianapolis Star*, May 20, 1956, sect. 1, p. 1.
5. Cadou, "Novi Withdrawn from Race," *Indianapolis Star*, May 28, 1956, p. 1.
6. "Flood Routs 2,000 Families," *Indianapolis Star*, May 29, 1956, p. 1.
7. "500 to Run Tomorrow as Scheduled," *Indianapolis Star*, May 29, 1956, p. 1.
8. Shaplen, "The Hoosier Pied Piper, Part I," *Sports Illustrated*, May 26, 1958, p. 76.
9. Davidson and Shaffer, *Autocourse*, 138.
10. Cadou, "Flaherty Wins as Death Shuns Wreck-Strewn 500," *Indianapolis Star*, May 31, 1956, p. 1.
11. Popely, *Indianapolis 500 Chronicle*, 127.
12. Cadou, "Calls 'Em," *Indianapolis Star*, May 12, 1956, p. 15.

13. "New Tower Is Track Jewel," *Indianapolis Star*, May 30, 1957, p. 14.
14. Taylor, *Indy: Seventy-Five Years of Racing*, 139.
15. "New Tower Is Track Jewel," *Indianapolis Star*, May 30, 1957, p. 14.
16. O'Reilly, "Hulman Has More Big Plans for Speedway," *Indianapolis News*, May 2, 1957, p. 43.
17. Cadou, "Calls 'Em," *Indianapolis Star*, May 3, 1957, p. 31.
18. "Pat Flaherty Is Eager to Race after Accident," *Indianapolis Star*, May 30, 1957, p. 13.
19. Cadou, "Calls 'Em," *Indianapolis Star*, May 16, 1957, p. 41.
20. Cadou, "Speedway Mishap Kills Andrews in Farina Car," *Indianapolis Star*, May 16, 1957, p. 41.
21. Cadou, "O'Connor Wins 500 Pole," *Indianapolis Star*, May 19, 1957, p. 1.
22. Cadou, "Hanks' Record 135 MPH Wins; Jim Rathmann 2d, Bryan 3rd," *Indianapolis Star*, May 31, 1957, p. 1.
23. Collins, "'Old Sam' Just Has Himself a Good Cry," *Indianapolis Star*, May 31, 1957, p. 1.
24. Cadou, "Calls 'Em," *Indianapolis Star*, May 31, 1957, p. 22.
25. Eggert, "Flaherty Is Rejected as 500 Driver," *Indianapolis Star*, May 6, 1958, p. 27.
26. Cadou, "Rathmann on Pole as Records Fall," *Indianapolis Star*, May 18, 1958, sect. 1, p. 1.
27. Cadou, "Calls 'Em," *Indianapolis Star*, May 18, 1958, sect. 2, p. 2.
28. Cadou, "Calls 'Em," *Indianapolis Star*, May 30, 1958, p. 20.
29. Cadou, "Bryan Escapes Big Pileup, Wins '500'; O'Connor Killed," *Indianapolis Star*, May 31, 1958, p. 1.
30. Moore, "Special Year for Fengler," *Indianapolis Star*, May 29, 1971, p. 22.
31. Cadou, "Calls 'Em," *Indianapolis Star*, May 31, 1958, p. 13.
32. Davidson and Shaffer, *Autocourse*, 148.
33. Cadou, "Calls 'Em," *Indianapolis Star*, May 31, 1958, p. 13.
34. Dorson, *The Indy 500: An American Institution under Fire*, 39.
35. Cadou, "Speedway Opens for Practice," *Indianapolis Star*, May 1, 1959, p. 31.
36. Cadou, "Speedway Opens Race Season," *Indianapolis Star*, May 2, 1959, p. 14.
37. Cadou, "Trio Blisters Speedway at 144.4," *Indianapolis Star*, May 9, 1959, p. 1.
38. Cadou, "Calls 'Em," *Indianapolis Star*, May 22, 1959, p. 28.
39. Eggert, "Driver Burned in Race Test," *Indianapolis Star*, May 3, 1959, p. 1.
40. Eggert, "Early Arrivals Total 31 Cars," *Indianapolis Star*, May 5, 1959, p. 31.
41. Cadou, "Trio Blisters Speedway at 144.4," *Indianapolis Star*, May 9, 1959, p. 1.
42. Eggert, "Rathmann Roars around Track at 147," *Indianapolis Star*, May 12, 1959, p. 1.
43. Eggert, "Jerry Unser, Burned in Crash, Is Dead," *Indianapolis Star*, May 18, 1959, p. 19.
44. Cadou, "Calls 'Em," *Indianapolis Star*, May 17, 1959, sect. 4, p. 2.
45. Eggert, "Rookie Dies after Crash," *Indianapolis Star*, May 20, 1959, p. 1.
46. Cadou, "Thompson Wins '500' Pole," *Indianapolis Star*, May 17, 1959, p. 1.
47. Eggert, "Rookie Dies after Crash," *Indianapolis Star*, May 20, 1959, p. 24.
48. Dorson, *The Indy 500: An American Institution under Fire*, 13.
49. Cadou, "Calls 'Em," *Indianapolis Star*, May 30, 1959, p. 13.
50. Cadou, "Ward Wins, Sets Record," *Indianapolis Star*, May 31, 1959, p. 1.
51. Cadou, Skid Mars First '500' Tests," *Indianapolis Star*, May 2, 1960, p. 1.
52. Cadou, "Sachs 146.592 Wins Pole," *Indianapolis Star*, May 15, 1960, p. 1.
53. Cadou, "Rookie Sets Track Marks," *Indianapolis Star*, May 23, 1960, p. 1.
54. Fuson, "Few Hoosiers Ever See the Real Anton Hulman," *Indianapolis News*, February 6, 1961, p. 14.
55. "Jimmy Daywalt Gives Up Place in 500 Field," *Indianapolis Star*, May 26, 1960, p. 52.
56. Frank, "Tragic Race Stand Collapse Probed," *Indianapolis Star*, May 31, 1960, p. 1, 10.
57. Cavinder, "Race Crowd Provides Own Show," *Indianapolis Star*, May 19, 1959, p. 3.
58. Cadou, "Rathmann Outduels Ward," *Indianapolis Star*, May 31, 1960, p. 1.
59. "Hulman's Firm Foundation Keeps Racing Alive, Well," *Indianapolis Star*, June 4, 1978, sect. 5, p. 4; and Lucas Oil Raceway website www.lucasoilraceway.com.

Chapter 11

1. Eggert, "Bill Eggert's Speedway Diary," *Indianapolis Star*, May 29, 1961, p. 39.
2. "Turner's 140, Boyd's 139 First Day Bests," *Indianapolis Star*, May 2, 1961, p. 23.
3. "Lose 30 Hours of Practice," *Indianapolis Star*, May 9, 1961, p. 25.
4. Cadou, "Calls 'Em," *Indianapolis Star*, May 5, 1961, p. 2.
5. Cadou, "Novi Explodes, Rams Wall," *Indianapolis Star*, May 12, 1961, p. 1.
6. Cadou, "Calls 'Em," *Indianapolis Star*, May 12, 1961, p. 28.
7. Cadou, "Novi Explodes, Rams Wall," *Indianapolis Star*, May 12, 1961, p. 1.
8. "Ride for Pal Kills Tony," *Indianapolis Star*, May 13, 1961, p. 1.
9. Collins, "Bettenhausen Drove Like There

Was No Tomorrow," *Indianapolis Star*, May 13, 1961, p. 1.
10. Cadou, "Calls 'Em," *Indianapolis Star*, May 14, 1959, p. 41.
11. Collins, "Bettenhausen Drove Like There Was No Tomorrow," *Indianapolis Star*, May 13, 1961, p. 1.
12. Eggert, "Novi Withdrawn as Right Driver Is Unavailable," *Indianapolis Star*, May 16, 1961, p. 26.
13. Cadou, "Calls 'Em," *Indianapolis Star*, May 17, 1961, p. 23.
14. Eggert, "Experts Favoring Ward in 500-Mile Race," *Indianapolis Star*, May 28, 1961, sect. 4, p. 1.
15. Cadou, "Calls 'Em," *Indianapolis Star*, May 29, 1961, p. 45.
16. Cadou, "Calls 'Em," *Indianapolis Star*, May 30, 1961, p. 18.
17. Davidson and Shaffer, *Autocourse*, 158.
18. "Fame and Glory Were Theirs," *Indianapolis Star Magazine*, May 29, 1961, p. 13.
19. Cadou, "A. J. Foyt Wins '500' Duel," *Indianapolis Star*, May 31, 1961, p. 1.
20. Cadou, "Calls 'Em," *Indianapolis Star*, May 31, 1961, p. 17.
21. Collins, "'500' Broadcast Sent around World," *Indianapolis Star*, May 29, 1961, p. 43.
22. Cadou, "Top Pilots Honored at USAC Award Fete," *Indianapolis Star*, May 9, 1961, p. 26.
23. "Fame and Glory Were Theirs," *Indianapolis Star Magazine*, May 29, 1961, p. 13.

Chapter 12

1. Davidson and Shaffer, *Autocourse*, 83.
2. "Track Straightaway Resurfaced," *Indianapolis Star*, May 29, 1962, p. 34.
3. Cadou, "Jones Hits 148 But He's Going Down Those Straightaways Like a Bomb," *Indianapolis Star*, May 4, 1962, p. 26.
4. Cadou, "Calls 'Em," *Indianapolis Star*, May 12, 1962, p. 23.
5. Cadou, "Jones Cracks 150 Barrier," *Indianapolis Star*, May 13, 1962, p. 1.
6. Davidson and Shaffer, *Autocourse*, 163.
7. Cadou, "Jones Cracks 150 Barrier," *Indianapolis Star*, May 13, 1962, p. 1.
8. Cadou, "4 Bumped from Fastest '500' Field," *Indianapolis Star*, May 21, 1962, p. 1.
9. Cadou, "Rodger Ward Wins 2nd '500,'" *Indianapolis Star*, May 31, 1962, p. 1.
10. Eggert, "Coin Flip, Broken Line Change Outcome of Race," *Indianapolis Star*, May 31, 1962, p. 39.
11. Cadou, "Rodger Ward Wins 2nd '500,'" *Indianapolis Star*, May 31, 1962, p. 1.
12. Ibid.
13. Cadou, "Foyt Goes 146 Testing Wider Speedway Tires," *Indianapolis Star*, May 10, 1963, p. 53.
14. "McElreath Hits 150.451 at Speedway," *Indianapolis Star*, May 8, 1963, p. 26.
15. Ibid.
16. Eggert, "Jones Hits Record 152 Lap," *Indianapolis Star*, May 12, 1963, p. 48.
17. Eggert, "Lotus-Ford Nursing 1-Stop Plan," *Indianapolis Star*, May 16, 1963, p. 48.
18. Cadou, "Foyt Goes 146 Testing Wider Speedway Tires," *Indianapolis Star*, May 10, 1963, p. 53.
19. "500 Mile Qualifiers," *Indianapolis Star*, May 27, 1963, p. 23.
20. Cadou, "Fastest '500' Set to Go," *Indianapolis Star*, May 30, 1963, p. 1.
21. Cadou, "Calls 'Em," *Indianapolis Star*, May 30, 1963, p. 21.
22. Cadou, "Jones Wins Fastest '500,'" *Indianapolis Star*, May 31, 1963, p. 1.
23. Cadou, "Calls 'Em," *Indianapolis Star*, May 31, 1963, p. 25.
24. Ibid.
25. Cadou, "Jones Wins Fastest '500,'" *Indianapolis Star*, May 31, 1963, p. 1.
26. Popely, *Indianapolis 500 Chronicle*, p. 169.
27. Moore, "New Speedway Creation by Yunick Has Driver in Outside Component," *Indianapolis Star*, May 2, 1964, p. 26.
28. "Three Wheel Steering Put on Thompson Cars," *Indianapolis Star*, May 4, 1964, p. 29.
29. Moore, "Meyer to Try Out Aluminum Offy," *Indianapolis Star*, May 8, 1964, p. 36.
30. Cadou and Stultz, "Clark on Pole," *Indianapolis Star*, May 17, 1964, p. 1.
31. Moore, "500 May Lose Foreign Drivers in '65," *Indianapolis Star*, May 21, 1964, p. 1.
32. Moore, "Oil Leakage Riles Speedway Officials," *Indianapolis Star*, May 23, 1964, p. 28.
33. "Closed-Circuit Setup Elaborate," *Indianapolis Star*, May 31, 1964, p. 48.
34. Collins, "Foyt Victor in Tragic 500," *Indianapolis Star*, May 31, 1964, p. 1.
35. Davidson and Shaffer, *Autocourse*, 173.
36. Collins, "Foyt Victor in Tragic 500," *Indianapolis Star*, May 31, 1964, p. 1.
37. Davidson and Shaffer, *Autocourse*, 173.
38. Kramer, *Indianapolis Motor Speedway 100 Years of Racing*, 174.
39. The Beatles Bible website, www.beatlesbible.com.
40. Marquette, "Hurtubise Gets Hero's Welcome from Race Fans," *Indianapolis Star*, May 3, 1965, p. 29.
41. "Pit Pass," *Indianapolis Star*, May 15, 1965, sect. 4, p. 2.
42. Davidson and Shaffer, *Autocourse*, 174.
43. "Pit Pass," *Indianapolis Star*, May 15, 1965, sect. 4, p. 2.

44. Marquette, "Competition Flaring at Speedway," *Indianapolis Star*, May 14, 1965, p. 20.
45. Moore, "Tire Can Alter '65 Complexion," *Indianapolis Star*, May 18, 1965, p. 21.
46. Marquette and Moore, "Goodyear Solves 500 Tire Trouble," *Indianapolis Star*, May 19, 1965, p. 29.
47. "Buffed Tires Out Despite Protests," *Indianapolis Star*, May 22, 1965, p. 26.
48. "Foyt's 161.233 Takes Pole," *Indianapolis Star*, May 16, 1965, p. 1.
49. "New Era Booms at Speedway Now; Rear Engine Autos Push Offy," *Indianapolis Star*, May 29, 1964, p. 41.
50. Moore, "Modern Engine Needed to Save Offy's Prestige," *Indianapolis Star*, May 18, 1964, p. 18.
51. "Speedway Was at Peace during War Years," *Indianapolis Star*, May 27, 1995, p. s7.
52. "Hulman Honored," *Indianapolis Star*, May 24, 1965, p. 30.
53. Davidson and Shaffer, *Autocourse*, 176.
54. Ibid., 83, 84.
55. Kramer, *Indianapolis Motor Speedway 100 Years of Racing*, 155, 156.

Chapter 13

1. "Balloon Event Highlight Today," *Indianapolis Star*, May 15, 1966, p. 1.
2. Ralph Kramer, Indianapolis Motor Speedway: 100 Years of Racing, 184.
3. Overpeck, "Mario Sets Pole Records; Chuck Rodee Crashes, Dies," *Indianapolis Star*, May 15, 1966, p 1
4. "5,000 Musicians To Open Race Day Program," *Indianapolis Star*, May 29, 1966, p. 1.
5. Ibid.
6. Overpeck, "Hill Wins Disputed '500,'" *Indianapolis Star*, May 31, 1966, p. 1.
7. "Pileup Began After I Was Hit: Foster," *Indianapolis Star*, May 31, 1966, p. 1.
8. Ibid, p 12
9. Davidson and Shaffer, *Autocourse*, p. 180.
10. Overpeck, "Hill Wins Disputed '500,'" *Indianapolis Star*, May 31, 1966, p. 1.
11. "Clark's Owner Demands Proof," *Indianapolis Star*, May 31, 1966, p 36.
12. Overpeck, "Race Protest Dropped, Hill Still It," *Indianapolis Star*, June 1, 1966, p. 28.
13. Davidson and Shaffer, *Autocourse*, 181.
14. Indiana University archives.
15. Overpeck, "Andretti Gets '500' Pole," *Indianapolis Star*, May 14, 1967, p. 1.
16. Marquette, "500 Pilots Protest Turbine Exhaust," *Indianapolis Star*, May 27, 1967, p. 30.
17. Overpeck, "32 To Resume '500' Today," *Indianapolis Star*, May 31, 1967, p. 1.
18. "Pit Pass," *Indianapolis Star*, June 1, 1967, p. 50.
19. Overpeck, "Foyt Grabs 3D '500' Win," *Indianapolis Star*, June 1, 1967, p. 1.
20. Marquette, "'I thought I Was Out Of It' Foyt Admits," *Indianapolis Star*, June 1, 1967, p. 1.
21. Ibid., p. 7
22. Overpeck, "Foyt Grabs 3d 500 Win," *Indianapolis Star*, June 1, 1967, p. 1.
23. "Foyt Collects Record Total Of $171,277," *Indianapolis Star*, June 1, 1967, p. 1.
24. Snodgrass, "Hulman's 500 Richest, Best-Run Race," *Indianapolis Star*, May 24. 1975, p. 32.
25. Marquette, "Rookie Pilot Spence Slams Turbine into Wall, Dies of Injuries to Head," *Indianapolis Star*, May 8, 1968, p. 36.
26. Overpeck, "Suspension, Steering Metal Wrong Type," *Indianapolis Star*, May 12, 1968, Sect. 4, p. 1.
27. Davidson & Shaffer, *Autocourse*, 188.
28. Overpeck, "A Go-Go Mario Captures '500,'" *Indianapolis Star*, May 31, 1969, p. 1.
29. Overpeck, "Unser Wins in '500' Duel," *Indianapolis Star*, May 31, 1968, p 1
30. Overpeck, "A Go-Go Mario Captures '500,'" *Indianapolis Star*, May 31, 1969, p. 14.
31. "Turbine 'Popped' the USACed," *Indianapolis Star*, May 26, 1969, p. 27.
32. Overpeck, "A Go-Go Mario Captures '500,'" *Indianapolis Star*, May 31, 1969, p. 1.
33. Overpeck, "Mario's Extra Radiator Stirs Row," *Indianapolis Star*, May 29, 1969, p. 1.
34. Popely, Indianapolis 500 Chronicle, 208.
35. Overpeck, "A Go-Go Mario Captures '500,'" *Indianapolis Star*, May 31, 1969, p. 1.
36. Davidson, "Racing Film 'Winning' Offered Hulman Shot At Being Actor," *Indianapolis Star*, May 18, 2000, p. D-9.
37. Cavinder, "Tony Hulman, Hoosier in Profile" *Star Magazine*, May 28, 1972, p 6
38. Marquette, Al Unser Wins "Screamer'," *Indianapolis Star*, May 17, 1970, p 1
39. Cadou, "Beer To Come Foaming Back—Legally—Come Memorial Day," *Indianapolis Star*, May 26, 1970, p. 1.
40. Marquette, "Al Unser Captures 500," *Indianapolis Star*, May 31, 1970, p. 1.
41. Cadou, "1971 Race To Be Run On May 29," *Indianapolis Star*, May 27, 1970, p. 1.
42. "Pit Pass," *Indianapolis Star*, May 8, 1971, p. 28.
43. Moore, "Drivers Union Not Needed: Foyt," *Indianapolis Star*, May 19 1971, p. 39.
44. Marquette, "33 Positions Still Open In Field as '500' Race Trials Rained Out," *Indianapolis Star*, May 14, 1971, p. 1.
45. Burford and Gelarden, "Tornado Rips East Side, 26 Hurt," *Indianapolis Star*, May 15, 1971, p. 1.
46. Marquette, "Revson Springs Pole Surprise," *Indianapolis Star*, May 17, 1971, p. 1.

47. "Yellow Speed Set At 80," *Indianapolis Star*, May 26, 1971, p. 35.
48. "500 'Live' On Radio Only," *Indianapolis Star*, May 29, 1971, p. 12.
49. Marquette, "Home TV of Speedway Classic Could Backfire On Hulman," *Indianapolis Star*, May 29, 1971, p. 31.
50. Keating, "Pace Car Hits Temporary Stand," *Indianapolis Star*, May 30,1971, p. 1.
51. Marquette, "Lighting Strikes Twice For Al," *Indianapolis Star*, May 30, 1971, p. 1.
52. Davidson and Shaffer, *Autocourse*, 199.
53. Marquette, "Bobby Unser's 195.940 Leading Pole Dash," *Indianapolis Star*, May 15, 1972, p 1
54. Marquette, "Malloy 33d Driver to Die At Speedway," *Indianapolis Star*, May 19, 1972, p 39.
55. "Pit Pass," *Indianapolis Star*, May 5, 1971, p 43
56. "Fengler Drops Bomb, Drivers Explode" *Indianapolis Star*, May 25, 1972, p 55
57. Marquette, "Donohue Captures '500 Plum; Expected To Get $200,000," *Indianapolis Star*, May 28, 1972, p. 1.
58. Bevens, "Grant Thinks He Won; To Protest," *Indianapolis Star*, May 28, 1972, Sect 4, p. 1.
59. "Mixed Reviews On Yellow Light," *Indianapolis Star*, May 28, 1972, Sect. 4, p. 2.
60. Moore, "Tech Boss, DelRoy, To Ask For Changes," *Indianapolis Star*, May 11, 1972, p. 45.
61. "Pit Pass," *Indianapolis Star*, May 27, 1972, Sect. 3, p. 5.

Chapter 14

1. Cavinder, "Tony Hulman, Hoosier in Profile," *Star Magazine*, May 28, 1972, p. 6.
2. Beck, "Hulman Group Takes Over Ontario Track," *Indianapolis Star*, April 11, 1973, p. 1.
3. Collins, "Sports over Lightly," *Indianapolis Star*, May 11, 1973, p. 41.
4. Beck, "Hulman Group Takes Over Ontario Track," *Indianapolis Star*, April 11, 1973, p. 1.
5. "Pit Pass," *Indianapolis Star*, May 26, 1973, p. 28.
6. Merrill, *The Oil Crisis of 1973–1974*, 13.
7. Ibid., 22.
8. Marquette, "USAC Readies ACCUS Exit," *Indianapolis Star*, May 12, 1973, p. 31.
9. Marquette, "Rutherford Grabs 500 Pole; Crash in Practice Kills Pollard," *Indianapolis Star*, May 15, 1973, p. 1.
10. "Andy Proposes Limit on Fuel," *Indianapolis Star*, May 20, 1973, sect. 4, p. 3.
11. Marquette, "12 Car Crash Injures 13 Fans, Walther as Rain Postpones Race," *Indianapolis Star*, May 29, 1973, p. 1.
12. Marquette, "Johncock Wins Troubled Race; Savage Hurt in Flaming Crash," *Indianapolis Star*, May 30, 1973, p. 1.
13. "Emergency Truck Kills Mechanic in Pits," *Indianapolis Star*, May 31, 1973, p. 1.
14. Marquette, "Johncock Wins Troubled Race; Savage Hurt in Flaming Crash," *Indianapolis Star*, May 30, 1973, p. 1.
15. Daniels, Moore, Eggert and Cadou, *75 Years of the Indianapolis 500*, "1973."
16. Overpeck, "Speedway Changes Run More than $300,000," *Indianapolis Star*, May 25, 1974, p. 38.
17. www.dalube.com (D. A. Lubricants website).
18. Moore, "New Speedway Opens Tomorrow," *Indianapolis Star*, May 5, 1974, sect. 3, p. 1.
19. Marquette, "Bobby Unser's Eagle Flies— 188.294 MPH," *Indianapolis Star*, May 7, 1974, p. 29.
20. "Pit Pass," *Indianapolis Star*, May 7, 1974, p. 23.
21. Marquette, "Bobby Unser's Eagle Flies— 188.294 MPH," *Indianapolis Star*, May 7, 1974, p. 29.
22. Marquette, "Pole May Not Be to the Swiftest," *Indianapolis Star*, May 11, 1974, p. 24.
23. Marquette, "Foyt's 191.6 MPH Holds Pole," *Indianapolis Star*, May 12, 1974, sect. 1, p. 1.
24. Marquette, "Pole May Not Be to the Swiftest," *Indianapolis Star*, May 11, 1974, p. 24.
25. Marquette, "Foyt's 191.6 MPH Holds Pole," *Indianapolis Star*, May 12, 1974, sect. 1, p. 1.
26. Beasley, "14 Held in Melee," *Indianapolis Star*, May 12, 1974, sect. 1, p. 1.
27. Overpeck, "Bignotti Turbo Controversy Rages," *Indianapolis Star*, May 13, 1974, p. 22.
28. Marquette, "'Great Blower' Battle," *Indianapolis Star*, May 14, 1974, p. 23.
29. Marquette, "A. J. Foyt Still on '500' Pole," *Indianapolis Star*, May 19, 1974, sect. 1, p. 1.
30. Moore, "Judge Gives Race Green Flag," *Indianapolis Star*, May 24, 1974, p. 10.
31. Marquette, "500 Discontent Continues," *Indianapolis Star*, May 20, 1974, p. 23.
32. Overpeck, "Speedway Warned: See You in Court," *Indianapolis Star*, May 21, 1974, p. 24.
33. Gelarden, "500 Suit Still Unresolved," *Indianapolis Star*, May 23, 1974, p. 1.
34. Moore, "Judge Gives Race Green Flag," *Indianapolis Star*, May 24, 1974, p. 1.
35. "USAC Nixes Appeal from Car Owners," *Indianapolis Star*, May 25, 1974, p. 25.
36. "500 Race Suit Going to Trial," *Indianapolis Star*, May 1, 1975, p. 37.
37. "1974 Indianapolis 500 Set, Sunday May 26," *Indianapolis Star*, May 23, 1973, p. 52.
38. Marquette, "Rutherford's 11th Try Wins 500," *Indianapolis Star*, May 27, 1974, p. 1.
39. Davidson and Shaffer, *Autocourse*, 211.

40. Marquette, "Foyt Captures 4th '500' Pole," *Indianapolis Star*, May 11, 1975, p. 1.
41. Marquette, "Bobby U. Wins Rain-Cut '500,'" *Indianapolis Star*, May 26, 1975, p. 1.
42. "Pit Pass," *Indianapolis Star*, May 9, 1976, sect. 3, p. 4.
43. Moore, "Speedway Opens for Practice Saturday," *Indianapolis Star*, May 2, 1976, sect. 3, p. 1.
44. Marquette, "Of All Things, a Wrong Way Turn by Speedway Owner," *Indianapolis Star*, May 1, 1976, p. 25.
45. Marquette, "No Ms-Take: Jan to Drive," *Indianapolis Star*, May 4, 1976, p. 28.
46. Davidson and Shaffer, *Autocourse*, 213.
47. Miller, "Rookie Hurdles 2 Speedway Fences," *Indianapolis Star*, May 12, 1976, p. 45.
48. "Driver's Howl: Don't Fence Me In!" *Indianapolis Star*, May 14, 1976, p. 52.
49. Moore, "Changes at Track Seen Acceptable by 500 Drivers," *Indianapolis Star*, May 25, 1976, p. 21.
50. Marquette, "Weather Again Cuts '500' Short," *Indianapolis Star*, May 31, 1976, p. 1.
51. Moore, "Speedway Geared for 61st Opening," *Indianapolis Star*, May 1, 1977, sect. 2, p. 1.
52. Overpeck, "Cagle Has Dedicated His Life to Speedway," *Indianapolis Star*, May 28, 1977, p. A-3.
53. Moore, "Speedway Geared For 61st Opening," *Indianapolis Star*, May 1, 1977, sect. 2, p. 1.
54. Davidson and Shaffer, *Autocourse*, 216.
55. "'Voice of Indianapolis 500,' Sid Collins, Found Dead," *Indianapolis Star*, May 3, 1977, p. 1.
56. Moore, "Speedway Geared For 61st Opening," *Indianapolis Star*, May 1, 1977, sect. 2, p. 1.
57. Moore, "Mario Makes Month of May Merrier," *Indianapolis Star*, May 12, 1977, p. 58.
58. Moore, "Guthrie Tops 185 MPH; Fastest on Opening Day," *Indianapolis Star*, May 8, 1977, sect. 2, p. 1.
59. Snodgrass, "Women at Indy Not Probable," *Indianapolis Star*, May 26, 1973, p. 64.
60. Moore, "Heavies Making Presence Known," *Indianapolis Star*, May 9, 1977, p. 24.
61. Miller, "Rutherford's on the Run—196.850," *Indianapolis Star*, May 10, 1977, p. 22.
62. Moore, "Mario Makes Month of May Merrier," *Indianapolis Star*, May 12, 1977, p. 58.
63. Moore, "Rutherford Joins the Club: 200.624," *Indianapolis Star*, May 13, 1977, p. 33.
64. Miller, "Sneva Grabs Pole with 198.884," *Indianapolis Star*, May 15, 1977, sect. 1, p. 1.
65. Overpeck, "Sneva Did the Job When It Counted," *Indianapolis Star*, May 15, 1977, sect. 2, p. 1.
66. "A. J. Foyt Adds Another Record," *Indianapolis Star*, May 15, 1977, sect. 2, p. 1.
67. Miller, "Janet Paces 8 into '500,'" *Indianapolis Star*, May 23, 1977, p. 23.
68. Overpeck, "Bumped Salt Walther 'Buys' a Spot in Race," *Indianapolis Star*, May 24, 1977, p. 1.
69. Overpeck, "Puterbaugh Will Drive in '500,'" *Indianapolis Star*, May 25, 1977, p. 1.
70. Collins, "Big Walther Flap a Thorne-y Stunt," *Indianapolis Star*, May 26, 1977, p. 47.
71. 500 Festival website, www.500festival.com.
72. Davidson and Shaffer, *Autocourse*, 218.
73. Miller, "Super Tex '500' Winner 4th Time," *Indianapolis Star*, May 29, 1977, p. 1.
74. Overpeck, "Foyt's Victory Was Popular One," *Indianapolis Star*, May 29, 1977, p. 1.
75. "Coyote Rolls into Museum," *Indianapolis Star*, May 29, 1977, p. 34.
76. Dorson, *The Indy 500: An American Institution Under Fire*, 38.

Chapter 15

1. "'Auto Racing Hall of Fame' Contemplated," *Indianapolis Star*, May 28, 1947, p. 20.
2. Cotton, "Speedway May Become Year-Round 'Mecca' for Race Fans with New 'Shrine to Speed,'" *Indianapolis Star*, May 30, 1949, p. 4 supplement.
3. Riggs, "Racing's Repository," *Automobile Quarterly*, vol. 41, no 3, 2001, p. 85.
4. "The New Speedway Museum," *Indianapolis Star Magazine*, April 18, 1976, p. 26.
5. Riggs, "Racing's Repository," *Automobile Quarterly*, Vol. 41, No 3, p. 86.
6. "Speedway Boasts 'New Look' Offices, Museum," *Indianapolis Star*, May 30, 1956, p. 12.
7. Riggs, "Racing's Repository," *Automobile Quarterly*, Vol. 41, No 3, p. 86.
8. "500's Great Moments Relived in New Speedway Museum," *Indianapolis Star*, May 30, 1956, p. 5.
9. Riggs, "Racing's Repository," *Automobile Quarterly*, Vol. 41, No 3, p. 86.
10. "500's Great Moments Relived in New Speedway Museum," *Indianapolis Star*, May 30, 1956, p. 5.
11. Riggs, "Racing's Repository," *Automobile Quarterly*, Vol. 41, No 3, p. 86.
12. "500's Great Moments Relived in New Speedway Museum," *Indianapolis Star*, May 30, 1956, p. 5.
13. Scott & Gray, *Indy Racing before the 500*, 65, 66, 70.
14. "Speedway Museum Packs 'Em In," *Indianapolis Star*, May 29, 1959, p. 12.
15. Riggs, "Racing's Repository," *Automobile Quarterly*, Vol. 41, No 3, p. 86.
16. Eggert, "Parnelli Sets 153.139 Mark," *Indianapolis Star*, May 16, 1963, p. 48.
17. "Motor Speedway Museum," *Indianapolis Star Magazine*, May 19, 1963, p. 16.
18. Davidson & Shaffer, *Autocourse*, 33.
19. Fisher, *The Pacesetter*, 58.

20. Riggs, "Racing's Repository," *Automobile Quarterly*, Vol. 41, No 3, p. 87.
21. Ibid.
22. Ibid., 88.
23. "Pit Pass," *Indianapolis Star*, May 22, 1967, p. 32.
24. "1937 Car 30 Years Ahead of Time," *Indianapolis Star*, May 29, 1971, p. 30.
25. Riggs, "Racing's Repository," *Automobile Quarterly*, Vol. 41, No 3, p. 89.
26. "The New Speedway Museum," *Indianapolis Star Magazine*, April 18, 1976, p. 26.
27. "Tony's Tradition Will Never Die," *Indianapolis Star*, May, 27, 1978, p. 16.
28. Cavinder, "Tony Hulman, Hoosier in Profile," *Star Magazine*, May 28, 1972, p. 6.
29. Cavinder, "A Slow Trip Around a Fast Oval," *Indianapolis Star Magazine*, May 26, 1963, p. 26.

Chapter 16

1. Baron, *Brewed in America*, 3.
2. Ibid., 31.
3. Ibid., 175.
4. Ostrander, *Hoosier Beer*, 161.
5. Elliott, *A History of Evansville and Vanderburgh County, Indiana*, 418.
6. Brant and Fuller, *A History of Vanderburgh County, Indiana*, 170.
7. Ostrander, *Hoosier Beer*, 161.
8. Brant, *History of Vanderburgh County, Indiana*, 171.
9. Elliott, *A History of Evansville and Vanderburgh County, Indiana*, 418.
10. Brant, *History of Vanderburgh County, Indiana*, 171.
11. Elliott, *A History of Evansville and Vanderburgh County, Indiana*, 418.
12. Ibid., 419.
13. Brant, *History of Vanderburgh County, Indiana*, 170.
14. Ostrander, *Hoosier Beer*, 163.
15. Ibid., 161.
16. Brant, *History of Vanderburgh County, Indiana*, p. 170.
17. Baron, *Brewed in America*, 236.
18. Ostrander, *Hoosier Beer*, 170.
19. Baron, *Brewed in America*, 268.
20. Moody Publishing Company, *Moody's Manual of Railroad and Corporation Securities*, vol. 2, p. 1002.
21. Elliott, *A History of Evansville and Vanderburgh County, Indiana*, 419.
22. Ostrander, *Hoosier Beer*, 171.
23. *Power*, vol. 46, no 10, p. 310.
24. Baron, *Brewed in America*, 300.
25. Commager, *Documents of American History*, 133.
26. Ostrander, *Hoosier Beer*, 19.
27. Ibid., 166.
28. Baron, *Brewed in America*, 306.
29. Ibid., 321.
30. Ibid., 318.
31. Ibid., 323.
32. Ibid., 323.
33. Ibid., 326, 327.
34. Ibid., 334.
35. Ibid., 335.
36. "News and Views of the Breweries," *Modern Brewery Age*, November, 1949, p. 104.
37. "News and Views of the Breweries," *Modern Brewery Age*, May 1948, p. 96.
38. Baron, *Brewed in America*, 327, 328.
39. "News and Views of the Breweries," *Modern Brewery Age*, June 1948, p. 87.
40. "News and Views of the Breweries," *Modern Brewery Age*, April 1949, p. 86.
41. "News and Views of the Breweries," *Modern Brewery Age*, May 1949, p. 91.
42. "News and Views of the Breweries," *Modern Brewery Age*, June 1949, p. 84.
43. "News and Views of the Breweries," *Modern Brewery Age*, September 1949, p. 89.
44. Baron, *Brewed in America*, 331.
45. "News and Views of the Breweries," *Modern Brewery Age*, February 1950, p. 86.
46. "Hulman Buys Cook's Brewery," *Indianapolis Times*, January 17, 1950, p. 9.
47. Cloutier Oral History, 39, 40.
48. Ibid., 40.
49. Ibid., 41.
50. "Cook's Brewery to Close Friday," *Evansville Courier*, September 10, 1955, p. 1.
51. "News and Views of the Breweries," *Modern Brewery Age*, September 1955, p. 116.
52. Baron, *Brewed in America*, 343.
53. Ostrander, *Hoosier Beer*, 166.
54. Cloutier Oral History, 43.
55. Ostrander, *Hoosier Beer*, 166.

Chapter 17

1. Pendergrast, *For God, Country, and Coca-Cola*, 65.
2. Allen, *Secret Formula*, 106.
3. Pendergrast, *For God, Country, and Coca-Cola*, 74.
4. Ibid.
5. Allen, *Secret Formula*, 107.
6. Pendergrast, *For God, Country, and Coca-Cola*, 75.
7. Allen, *Secret Formula*, 107.
8. Pendergrast, *For God, Country, and Coca-Cola*, 76.
9. Allen, *Secret Formula*, 108.
10. "New $500,000 Coca-Cola Bottling Company Plant Will Be Open to Public Tuesday—Employs 125," *Indianapolis Star*, September 27, 1931, sect. 4, p. 36.
11. Allen, *Secret Formula*, 109.

12. "New $500,000 Coca-Cola Bottling Company Plant Will Be Open to Public Tuesday—Employs 125," *Indianapolis Star*, September 27, 1931, sect. 4, p. 36.
13. Pendergrast, *For God, Country, and Coca-Cola*, 93.
14. Allen, *Secret Formula*, 111, 112.
15. *Terre Haute Tribune-Star* and McCormick, *Century: 100 Years in the Wabash Valley*, 4.
16. Ibid., 14.
17. Pendergrast, *For God, Country, and Coca-Cola*, 106.
18. Allen, *Secret Formula*, 112, 113.
19. "New $500,000 Coca-Cola Bottling Company Plant Will Be Open to Public Tuesday—Employs 125," *Indianapolis Star*, September 27, 1931, sect. 4, p. 36.
20. Bodenhamer, Barrows and Vanderstel, *Encyclopedia of Indianapolis*, 454.
21. Dreyer, "Local Coca-Cola Plant Is Mechanized Marvel," *Indianapolis News*, August 3, 1954, p. 12.
22. Grabow, "Big Brother of Coca-Cola Put on Sale Here," *Indianapolis News*, January 16, 1956, p. 19.
23. McCarthy, "Mickey McCarthy Says," *Indianapolis News*, September 2, 1954, p. 25.
24. "Hulman Is Head of Coca-Cola Co.," *Indianapolis News*, January 4, 1965, p. 1.
25. Dorson, *The Indy Five Hundred: An American Institution Under Fire*, 175.
26. "Hulman Is Head of Coca-Cola Co," *Indianapolis News*, January 4, 1965, p. 1.
27. Dorson, *The Indy Five Hundred: An American Institution Under Fire*, 175.
28. Pendergrast, *For God, Country, and Coca-Cola*, 278.
29. Coca-Cola Company website, www.cocacola.com/heritage.
30. Ibid.
31. "Things Going for Coke," *Indianapolis News*, July 18, 1967, p. 21.
32. Corya, "Chance to See How Coke Is (and Was) Bottled," *Indianapolis News*, April 25, 1968, p. 50.
33. Pendergrast, *For God, Country, and Coca-Cola*, 310.
34. Ibid.
35. Allen, *Secret Formula*, 373.
36. Ibid., 390, 391.
37. Pendergrast, *For God, Country, and Coca-Cola*, 320, 339.
38. Bird, "Transport Manager Arrested," *Indianapolis News*, April 11, 1977, p. 1; and "More Arrests Due in Bottling Plant Thefts," *Indianapolis News*, April 12, 1977, p. 1.
39. "L.A. Group Buys Coca-Cola Plant," *Indianapolis News*, April 24, 1981, p. 1.
40. Wilkinson, "West Coast Firm Buys Coca-Cola Plant," *Indianapolis Star*, April 24, 1981, p. 46.
41. "Local Coke Plant Sold for 2nd Time," *Indianapolis Star*, May 2, 1981, p. 3.

Chapter 18

1. Smith, *Popped Culture*, 139.
2. Fish, *Orville Redenbacher*, 50.
3. Sherman, *Popcorn King*, 33.
4. Ibid., 12.
5. Ibid., 13.
6. Ibid., 15, 16.
7. Sherman, *Popcorn King*, 23.
8. Ibid., 34.
9. Fish, *Orville Redenbacher*, 50.
10. Sherman, *Popcorn King*, 34.
11. Fish, *Orville Redenbacher*, 50.
12. Ibid.
13. Ibid.
14. Sherman, *Popcorn King*, 15.
15. Smith, *Popped Culture*, 139.
16. Fish, *Orville Redenbacher*, 51.
17. Sherman, *Popcorn King*, 45.
18. Ibid., 47.
19. Ibid., 48.
20. Ibid., 54.
21. Ibid., 56.
22. Ibid., 49.
23. Ibid., 47.

Chapter 19

1. Taylor, *Indiana: A New Historical Guide*, 200.
2. Fuson, "Few Hoosiers Ever See the Real Anton Hulman," *Indianapolis News*, February 6, 1961, p. 14.
3. Markle and Collins, *The House of Hulman*, 342.
4. "Louisville after the Bombings" website, www.oldlouisville.com.
5. Digital photograph collection, University of Louisville, www.louisville.edu.
6. "Louisville after the Bombings" website, www.oldlouisville.com.
7. Emporis website, www.emporis.com.
8. "Inside Indianapolis," *Indianapolis Times*, January 19, 1946, p. 7.
9. Nation, "Anton Hulman Jr. 1901–1977," *The Spectator*, November 5, 1977, p. 6.
10. Salter, "Terre Haute House Coming Down," *Tribune-Star*, September 16, 2005, p. A-1, A-4.
11. Answers.com website, www.answers.com; and McCormick, *Terre Haute, Queen City*, 134.
12. Nation, "Anton Hulman Jr. 1901–1977," *The Spectator*, November 5, 1977, p. 6.
13. "Hulman Dynasty 1850–1997," *Tribune-Star*, May 26, 1997, special section.
14. *Terre Haute Tribune-Star* and McCormick, *Century: 100 Years in the Wabash Valley*, 61.

15. www.wthi-tv.com.
16. Ibid.
17. Cloutier Oral History, 44.
18. Indiana Energy website, www.indianaenergy.com.
19. Answers.com website, www.answers.com.
20. Cloutier Oral History, 44.
21. Indiana Historical Society website, www.indianahistory.org.
22. "Hulman Dynasty 1860–1997," May 25, 1997, special section.
23. Indiana Historical Society website, www.indianahistory.org.

Chapter 20

1. Bloxsome, *Rose: The First 100 Years*, 9.
2. Ibid., 10.
3. Ibid., 9.
4. Ibid., 10.
5. McCormick, *Terre Haute, Queen City*, 28.
6. Bloxsome, *Rose: The First 100 Years*, 10.
7. Ibid., 9.
8. Ibid., 13.
9. Bloxsome, *Rose: The First 100 Years*, 17.
10. Ibid., 18.
11. Ibid., 21.
12. Bloxsome, *Rose: The First 100 Years*, 28, 29.
13. McAllister, *Centennial History of Indiana State University*, 4.
14. Ibid., 5.
15. Ibid., 10.
16. Ibid., 11.
17. Bloxsome, *Rose: The First 100 Years*, 74.
18. Ibid., 91.
19. Ibid., 93.
20. Ibid., 90.
21. Ibid., 102.
22. McAllister, *Centennial History of Indiana State University*, 17, 68.
23. Bloxsome, *Rose: The First 100 Years*, 128.
24. Ibid., 161.
25. Ibid., 162.
26. McAllister, *Centennial History of Indiana State University*, 17, 68.
27. Bloxsome, *Rose: The First 100 Years*, 162.
28. "Hulman Gift to Rose Poly," *Terre Haute Tribune*, January 6, 1971, p. 1.
29. Bloxsome, *Rose: The First 100 Years*, 162.
30. Wilkinson, "Hulmans Give Foundation's Huge Assets to Rose Poly," *Indianapolis Star*, January 7, 1971, p. 24.
31. Bloxsome, *Rose: The First 100 Years*, 162.
32. "Rose-Hulman: Another Exciting Hundred Years," *Terre Haute Times*, March 3, 1973, p. 1.
33. "Sycamores, Purdue to Christen ISU Arena," *Indianapolis Star*, December 13, 1973, p. 65.
34. McCormick, *Terre Haute, Queen City*, 153.

Chapter 21

1. *Terre Haute Tribune-Star* and McCormick, *Century: 100 Years in the Wabash Valley*, 47.
2. Freeman, "Abandoned & Little Known Airfields," www.airfields_freeman.com.
3. "Terre Haute Civic Leader Gives $100,000 to City," *Indianapolis Star*, March 23, 1943, p. 7.
4. Cole, "Hulman Falters at Speech-Making, but Does Top Job in Business World," *Indianapolis Star*, June 15, 1947, p. 5.
5. "Inside Indianapolis," *Indianapolis Times*, January 19, 1946, p. 7.
6. McCormick, *Terre Haute, Queen City*, 124.
7. "Inside Indianapolis," *Indianapolis Times*, January 19, 1946, p. 7.
8. "Fire Destroys Hulman Lodge at Terre Haute," *Indianapolis Star*, March 14, 1965, sect. 3, p. 24.
9. Andrews, Ronald, "History of Markle's Mill," www.randrews4.com.
10. *Terre Haute Tribune-Star* and McCormick, *Century: 100 Years in the Wabash Valley*, 61.
11. Cole, "Hulman Falters at Speech-Making, but Does Top Job in Business World," *Indianapolis Star*, June 15, 1947, p. 5.
12. "The Hulmans Coming to America (Tony's Touch Impacts Terre Haute and Beyond)," *Terre Haute Tribune-Star*, May 26, 1997, special section, p. 4.
13. Taylor, *Indiana: A New Historical Guide*, 276.
14. "Hulmans Give Funds, Land to Terre Haute," *Indianapolis Star*, April 25, 1973, p. 1.
15. Blacketer, "Golf Course Land Gift Completed," *Terre Haute Tribune*, October 25, 1974, p. 1.
16. "Flood Control Commission Re-Elects Hulman," *Indianapolis Star*, January 26, 1952, p. 13.
17. Indiana Department of Natural Resources website, www.in.gov/dnr/parklake/2960.
18. "8,100-Acre State Park Assured," *Indianapolis Star*, August 24, 1949, p. 1.
19. Indiana Department of Natural Resources website, www.in.gov/dnr/parklake/2960.
20. "Hulman State Conservation Unit Head," *Indianapolis Star*, December 27, 1962, p. 12.
21. "8,100-Acre State Park Assured," *Indianapolis Star*, August 24, 1949, p. 1.
22. "Hulman Named on U.S. Health Advisory Board," *Indianapolis Star*, September 27, 1957, p. 22.

Chapter 22

1. Chandler, *Henry Flagler*, 7.
2. Ibid., 15.
3. Ibid., 17.
4. Ibid., 31.
5. Ibid., 29, 30.
6. Ibid., 42, 43.
7. Ibid., 51.
8. Ibid., 56.
9. Ibid., 58.
10. Ibid., 62.
11. Ibid., 70.
12. Ibid., 85.
13. Ibid., 88.
14. Ibid., 90, 95.
15. Ibid., 96, 97, 102, 104.
16. Beebe, *Mansions on Rails*, 20, 21.
17. Ibid., 22.
18. Welch, *Cars by Pullman*, 38.
19. Ibid., 38.
20. Beebe, *Mansions on Rails*, 21.
21. Ibid., 22.
22. White, *The American Railroad Passenger Car*, 651, 652.
23. Ibid., 654.
24. Beebe, *Mansions on Rails*, 104.
25. Delaware Federal Writer's Project, *Delaware, a Guide to the First State*, 310.
26. White, *The American Railroad Passenger Car*, 354.
27. Ibid., 354, 355.
28. Indiana Transportation Museum website, www.itm.org/fec90.
29. Waldon, "Face-Lifted Queen of Rails Delivered to Hulmans," *Indianapolis Star*, September 7, 1969, sect. 6, p. 4.
30. Ibid.
31. "Palatial Private Railroad Cars Again Rolling on Nation's Tracks," *Indianapolis Star*, June 1, 1965, sect. 2, p. 8.
32. Waldon, "Face-Lifted Queen of Rails Delivered to Hulmans," *Indianapolis Star*, September 7, 1969, sect. 6, p. 4.
33. Toles, "Palaces on Wheels," *Railway Magazine*, vol. 116, July 1970, p. 400.

Chapter 23

1. *Terre Haute Tribune-Star* and McCormick, *Century: 100 Years in the Wabash Valley*, 1, 14.
2. Ibid., 1.
3. Taylor, *Indiana: A New Historical Guide*, p. 270.
4. "Open House in Terre Haute," *Time*, February 21, 1969, p. 20.
5. Salstrom, *Appalachia's Path to Dependency: Rethinking a Region's Economic History*, 89.
6. *Terre Haute Tribune-Star* and McCormick, *Century: 100 Years in the Wabash Valley*, 39.
7. Ibid., 25.
8. Ibid., 38.
9. "Triumph in Terre Haute," *Kiplinger Personal Finance*, February 1947, 33–35.
10. "The Big, Big Bettors, Hide, Hide and Hide," *Life*, September 1, 1958, p. 17.
11. Ibid., 18.
12. Riley, "A Tale of One, or Maybe Two, Indiana Cities," *Muncie Star-Press*, February 8, 1998, p. 2D.
13. Wyden, "Indiana's Delinquent City," *Saturday Evening Post*, February 11, 1961, p. 26.
14. Cloutier Oral History, p. 48, 49.
15. Ibid., 47, 48.
16. Wyden, "Indiana's Delinquent City," *Saturday Evening Post*, February 11, 1961, 63.
17. Cloutier Oral History, 50, 51.
18. Wyden, "Indiana's Delinquent City," *Saturday Evening Post*, February 11, 1961, 63.
19. Ibid.
20. Ibid.
21. Ibid., 64.
22. Ibid., 27.

Chapter 24

1. Claus, "Hulman Never Forgot Birthplace," *Terre Haute Tribune*, October 28, 1977, p. 14.
2. "Tony Hulman, Mr. 500, Dies," *Indianapolis Star*, October 28, 1977, p. 1.
3. "Terre Haute Services Monday for Hulman," *Indianapolis Star*, October 29, 1977, p. 1.
4. "Final Tribute Paid Hulman by Associates and Friends," *Indianapolis Star*, November 1, 1977, p. 1.
5. Nation, "Anton Hulman Jr. 1901–1977," *The Spectator*, November 5, 1977, p. 6, 11.
6. "Tony Hulman Laid to Rest," Nov. 1, 1977, *Terre Haute Tribune*, p. 3.
7. "Final Tribute Paid Hulman by Associates and Friends," *Indianapolis Star*, November 1, 1977, p. 1.
8. "Hulman Named Director of Indiana National," *Indianapolis News*, October 13, 1954, p. 53.
9. Motorsports Hall of Fame of America website, www.mshf.com.

Bibliography

Books

Allen, Frederick. *Secret Formula: How Brilliant Marketing and Relentless Salesmanship Made Coca-Cola the Best Known Product in the World.* New York: HarperBusiness, 1994.

Baron, Stanley, & James Harvey Young. *Brewed in America: A History of Beer and Ale in the United States.* Boston: Little, Brown, 1962.

Beebe, Lucius. *Mansions on Rails: The Folklore of the Private Railway Car.* Berkeley, CA: Howell-North, 1959.

Blanchard, Charles. *The History of the Catholic Church in Indiana.* Logansport, IN: A. W. Bowen, 1898.

Bloemker, Al. *500 Miles to Go: The History of the Indianapolis Motor Speedway.* New York: Coward-McCann, 1961.

Bloxsome, John L. *Rose: The First 100 Years.* Terre Haute, IN: Rose-Hulman Institute of Technology, 1973.

Bodenhamer, David J., Robert C. Barrows, and David Gordon Vanderstel. *Encyclopedia of Indianapolis.* Bloomington: Indiana University Press, 1994.

Brant and Fuller. *A History of Vanderburgh County Indiana: From the Earliest Times to the Present, with Biographical Sketches, Reminiscences, Etc.* Evansville, IN: Unigraphic, 1979.

Chandler, David Leon. *Henry Flagler: The Astonishing Life and Times of the Visionary Robber Baron Who Founded Florida.* New York: Macmillan, 1986.

Clark, Marjorie R., and S. Fanny Simon. *The Labor Movement in America.* New York: Norton, 1938.

Clymer, Floyd. *Floyd Clymer's Indianapolis 500 Race History: A Complete Detailed History of Every Race since 1909.* Los Angeles: Floyd Clymer, 1946.

Cohane, Tim. *The Yale Football Story.* New York: Putnam, 1938.

Commager, Michael Steele. *Documents of American History.* New York: Appleton-Century-Crofts, 1968.

Daniels, Ted, George Moore, William Eggert, and Jep Cadou. *75 Years of the Indianapolis 500.* Indianapolis: Indianapolis Star, 1986.

Davidson, Donald. "The Formation of USAC." Foreword to *United States Auto Club: 50 Years of Speed and Glory*, by Dick Wallen, Dan Fleisher, and Michael Harker. Glendale, AZ: Dick Wallen's Racing Classics, 2006.

Davidson, Donald, and Rick Shaffer. *Autocourse: Official History of the Indianapolis 500.* Silverstone, Northants, UK: Crash Media Group, 2006.

Deutsch, Tracey. *Building a Housewife's Paradise: Gender, Politics and American Grocery Stores in the Twentieth Century.* Chapel Hill: University of North Carolina Press, 2010.

Dorson, Ron. *The Indy 500: An American*

Institution Under Fire. New Port Beach, CA: Bond/Parkhurst Books, 1974.

Elliott, Joseph P. *A History of Evansville and Vanderburgh County, Indiana; a complete and concise account from the earliest times to the present; embracing reminiscences of the pioneers and biographical sketches*. Evansville, IN: Keller Print/Unigraphic, 1897, 1970.

Fish, Kevin R. "Orville Redenbacher, More than Popcorn." *Traces of Indiana and Midwestern History*, Winter 2006, p. 50.

Fisher, Jerry. *The Pacesetter: The Untold Story of Carl G. Fisher*. Ft. Bragg, CA: Lost Coast Press, 1998.

Furer, Howard B. *The Germans in America, 1607-1970: A Chronology & Fact Book*. Dobbs Ferry, NY: Oceana Books, 1973.

Goebel, Dorothy Burne. *William Henry Harrison: A Political Biography*. Philadelphia: Porcupine Press, 1974.

Kramer, Ralph. *Indianapolis Motor Speedway: 100 Years of Racing*. Iola, WI: Krause, 2009.

Levinson, Marc. *The Great A&P and the Struggle for Small Business in America*. New York: Hill & Wang, 2011.

Lewis, David A. *Eddie Rickenbacker: An American Hero in the Twentieth Century*. Baltimore, MD: Johns Hopkins University Press, 2005.

Leyes, Richard A., and William A. Fleming (National Air and Space Museum). *The History of North American Small Gas Turbine Aircraft Engines*. Reston, VA: Smithsonian Institute, 1999.

McAllister, Jean Anne, and Lloyd Long. *Centennial History of Indiana State University, 1870-1970*. Terre Haute: Indiana State University Sycamore, 1970.

McCormick, Mike. *Terre Haute, Queen City of the Wabash*. Charleston, SC: Arcadia, 2005.

Merrill, Karen R. *The Oil Crisis of 1973-1974: A Brief History with Documents*. Boston: Bedford, St. Martin's, 2007.

Meserole, William H., and Charles H. Sevin. *Effective Grocery Wholesaling*. Washington, DC: Department of Commerce, U.S. Printing Office, 1941.

Moody Manual Company. *Moody's Manual of Railroad and Corporation Securities*. New York: Moody Publishing, 1905.

Orr, Frank, and Terre Haute Northwest Territory Celebration Committee. *The Wabash Valley Remembers, 1787-1938: A Chronicle, One Hundred and Fifty Years of Progress*. Terre Haute, IN, 1938.

Ostrander, Bob, and Derrick Morris. *Hoosier Beer: Tapping into Indiana Brewing History*. Charleston, SC: History Press, 2011.

Pendergrast, Mark. *For God, Country, and Coca-Cola: The Unauthorized History of the Great American Soft Drink and the Company That Makes It*. New York: Scribner, 1993.

Popely, Rick, and L. Spencer Riggs. *Indianapolis 500 Chronicle*. Lincolnwood, IL: Publications International, 1998.

Roznowski, Tom. *An American Hometown: Terre Haute, Indiana, 1927*. Bloomington: Indiana University Press, 2009.

Saint Anthony Hospital, Poor Sisters of St. Francis Seraph, of the Perpetual Adoration. *Diamond Jubilee: St. Anthony's Hospital, 1882-1957, 75 Years of Service to the Sick*. Terre Haute, IN: Saint Anthony's Hospital, 1957.

Salstrom, Paul. *Appalachia's Path to Dependency Rethinking a Region's Economic History 1730-1940*. Lexington: University Press of Kentucky, 1994.

Scott, D. Bruce, and Hetty Gray. *Indy: Racing before the 500*. Batesville: Indiana Reflections LLC, 2005.

Shaw, Wilbur. *Gentlemen, Start Your Engines*. New York: Coward-McCann, 1955.

Sherman, Len. *Popcorn King: How Orville Redenbacher and His Popcorn Charmed America*. Arlington, TX: Summit Publishing, 1996.

Smith, Andrew F. *Popped Culture: A Social History of Popcorn in America*. Columbia: University of South Carolina Press, 1999.

Sonnenberg, Paul, and William A. Schoenberger. *Allison: Power of Excellence. 1915-1990*. Malibu, CA: Coastline, 1990.

St. Benedict's Church. *Centennial of the Parish of St. Benedict, Terre Haute, Indiana*. Terre Haute, 1965.

Taylor, Rich. *Indy: Seventy-Five Years of Racing's Greatest Spectacle*. New York: St. Martin's, 1991.

Taylor, Robert M., and Indiana Historical Society. *Indiana: A New Historical Guide*. Indianapolis: Indiana Historical Society Press, 1989.

Taylor, Robert M., Connie A. McBirney, and Indiana Historical Society. *Peopling Indiana: The Ethnic Experience*. Indianapolis: Indiana Historical Society Press, 1996.

Terre Haute Tribune-Star and Mike McCormick. *Century: 100 Years in the Wabash Valley*. Terre Haute, IN: *Terre Haute Tribune-Star*, 2000.

Welch, Joe, Bill Howes, and Kevin J. Holland. *The Cars of Pullman*. Minneapolis, MN: Voyager Press, 2010.

White, John H., Jr. *The American Railroad*

Passenger Car. Baltimore, MD: Johns Hopkins University Press, 1978.
Yates, Brock. *Against Death and Time: One Fatal Season in Racing's Glory Years.* New York: Thunder Mouth Press, 2004.
Zahorchak, Fr. Michael J., and Joe Mattox. *The History of St. Joseph & Calvary Cemeteries, Terre Haute, Indiana.* Terre Haute, IN: Joe Mattox, 1994.

Newspaper and Magazine Articles

"AAA Quits Racing as Criticism Mounts." *Indianapolis News*, August 3, 1955, p. 1.
"AAA Rule Keeps Holland from Try at More Laurels." *Indianapolis Star*, May 30, 1951, p. 44.
"A. J. Foyt Adds Another Record." *Indianapolis Star*, May 15, 1977, sect. 2, p. 1.
"Accept U.S. Ceiling on Wage Boost." *Indianapolis Star*, May 15, 1952, p. 1.
Anderson, Frank. "Crankshaft Ills in 10 Cars Bared." *Indianapolis Star*, May 26, 1954, p. 1.
_____. "Speedway Grows Safety Conscious." *Indianapolis Star*, May 10, 1953, sect. 4, p. 3.
"Andy Proposes Limit On Fuel." *Indianapolis Star*, May 20, 1973, sect. 4, p. 3.
Angelopoulous, Angelo. "New Organization Gives Auto Racing Folks Assurance." *Indianapolis News*, August 11, 1955, p. 44.
"Anton Hulman Jr.: The Story of a Shy Tycoon." *Indianapolis Times*, May 25, 1962, p. 8.
"'Auto Racing Hall of Fame' Contemplated." *Indianapolis Star*, May 28, 1947, p. 20.
"Ayulo Dies of Speedway Crash Hurts." *Indianapolis Star*, May 18, 1955, p. 1.
"Balloon Event Highlight Today." *Indianapolis Star*, May 15, 1966, p. 1.
Beal, Charles A. "Ayulo Hits Wall at 139 mph." *Indianapolis Star*, May 17, 1955, p. 1.
_____. "Ward's Skid Out of Southeast Turn Caused Crash That Killed Vukovich." *Indianapolis Star*, May 31, 1955, p. 1.
Beasley, Michael. "14 Held in Melee." *Indianapolis Star*, May 12, 1974, sect. 1, p. 1.
Beck, Tom. "Hulman Group Takes Over Ontario Track." *Indianapolis Star*, April 11, 1973, p. 1.
Bevens, Jeff. "Grant Thinks He Won; To Protest." *Indianapolis Star*, May 28, 1972, sect. 4, p. 1.
Bird, Paul. "Transport Manager Arrested." *Indianapolis News*, April 11, 1977, p. 1.
Blacketer, Colleen. "Golf Course Land Gift Completed." *Terre Haute Tribune*, October 25, 1974, p. 1.
"Buffed Tires Out Despite Protests." *Indianapolis Star*, May 22, 1965, p. 26.
Burford, Victor L., and Joseph R. Gelarden. "Tornado Rips East Side, 26 Hurt." *Indianapolis Star*, May 15, 1971, p. 1.
Cadou, Jep, Jr. "A. J. Foyt Wins '500' Duel." *Indianapolis Star*, May 31, 1961, p. 1.
_____. "Beer to Come Foaming Back—Legally—Come Memorial Day." *Indianapolis Star*, May 26, 1970, p. 1.
_____. "Bryan Escapes Big Pileup, Wins '500'; O'Connor Killed." *Indianapolis Star*, May 31, 1958, p. 1.
_____. "Calls 'Em." *Indianapolis Star*, May 4, 1954, p. 28.
_____. "Calls 'Em." *Indianapolis Star*, May 14, 1954, p. 32.
_____. "Calls 'Em." *Indianapolis Star*, May 31, 1955, p. 18.
_____. "Calls 'Em." *Indianapolis Star*, June 19, 1955, sect. 2, p. 2.
_____. "Calls 'Em." *Indianapolis Star*, July 13, 1955, p. 25.
_____. "Calls 'Em." *Indianapolis Star*, July 14, 1955, p. 34.
_____. "Calls 'Em." *Indianapolis Star*, July 30, 1955, p. 15.
_____. "Calls 'Em." *Indianapolis Star*, August 4, 1955, p. 32.
_____. "Calls 'Em." *Indianapolis Star*, August 6, 1955, p. 15.
_____. "Calls 'Em." *Indianapolis Star*, August 11, 1955, p. 32.
_____. "Calls 'Em." *Indianapolis Star*, May 12, 1956, p. 15.
_____. "Calls 'Em." *Indianapolis Star*, May 3, 1957, p. 31.
_____. "Calls 'Em." *Indianapolis Star*, May 16, 1957, p. 41.
_____. "Calls 'Em." *Indianapolis Star*, May 31, 1957, p. 22.
_____. "Calls 'Em." *Indianapolis Star*, May 18, 1958, sect. 2, p. 2.
_____. "Calls 'Em." *Indianapolis Star*, May 30, 1958, p. 20**.
_____. "Calls 'Em." *Indianapolis Star*, May 31, 1958, p. 13.
_____. "Calls 'Em." *Indianapolis Star*, May 14, 1959, p. 41.
_____. "Calls 'Em." *Indianapolis Star*, May 17, 1959, sect. 4, p. 2.
_____. "Calls 'Em." *Indianapolis Star*, May 22, 1959, p. 28.
_____. "Calls 'Em." *Indianapolis Star*, May 30, 1959, p. 13.

Bibliography

———. "Calls 'Em." *Indianapolis Star*, May 5, 1961, p. 23.
———. "Calls 'Em." *Indianapolis Star*, May 12, 1961, p. 28.
———. "Calls 'Em." *Indianapolis Star*, May 17, 1961, p. 23.
———. "Calls 'Em." *Indianapolis Star*, May 29, 1961, p. 45.
———. "Calls 'Em." *Indianapolis Star*, May 30, 1961, p. 18.
———. "Calls 'Em." *Indianapolis Star*, May 31, 1961, p. 17.
———. "Calls 'Em." *Indianapolis Star*, May 12, 1962, p. 23.
———. "Calls 'Em." *Indianapolis Star*, May 30, 1963, p. 21.
———. "Calls 'Em." *Indianapolis Star*, May 31, 1963, p. 25.
———. "Fastest '500' Set to Go." *Indianapolis Star*, May 30, 1963, p. 1.
———. "'500' to Run Tomorrow as Scheduled." *Indianapolis Star*, May 29, 1956, p. 1.
———. "500 Will Run—Hulman; SCCA Sponsorship Seen." *Indianapolis Star*, August 4, 1955, p. 1.
———. "Flaherty Wins as Death Shuns Wreck-Strewn 500." *Indianapolis Star*, May 31, 1956, p. 1.
———. "Flaherty Wins Pole at 145.5." *Indianapolis Star*, May 20, 1956, sect. 1, p. 1.
———. "4 Bumped from Fastest '500' Field." *Indianapolis Star*, May 21, 1962, p. 1.
———. "Foyt Goes 146 Testing Wider Speedway Tires." *Indianapolis Star*, May 10, 1963, p. 53.
———. "'Hanks' Record 135 MPH Wins; Jim Rathmann 2d, Bryan 3rd." *Indianapolis Star*, May 31, 1957, p. 1.
———. "Hoyt Wins Pole at 140.045." *Indianapolis Star*, May 15, 1955, p. 1.
———. "Jones Cracks 150 Barrier." *Indianapolis Star*, May 13, 1962, p. 1.
———. "Jones Hits 148.5 Practice Lap." *Indianapolis Star*, May 4, 1962, p. 26.
———. "Jones Wins Fastest '500.'" *Indianapolis Star*, May 31, 1963, p. 1.
———. "McGrath Shatters Record." *Indianapolis Star*, May 16, 1955, p. 1.
———. "McGrath's 141 Takes Pole as Speedway Record Falls." *Indianapolis Star*, May 16, 1954, p. 1.
———. "1971 Race to Be Run on May 29." *Indianapolis Star*, May 27, 1970, p. 1.
———. "Novi Explodes, Rams Wall." *Indianapolis Star*, May 12, 1961, p. 1.
———. "Novi Withdrawn from Race." *Indianapolis Star*, May 28, 1956, p. 1.
———. "O'Connor Wins 500 Pole." *Indianapolis Star*, May 19, 1957, p. 1.
———. "Rathmann on Pole as Records Fall." *Indianapolis Star*, May 18, 1958, sect. 1, p. 1.
———. "Rathmann Outduels Ward." *Indianapolis Star*, May 31, 1960, p. 1.
———. "Rodger Ward Wins 2nd '500.'" *Indianapolis Star*, May 31, 1962, p. 1.
———. "Rookie Sets Track Marks." *Indianapolis Star*, May 23, 1960, p. 1.
———. "Sachs 146.592 Wins Pole." *Indianapolis Star*, May 15, 1960, p. 1.
———. "Skid Mars First '500' Tests." *Indianapolis Star*, May 2, 1960, p. 1.
———. "Speedway Mishap Kills Andrews in Farina Car." *Indianapolis Star*, May 16, 1957, p. 41.
———. "Speedway Opens for Practice." *Indianapolis Star*, May 1, 1959, p. 31.
———. "Speedway Opens Race Season." *Indianapolis Star*, May 2, 1959, p. 14.
———. "Thompson Wins '500' Pole." *Indianapolis Star*, May 17, 1959, p. 1.
———. "Top Pilots Honored at USAC Award Fete." *Indianapolis Star*, May 9, 1961, p. 26.
———. "Trio Blisters Speedway at 144.4." *Indianapolis Star*, May 9, 1959, p. 1.
———. "Vukovich Wins Record 500." *Indianapolis Star*, June 1, 1954, p. 1.
———. "Vuky Serves Notice, Turns Lap at 141.2 mph." *Indianapolis Star*, May 13, 1955, p. 34.
———. "Ward Wins, Sets Record." *Indianapolis Star*, May 31, 1959, p. 1.
Cadou, Jep, Jr., and Max Stultz. "Clark on Pole." *Indianapolis Star*, May 17, 1964, p. 1.
Cavinder, Fred D. "Race Crowd Provides Own Show." *Indianapolis Star*, May 19, 1959, p. 3.
———. "A Slow Trip around a Fast Oval." *Indianapolis Star Magazine*, May 26, 1963, p. 26.
———. "Tony Hulman, Hoosier in Profile." *Star Magazine*, May 28, 1972, p. 6.
"The Changing Face of the Speedway." *Indianapolis Star*, May 9, 1993, p. K-8.
"Chet Miller's Tragic Accident Raised Toll to 53." *Indianapolis Star*, May 30, 1953, p. 6 supplement.
"Clark's Owner Demands Proof." *Indianapolis Star*, May 31, 1966, p. 36.
Claus, Jimmy. "Hulman Never Forgot Birthplace." *Terre Haute Tribune*, October 28, 1977, p. 14.
"Closed-Circuit Setup Elaborate." *Indianapolis Star*, May 31, 1964, p. 48.
"Cochran Puts Wheels in Motion to Save Speedway from Ruin." *Indianapolis Star*, May 9, 1993, p. K-4.

Collins, Bob. "Bettenhausen Drove Like There Was No Tomorrow." *Indianapolis Star*, May 13, 1961, p. 1.
_____. "Big Walther Flap a Thorne-y Stunt." *Indianapolis Star*, May 26, 1977, p. 47.
_____. "Foyt Victor in Tragic 500." *Indianapolis Star*, May 31, 1964, p. 1.
_____. "Memories Galore: Ol Indy and Me Go Back a Long Way." *Indianapolis Star*, May 25, 1991, p. D-4.
_____. "'Old Sam' Just Has Himself a Good Cry." *Indianapolis Star*, May 31, 1957, p. 1.
_____. "Sports over Lightly." *Indianapolis Star*, May 11, 1973, p. 41.
Collins, Sid. "'500' Broadcast Sent around World." *Indianapolis Star*, May 29, 1961, p. 43.
"Connor Turns 153 MPH Lap in Tolan Car." *Indianapolis Star*, May 3, 1953, sect. 4, p. 1.
"Cook's Brewery to Close Friday." *Evansville Courier*, September 10, 1955, p. 1.
Corya, Robert. "Chance to See How Coke Is (and Was) Bottled." *Indianapolis News*, April 25, 1968, p. 50.
Cotton, Edward W. "Grandstand Crash Sudden, Terrifying." *Indianapolis Star*, May 15, 1949, sect. 4, p. 1.
_____. "Speedway May Become Year-Round 'Mecca' for Race Fans with New 'Shrine to Speed.'" *Indianapolis Star*, May 30, 1949, p. 4 supplement.
"Coyote Rolls into Museum." *Indianapolis Star*, May 29, 1977, p. 34.
Davidson, Donald. "Racing Film 'Winning' Offered Hulman Shot at Being 'Actor.'" *Indianapolis Star*, May 18, 2000, p. D-9.
Dollase, Mark. "Can You Still Call Her a Girl When She's Eighty-Seven Years Old?" *Indiana Preservationist*, vol. 1, January/February 1993, p. 10, 11.
Dreyer, Gerald. "Local Coca-Cola Plant Is Mechanized Marvel." *Indianapolis News*, August 3, 1954, p. 12.
"Driver Jerry Hoyt Dies of Race Crash Injury." *Indianapolis Star*, July 12, 1955, p. 13.
"Driver's Howl: Don't Fence Me In!" *Indianapolis Star*, May 14, 1976, p. 52.
Eggert, Bill. "Coin Flip, Broken Line Change Outcome of Race." *Indianapolis Star*, May 31, 1962, p. 39.
_____. "Driver Burned in Race Test." *Indianapolis Star*, May 3, 1959, p. 1.
_____. "Early Arrivals Total 31 Cars." *Indianapolis Star*, May 5, 1959, p. 31.
_____. "Experts Favoring Ward in 500-Mile Race." *Indianapolis Star*, May 28, 1961, sect. 4, p. 1.
_____. "Flaherty Is Rejected as 500 Driver." *Indianapolis Star*, May 6, 1958, p. 27.
_____. "Jerry Unser, Burned in Crash, Is Dead." *Indianapolis Star*, May 18, 1959, p. 19.
_____. "Jones Hits Record 152 Lap." *Indianapolis Star*, May 12, 1963, p. 48.
_____. "Lotus-Ford Nursing 1-Stop Plan." *Indianapolis Star*, May 16, 1963, p. 48.
_____. "New '500' Rules in Making?" *Indianapolis Star*, May 1, 1956, p. 22.
_____. "Novi Withdrawn as Right Driver Is Unavailable." *Indianapolis Star*, May 16, 1961, p. 26.
_____. "Parnelli Sets 153.139 Mark." *Indianapolis Star*, May 16, 1963, p. 48.
_____. "Rathmann Roars around Track at 147." *Indianapolis Star*, May 12, 1959, p. 1.
_____. "Rookie Dies after Crash." *Indianapolis Star*, May 20, 1959, p. 24.
_____. "2 Cars Crack Lap Record." *Indianapolis Star*, May 14, 1956, p. 1.
"8,100-Acre State Park Assured." *Indianapolis Star*, August 24, 1949, p. 1.
"Emergency Truck Kills Mechanic in Pits." *Indianapolis Star*, May 31, 1973, p. 1.
"Fame and Glory Were Theirs." *Indianapolis Star Magazine*, May 29, 1961, p. 13.
"Fengler Drops Bomb, Drivers Explode." *Indianapolis Star*, May 25, 1972, p. 55.
"Final Tribute Paid Hulman by Associates and Friends." *Indianapolis Star*, November 1, 1977, p. 1.
"Fire Destroys Hulman Lodge at Terre Haute." *Indianapolis Star*, March 14, 1965, sect. 3, p. 24.
"500 'Live' On Radio Only." *Indianapolis Star*, May 29, 1971, p. 12.
"500 Mile Qualifiers." *Indianapolis Star*, May 27, 1963, p. 23.
"500 Race Suit Going to Trial." *Indianapolis Star*, May 1, 1975, p. 37.
"500's Great Moments Relived in New Speedway Museum." *Indianapolis Star*, May 30, 1956, p. 5.
"5,000 Musicians to Open Race Day Program." *Indianapolis Star*, May 29, 1966, p. 1.
"Flood Control Commission Re-Elects Hulman." *Indianapolis Star*, January 26, 1952, p. 13.
"Flood Routs 2,000 Families." *Indianapolis Star*, May 29, 1956, p. 1.
"Foyt Collects Record Total of $171,277." *Indianapolis Star*, June 1, 1967, p. 1.
"Foyt's 161.233 Takes Pole." *Indianapolis Star*, May 16, 1965, p. 1.
Frank, Edward H. "Tragic Race Stand Collapse

Probed." *Indianapolis Star*, May 31, 1960, p. 1, 10.
Fuson, Wayne. "Few Hoosiers Ever See the Real Anton Hulman." *Indianapolis News*, February 6, 1961, p. 14.
_____. "Tony Hulman—Savior of the 500 Speedway Track." *Indianapolis News*, October 28, 1977, p. 1.
Gelarden, R. Joseph. "500 Suit Still Unresolved." *Indianapolis Star*, May 23, 1974, p. 1.
Grabow, Bart. "Big Brother of Coca-Cola Put on Sale Here." *Indianapolis News*, January 16, 1956, p. 19.
Harrison, Harold. "AAA Refuses to Reopen Race Entries to Let in ASPAR Car." *Indianapolis Star*, May 8, 1947, p. 1.
_____. "Horn Wins Pole Position." *Indianapolis Star*, May 18, 1947, p. 1.
_____. "Novi Veteran Smacks into North Turn Wall." *Indianapolis Star*, May 17, 1948, p. 1.
_____. "Race Trials Start Today." *Indianapolis Star*, May 17, 1947, p. 1.
_____. "6 Wheeler Qualifies; Race Field Now 23." *Indianapolis Star*, May 22, 1948, p. 1.
_____. "Two More Qualify, in Special Trials; Waiver OK Needed." *Indianapolis Star*, May 30, 1947, p. 1.
_____. "Way Cleared For ASPAR." *Indianapolis Star*, May 23, 1947, p. 1.
"He Died Trying." *Indianapolis Star* (editorial), May 18, 1955, p. 20.
"Hoosier at Speedway Wheel." *Indianapolis Star*, November 16, 1945, p. 14.
"Hoyt Hurt Badly in Western Race." *Indianapolis Star*, July 11, 1955, p. 1.
"Hulman Buys Cook's Brewery." *Indianapolis Times*, January 17, 1950, p. 9.
"The Hulman Dynasty, 1850–1997." *Terre Haute Tribune-Star*, May 26, 1997, special section.
"Hulman Gift to Rose Poly." *Terre Haute Tribune*, January 6, 1971, p. 1.
"Hulman Helps U.S. Team Win Tuna Fishing Title." *Indianapolis Times*, September 11, 1949, p. 1.
"Hulman Honored." *Indianapolis Star*, May 24, 1965, p. 30.
"Hulman Is Head of Coca-Cola Co." *Indianapolis News*, January 4, 1965, p. 1.
"Hulman Named Director of Indiana National." *Indianapolis News*, October 13, 1954, p. 53.
"Hulman Named on U.S. Health Advisory Board." *Indianapolis Star*, September 27, 1957, p. 22.
"Hulman State Conservation Unit Head." *Indianapolis Star*, December 27, 1962, p. 12.

"The Hulmans Coming to America (Tony's Touch Impacts Terre Haute and Beyond)." *Terre Haute Tribune-Star*, May 26, 1997, special section.
"Hulman's Firm Foundation Keeps Racing Alive, Well." *Indianapolis Star*, June 4, 1978, sect. 5, p. 4.
"Hulmans Give Funds, Land to Terre Haute." *Indianapolis Star*, April 25, 1973, p. 1.
Hunt, Lester M. "One in Serious Condition after 20 Foot Plunge." *Indianapolis Star*, May 15, 1949, p. 1.
Hynes, Beatrice. "WIBC to Radio Speedway Race." *Indianapolis Star*, May 30, 1951, p. 36.
"Increased Speed Claimed for New Contoured Shoes." *Indianapolis Star*, May 30, 1951, p. 33.
"Inside Indianapolis." *Indianapolis Times*, January 19, 1946, p. 7.
"Jimmy Daywalt, Gives Up Place in 500 Field." *Indianapolis Star*, May 26, 1960, p. 52.
Keating, Thomas R. "Pace Car Hits Temporary Stand." *Indianapolis Star*, May 30, 1971, p. 1.
_____. "Speedway Resurrection." *Indianapolis Star*, October 31, 1977, p. 21.
"L.A. Group Buys Coca-Cola Plant." *Indianapolis News*, April 23, 1981, p. 1.
Lamm, Corky. "Heavy Footers Set for 500." *Indianapolis Star*, May 30, 1953, p. 1.
_____. "Vukovich Captures 500." *Indianapolis Star*, May 31, 1953, sect. 4, p. 1.
_____. "Vukovich Wins Hottest Race, Scarborough Dies." *Indianapolis Star*, May 31, 1953, p. 1.
"Local Coke Plant Sold for 2nd Time." *Indianapolis Star*, May 2, 1981, p. 30.
"Lose 30 Hours of Practice." *Indianapolis Star*, May 9, 1961, p. 25.
Marquette, Ray. "A. J. Foyt Still on '500' Pole." *Indianapolis Star*, May 19, 1974, sect. 1, p. 1.
_____. "Al Unser Captures 500." *Indianapolis Star*, May 31, 1970, p. 1.
_____. "Al Unser Wins 'Screamer.'" *Indianapolis Star*, May 17, 1970, p. 1.
_____. "Bobby U. Wins Rain-Cut '500.'" *Indianapolis Star*, May 26, 1975, p. 1.
_____. "Bobby Unser's Eagle Flies—188.294 MPH." *Indianapolis Star*, May 7, 1974, p. 29.
_____. "Bobby Unser's 195.940 Leading Pole Dash." *Indianapolis Star*, May 15, 1972, p. 1.
_____. "Donohue Captures '500 Plum; Expected to Get $200,000." *Indianapolis Star*, May 28, 1972, p. 1.
_____. "500 Discontent Continues." *Indianapolis Star*, May 20, 1974, p. 23.
_____. "500 Pilots Protest Turbine Exhaust." *Indianapolis Star*, May 27, 1967, p. 30.

_____. "Foyt Captures 4th '500' Pole." *Indianapolis Star*, May 11, 1975, p. 1.
_____. "Foyt's 191.6 MPH Holds Pole." *Indianapolis Star*, May 12, 1974, sect. 1, p. 1.
_____. "'Great Blower' Battle." *Indianapolis Star*, May 14, 1974, p. 23.
_____. "Home TV of Speedway Classic Could Backfire on Hulman." *Indianapolis Star*, May 29, 1971, p. 31.
_____. "Hurtubise Gets Hero's Welcome from Race Fans." *Indianapolis Star*, May 3, 1965, p. 29.
_____. "'I Thought I Was Out of It' Foyt Admits." *Indianapolis Star*, June 1, 1967, p. 1.
_____. "Johncock Wins Troubled Race; Savage Hurt in Flaming Crash." *Indianapolis Star*, May 30, 1973, p. 1.
_____. "Lighting Strikes Twice for Al." *Indianapolis Star*, May 30, 1971, p. 1.
_____. "Malloy 33d Driver to Die at Speedway." *Indianapolis Star*, May 19, 1972, p. 39.
_____. "No Ms-Take: Jan to Drive." *Indianapolis Star*, May 4, 1976, p. 28.
_____. "Of All Things, a Wrong Way Turn by Speedway Owner." *Indianapolis Star*, May 1, 1976, p. 25.
_____. "Pole May Not Be to the Swiftest." *Indianapolis Star*, May 11, 1974, p. 24.
_____. "Revson Springs Pole Surprise." *Indianapolis Star*, May 17, 1971, p. 1.
_____. "Rookie Pilot Spence Slams Turbine into Wall, Dies of Injuries to Head." *Indianapolis Star*, May 8, 1968, p. 36.
_____. "Rutherford Grabs 500 Pole; Crash in Practice Kills Pollard." *Indianapolis Star*, May 15, 1973, p. 1.
_____. "Rutherford's 11th Try Wins 500." *Indianapolis Star*, May 27, 1974, p. 1.
_____. "33 Positions Still Open in Field as '500' Race Trials Rained Out." *Indianapolis Star*, May 14, 1971, p. 1.
_____. "Tire Competition Flaring at Speedway." *Indianapolis Star*, May 14, 1965, p. 20.
_____. "12 Car Crash Injures 13 Fans, Walther as Rain Postpones Race." *Indianapolis Star*, May 29, 1973, p. 1.
_____. "USAC Readies ACCUS Exit." *Indianapolis Star*, May 12, 1973, p. 31.
_____. "Weather Again Cuts '500' Short." *Indianapolis Star*, May 31, 1976, p. 1.
Marquette, Ray, and George Moore. "Goodyear Solves 500 Tire Trouble." *Indianapolis Star*, May 19, 1965, p. 29.
McCarthy, Mickey. "Mickey McCarthy Says." *Indianapolis News*, September 2, 1954, p. 25.
"McElreath Hits 150.451 at Speedway." *Indianapolis Star*, May 8, 1963, p. 26.

Miller, Robin. "Janet Paces 8 Into '500." *Indianapolis Star*, May 23, 1977, p. 23.
_____. "Rutherford's on the Run—196.850." *Indianapolis Star*, May 10, 1977, p. 22.
_____. "Rookie Hurdles 2 Speedway Fences." *Indianapolis Star*, May 12, 1976, p. 45.
_____. "Sneva Grabs Pole with 198.884." *Indianapolis Star*, May 15, 1977, sect. 1, p. 1.
_____. "Super Tex '500' Winner 4th Time." *Indianapolis Star*, May 29, 1977, p. 1.
Mills, Jack. "Tony Hulman Is Mr. Speedway." *Indianapolis Times*, May 28, 1959, p. 3.
Mittman, Dick. "1947 500 Had Similar Drivers' Split." *Indianapolis Star*, May 24, 1996, p. S-22.
"Mixed Reviews on Yellow Light." *Indianapolis Star*, May 28, 1972, sect. 4, p. 2.
"Monthly Record of New Events." *Harper's New Monthly Magazine*, vol. 17, 1858, p. 829.
Moore, George. "Changes at Track Seen Acceptable by 500 Drivers." *Indianapolis Star*, May 25, 1976, p. 21.
_____. "Drivers Union Not Needed: Foyt." *Indianapolis Star*, May 19, 1971, p. 39.
_____. "500 Discontent Continues." *Indianapolis Star*, May 20, 1974, p. 23.
_____. "500 May Lose Foreign Drivers in '65." *Indianapolis Star*, May 21, 1964, p. 1.
_____. "Guthrie Tops 185 MPH; Fastest on Opening Day." *Indianapolis Star*, May 8, 1977, sect. 2, p. 1.
_____. "Heavies Making Presence Known." *Indianapolis Star*, May 9, 1977, p. 24.
_____. "Judge Gives Race Green Flag." *Indianapolis Star*, May 24, 1974, p. 1.
_____. "Mario Makes Month of May Merrier." *Indianapolis Star*, May 12, 1977, p. 58.
_____. "Meyer to Try Out Aluminum Offy." *Indianapolis Star*, May 8, 1964, p. 36.
_____. "Modern Engine Needed to Save Offy's Prestige." *Indianapolis Star*, May 18, 1964, p. 18.
_____. "New Speedway Creation by Yunick Has Driver in Outside Component." *Indianapolis Star*, May 2, 1964, p. 26.
_____. "New Speedway Opens Tomorrow." *Indianapolis Star*, May 5, 1974, sect. 3, p. 1.
_____. "Oil Leakage Riles Speedway Officials." *Indianapolis Star*, May 23, 1964, p. 28.
_____. "Rutherford Joins the Club: 200.624." *Indianapolis Star*, May 13, 1977, p. 33.
_____. "Special Year for Fengler." *Indianapolis Star*, May 29, 1971, p. 22.
_____. "Speedway Geared for 61st Opening." *Indianapolis Star*, May 1, 1977, sect. 2, p. 1.
_____. "Speedway Opens for Practice Satur-

day." *Indianapolis Star*, May 2, 1976, sect. 3, p. 1.

_____. "Tech Boss, DelRoy, to Ask for Changes." *Indianapolis Star*, May 11, 1972, p. 45.

_____. "Tire Can Alter '65 Complexion." *Indianapolis Star*, May 18, 1965, p. 21.

"More Arrests Due in Bottling Plant Thefts." *Indianapolis News*, April 12, 1977, p. 1.

"Motor Speedway Museum." *Indianapolis Star Magazine*, May 19, 1963, p. 16.

"Nalon's Novi Fastest of 14 Qualifiers; Mays 2d, McGrath, 3d." *Indianapolis Star*, May 15, 1949, sect. 7, p. 1.

Nation, Fred J. "Anton Hulman Jr. 1901–1977." *The Spectator*, November 5, 1977, p. 6, 11.

"Nazaruk, Picked to Drive in '500,' Dies in Eastern Sprint Car Crash." *Indianapolis Star*, May 2, 1955, p. 1.

"New Era Booms at Speedway Now; Rear Engine Autos Push Offy." *Indianapolis Star*, May 29, 1964, p. 41.

"New $500,000 Coca-Cola Bottling Company Plant Will Be Open to Public Tuesday—Employs 125." *Indianapolis Star*, September 27, 1931, sect. 4, p. 36.

"New Grandstand Rises." *Indianapolis Star*, May 30, 1951, p. 26.

"The New Speedway Museum." *Indianapolis Star Magazine*, April 18, 1976, p. 26.

"New Speedway Owner Plans Face-Lifting Job at Track." *Indianapolis News*, November 15, 1945, p. 1.

"New Tower Is Track Jewel." *Indianapolis Star*, May 30, 1957, p. 14.

"News and Views of the Breweries." *Modern Brewery Age*, May 1948, p. 96.

"News and Views of the Breweries." *Modern Brewery Age*, June 1948, p. 96.

"News and Views of the Breweries." *Modern Brewery Age*, February 1949, p. 89.

"News and Views of the Breweries." *Modern Brewery Age*, April 1949, p. 86.

"News and Views of the Breweries." *Modern Brewery Age*, May 1949, p. 91.

"News and Views of the Breweries." *Modern Brewery Age*, June 1949, p. 84.

"News and Views of the Breweries." *Modern Brewery Age*, September 1949, p. 89.

"News and Views of the Breweries." *Modern Brewery Age*, November 1949, p. 104.

"News and Views of the Breweries." *Modern Brewery Age*, February 1950, p. 86.

"News and Views of the Breweries." *Modern Brewery Age*, September 1955, p. 116.

"1937 Car 30 Years Ahead of Time." *Indianapolis Star*, May 29, 1971, p. 30.

"1974 Indianapolis 500 Set, Sunday May 26." *Indianapolis Star*, May 23, 1973, p. 52.

"183 Inch Type Is Likely to Prove Leader." *Indianapolis Star*, June 1, 1918, sect. 3, p. 25.

O'Reilly, Don. "Hulman Has More Big Plans for Speedway." *Indianapolis News*, May 2, 1957, p. 43.

Overpeck, Dave. "A Go-Go Mario Captures '500.'" *Indianapolis Star*, May 31, 1969, p. 1.

_____. "Andretti Gets '500' Pole." *Indianapolis Star*, May 14, 1967, p. 1.

_____. "Bignotti Turbo Controversy Rages." *Indianapolis Star*, May 13, 1974, p. 22.

_____. "Bumped Salt Walther 'Buys' a Spot in Race." *Indianapolis Star*, May 24, 1977, p. 1.

_____. "Cagle Has Dedicated His Life to Speedway." *Indianapolis Star*, May 28, 1977, p. A-3.

_____. "Foyt Grabs 3D '500' Win." *Indianapolis Star*, June 1, 1967, p. 1.

_____. "Foyt's Victory Was Popular One." *Indianapolis Star*, May 29, 1977, p. 1.

_____. "Hill Wins Disputed '500.'" *Indianapolis Star*, May 31, 1966, p. 1.

_____. "Mario's Extra Radiator Stirs Row." *Indianapolis Star*, May 29, 1969, p. 1.

_____. "Mario Sets Pole Records; Chuck Rodee Crashes, Dies." *Indianapolis Star*, May 15, 1966, p. 1.

_____. "Puterbaugh Will Drive in '500.'" *Indianapolis Star*, May 25, 1977, p. 1.

_____. "Race Protest Dropped, Hill Still It." *Indianapolis Star*, June 1, 1966, p. 28.

_____. "Sneva Did the Job When It Counted." *Indianapolis Star*, May 15, 1977, sect. 2, p. 1.

_____. "Speedway Changes Run More than $300,000." *Indianapolis Star*, May 25, 1974, p. 38.

_____. "Speedway Warned: See You in Court." *Indianapolis Star*, May 21, 1974, p. 24.

_____. "Suspension, Steering Metal Wrong Type." *Indianapolis Star*, May 12, 1968, sect. 4, p. 1.

_____. "32 to Resume '500' Today." *Indianapolis Star*, May 31, 1967, p. 1.

_____. "Unser Wins in '500' Duel." *Indianapolis Star*, May 31, 1968, p. 1.

"Palatial Private Railroad Cars Again Rolling on Nation's Tracks." *Indianapolis Star*, June 1, 1965, sect. 2, p. 8.

"Pat Flaherty Is Eager to Race after Accident." *Indianapolis Star*, May 30, 1957, p. 13.

Patton, W. Blaine. "Hepburn Shatters Trial Record with Blazing 133.944 MPH Run." *Indianapolis Star*, May 27, 1946, p. 1.

_____. "Hoosier Buys Speedway." *Indianapolis Star*, November 15, 1945, p. 1.

_____. "150,000 Jam Roadways; 60,000 at Speedway." *Indianapolis Star*, May 20, 1946, p. 1.

_____. "Robson Wins as Eight Finish." *Indianapolis Star*, May 31, 1946, p. 1.

_____. "Rudi Caracciola, European Race Champion, Badly Hurt in Crash into Speedway Wall." *Indianapolis Star*, May 29, 1946, p. 1.

_____. "Thousands See Speedway Preview." *Indianapolis Star*, May 19, 1946, sect. 1, p. 1.

"Pileup Began after I Was Hit: Foster." *Indianapolis Star*, May 31, 1966, p. 1.

"Pit Pass." *Indianapolis Star*, May 15, 1965, sect. 4, p. 2.

"Pit Pass." *Indianapolis Star*, May 22, 1967, p. 32.

"Pit Pass." *Indianapolis Star*, June 1, 1967, p. 50.

"Pit Pass." *Indianapolis Star*, May 5, 1971, p. 43.

"Pit Pass." *Indianapolis Star*, May 8, 1971, p. 28.

"Pit Pass." *Indianapolis Star*, May 27, 1972, sect. 3, p. 5.

"Pit Pass." *Indianapolis Star*, May 26, 1973, p. 28.

"Pit Pass." *Indianapolis Star*, May 7, 1974, p. 23.

"Pit Pass." *Indianapolis Star*, May 9, 1976, sect. 3, p. 4.

"Pop Will Be There as Usual." *Indianapolis Star*, May 28, 1948, p. 26 supplement.

Power, Fremont. "Tony Hulman—It Can't Be." *Indianapolis News*, October 31, 1977, p. 21.

"Qualifying Trials to Start May 18 for 500-Mile Race." *Indianapolis Star*, May 5, 1946, sect. 3, p. 41.

"Race Sabotage Probed." *Indianapolis Star*, May 29, 1949, p. 1.

"Racing Seeks New Sanction Body to Replace Existing AAA." *Indianapolis News*, August 4, 1955, p. 39.

"Rationing No Threat, Speedway Chief Claims." *Indianapolis Star*, May 6, 1952, p. 1.

"Ride for Pal Kills Tony." *Indianapolis Star*, May 13, 1961, p. 1.

Riggs, L. Spencer. "Racing's Repository, the Indianapolis Motor Speedway Hall of Fame Museum." *Automobile Quarterly*, vol. 41, no. 3, 2001, p. 85.

"Rookie Driver Critically Injured in Smashup." *Indianapolis Star*, May 3, 1949, p. 33.

"Rose-Hulman: Another Exciting Hundred Years." *Terre Haute Star*, March 3, 1973, p. 1.

"Rose Wins 500 Mile Race." *Indianapolis Star*, May 31, 1947, p. 1.

Salter, Stephanie. "Terre Haute House Coming Down." *Terre Haute Tribune-Star*, September 16, 2005, p. A-1, A-4.

"Scorching 141 Leads Field." *Indianapolis Star*, May 16, 1954, sect. 4, p. 1.

"Seek Solution to Race Deaths." *Indianapolis Star*, July 10, 1955, sect. 2, p. 4.

"71 Killed in Race Car Blast." *Indianapolis Star*, June 12, 1955, p. 1.

Shaplen, Robert. "The Hoosier Pied Piper, Part I." *Sports Illustrated*, May 26, 1958, p. 69.

_____. "The Hoosier Pied Piper, Part II." *Sports Illustrated*, June 2, 1958, p. 60.

"Shortage of Gas in City Acute." *Indianapolis Star*, May 9, 1952, p. 1.

"Six Wheeled Race-Car Dispels That 'Nothing New' Theory." *Indianapolis Star*, May 12, 1948, p. 29.

Snodgrass, Donna. "Hulman's 500 Richest, Best-Run Race." *Indianapolis Star*, May 24, 1975, p. 32.

_____. "Women at Indy Not Probable." *Indianapolis Star*, May 26, 1973, p. 64.

"Speedway Begins Probe as Abrasive Is Found in Engine of Ted Horn's Car." *Indianapolis Star*, May 28, 1949, p. 17.

"Speedway Boasts 'New Look' Offices, Museum." *Indianapolis Star*, May 30, 1956, p. 12.

"The Speedway Changes Hands." *Indianapolis News*, November 15, 1945, p. 10.

"Speedway Entry List Boosted to 50 Cars." *Indianapolis Star*, May 2, 1946, p. 22.

"Speedway Is Test Tube for Cummins Engine." *Indianapolis Star*, May 30, 1952, p. 48.

"Speedway Jam Is greatest in City's History." *Indianapolis Star*, May 31, 1946, p. 3.

"Speedway Museum Packs 'Em In." *Indianapolis Star*, May 29, 1959, p. 15.

"Speedway on Guard for Any 'Sabotage.'" *Indianapolis Star*, May 30, 1948, p. 1.

"Speedway Was at Peace during War Years." *Indianapolis Star*, May 27, 1995, p. s7.

Stranahan, Bob. "Agabashian Hits 139.104 mph." *Indianapolis Star*, May 18, 1952, p. 1.

_____. "Best Lap 137.049; Wins Pole." *Indianapolis Star*, May 12, 1951, p. 1.

_____. "Ferrari to Try for 500 Field." *Indianapolis Star*, May 7, 1953, p. 41.

_____. "'500 Cars Hitting 180 on Stretches; Some Could Reach 200 on Salt Flats.'" *Indianapolis Star*, May 24, 1950, p. 31.

_____. "Hollywood Gives Track, City a Boost." *Indianapolis Star*, May 30, 1950, p. 1.
_____. "Horn Hurt Critically during Test." *Indianapolis Star*, May 3, 1949, p. 1.
_____. "Lee Wallard Wins '500.'" *Indianapolis Star*, May 31, 1951, p. 1.
_____. "More 500 Cars Qualify." *Indianapolis Star*, May 25, 1952, p. 1.
_____. "Nalon Gets Sizzling Pole Slot with Sizzling 132.939." *Indianapolis Star*, May 15, 1949, p. 1.
_____. "Parsons 1st, Holland 2d." *Indianapolis Star*, May 31, 1950, p. 1.
_____. "Rose Wins Third '500' Mile Race." *Indianapolis Star*, June 1, 1948, p. 1.
_____. "Ruttman Wins in '500' Duel." *Indianapolis Star*, May 31, 1952, p. 1.
_____. "16 Year Veteran's Novi Strikes Wall; Trials Open Today." *Indianapolis Star*, May 16, 1953, p. 1.
_____. "Speedway Dealt Two Bad Blows." *Indianapolis Star*, May 2, 1951, p. 1.
_____. "Speedway Marks Topple." *Indianapolis Star*, May 14, 1950, p. 1.
_____. "Speedway's 'Big Push' On; Extra Practice Hour Ok'd." *Indianapolis Star*, May 14, 1952, p. 20.
_____. "Vukovich Paces 7 Qualifiers." *Indianapolis Star*, May 18, 1953, p. 1.
"Sycamores, Purdue to Christen ISU Arena." *Indianapolis Star*, December 13, 1973, p. 65.
"Television Broadcasts First Speedway Views." *Indianapolis Star*, May 29, 1949, p. 1.
"Terre Haute Civic Leader Gives $100,000 to City." *Indianapolis Star*, March 23, 1943, p. 7.
"Terre Haute Services Monday for Hulman." *Indianapolis Star*, October 29, 1977, p. 1.
"T-H Act May End Oil Strike." *Indianapolis Star*, May 13, 1952, p. 1.
"TH Means Tony Hulman of Terre Haute." *Indiana Business and Industry*, October 1966, p. 21.
"Things Going for Coke." *Indianapolis News*, July 18, 1967, p. 21.
"33 Race Fans Injured." *Indianapolis Star*, May 15, 1948, sect. 4, p. 1.
"Three Wheel Steering Put on Thompson Cars." *Indianapolis Star*, May 4, 1964, p. 29.
Toles, George E. "Palaces on Wheels." *Railway Magazine*, vol. 116, July 1970, p. 400.
"Tony Hulman Laid to Rest." *Terre Haute Tribune*, November 1, 1977, p. 3.
"Tony Hulman Lands a Beauty in International Tuna Tournament." *Indianapolis Times*, September 21, 1949, p. 15.
"Tony Hulman, Mr. 500, Dies." *Indianapolis Star*, October 28, 1977, p. 1.
"Tony Hulman, Speedway Owner, Planning Constantly for Improvement of Track." *Indianapolis Times*, May 29, 1950, p. 2 supplement.
"Tony's Tradition Will Never Die." *Indianapolis Star*, May 27, 1978, p. 16.
"Track Straightaway Resurfaced." *Indianapolis Star*, May 29, 1962, p. 34.
"Trials to Open Today for 500-Mile Classic." *Indianapolis Star*, May 18, 1946, p. 1.
"Train Shuttle to 500 Mapped in Bus Strike." *Indianapolis Star*, May 5, 1954, p. 1.
"Trains Operate to Speedway by Special Permit." *Indianapolis Star*, May 30, 1946, p. 2.
"Tuna a Sucker for Hoosier-Cured Sowbelly." *Indianapolis Times*, September 8, 1948, p. 1.
"Turbine 'Popped' the USACed." *Indianapolis Star*, May 26, 1969, p. 27.
"Turner's 140, Boyd's 139 First Day Bests." *Indianapolis Star*, May 2, 1961, p. 23.
"Ultimate Responsibility Is Hulman's but 'Family' Decides Many Things." *Indianapolis Star*, July 12, 1973, p. 1, 14.
"USAC Nixes Appeal from Car Owners." *Indianapolis Star*, May 25, 1974, p. 25.
"'Voice of Indianapolis 500,' Sid Collins, Found Dead." *Indianapolis Star*, May 3, 1977, p. 1.
"Vukovich, Miller Establish New Records." *Indianapolis Star*, May 25, 1952, sect. 4, p. 24.
"Vuky Proved to All He Could Win from Anywhere in Field." *Indianapolis Star*, May 3, 1955, p. 3.
Waldon, Mary. "Col. Herrington Sees Changing 500." *Indianapolis Star*, May 15, 1965, p. 8.
_____. "Face-Lifted Queen of Rails Delivered to Hulmans." *Indianapolis Star*, September 7, 1969, sect. 6, p. 4.
"Wilbur Shaw, 2 Others Died in Air Crash Near Decatur." *Indianapolis Star*, October 31, 1954, p. 1.
Wiley, Anna Bowles. "The Hulman-Fendrich Wedding: Folk Present Still Talking of Beautiful Ceremony." *Terre Haute Tribune*, October 6, 1926, p. 8.
Wilkins, Lloyd H. "Best Driver in the World Visits Speedway, Thinks It's Wonderful." *Indianapolis Star*, May 24, 1946, p. 15.
_____. "33 Racers Poised for Starting Bomb, Throngs Jam City." *Indianapolis Star*, May 30, 1946, p. 1.
Wilkinson, Ernest A. "Hulmans Give Foundation's Huge Assets to Rose Poly." *Indianapolis Star*, January 7, 1971, p. 24.
_____. "West Coast Firm Buys Coca-Cola

Plant." *Indianapolis Star*, April 24, 1981, p. 46.

Wolfe, Barbara. "Unprecedented Team Will Cover Action." *Indianapolis Star*, May 30, 1953, p. 19 supplement.

"Yellow Speed Set at 80." *Indianapolis Star*, May 26, 1971, p. 35.

"Zionsville Union Okays Pay Offer." *Indianapolis Star*, May 8, 1952, p. 1.

Websites

American Chemical Society website, www.acswebcontent.acs.org/landmarks/bakingpowder/development.html.

Andrews, Ronald. "History of Markle's Mill," www.randrews4.com.

Beatles Bible website, www.beatlesbible.com.

Coca-Cola website, www.Coca-Cola.com/heritage.

D. A. Lubricants website, www.dalube.com.

Emporis website, www.emporis.com/building/libertytower-dayton-oh-usa.

500 Festival website, www.500festival.com.

Freeman, Paul. "Abandoned & Little Known Airfields: Southern Indiana," www.airfieldsfreeman.com, 2002.

Independent Grocers Association website, www.iga.com.

Indiana Department of Natural Resources website, www.in.gov/dnr/parklake/2960.

Indiana Energy website, www.indianaenergy.com.

Indiana Transportation Museum website, www.itm.org/fec90.

"Louisville after the Bombing," website www.oldlouisville.com.

Lucas Oil Raceway website, www.lucasoilraceway.com.

Mittman, Dick. "Longtime IMS Superintendent Cagle Dies at 88, July 7, 2003," www.indianapolismotorspeedway.com.

Motorsports Hall of Fame of America website, www.mshf.com.

Songwriters Hall of Fame Website, www.songwritershalloffame.org.

University of Louisville website, digital photograph collection, www.louisville.edu.

WTHI website, www.wthi.com.

Miscellaneous

Cloutier Oral History, Indiana University Center for the Study of History and Memory.

Goldwaithe Oral History, Indiana University Center for the Study of History and Memory.

Indiana University, Bloomington, Indiana, archives.

Markle, A. R., and Gloria Collins, *The House of Hulman: 100 Years of Service 1850–1950*, Terre Haute, IN (unpublished).

"*The Hulman*," September 29, 1893, Scrapbook 97A, Vigo County Library Special Collection, p. 11.

Yale University Records, Torch Society.

Index

A & P 34, 37, 39, 167; *see also* Atlantic & Pacific Tea Company; Great Atlantic & Pacific Tea Company
Abbott, Horace 171
Agabashian, Freddie 73
Agajanian, J.C. 114
Ahlgreen, J.S. 37
Aitken, Johnny 80–81
Alexander McGregor Distillery 25–26, 173
Allison, James 4, 9–10, 13, 59, 79, 122
Allison Division of General Motors 16–17, 67, 139
Allison Engineering 10–11
Alton Box Board Company 201
American Automobile Association (AAA) 90–92
American Automobile Association (AAA) Contest Board 6, 56, 62–63, 72, 76, 80–82, 90–94, 155
American Bitumuls & Asphalt Company 113
American Broadcasting Company (ABC) 130
American Can Company 159
American Competition Committee for the United States (ACCUS) 135, 138
American Society for Professional Automobile Racing (ASPAR) 61–65
Amick, Richard (Red) 106
Andres, Emil 65
Andretti, Mario 121, 124, 126–127, 147
Andrews, Keith 100
Andrews, Park 81
Ascari, Alberto 86, 88
Atlantic & Pacific Tea Company 41, 44; *see also* A & P; Great Atlantic & Pacific Tea Company

Atlantic Commission Company 41
Automobile Competition Committee for the United States (ACCUS) 117
Ayulo, Manuel 86

Bailey, George 155
Barringer, George 60
Baur, Fred 28
Baynes, Paul 139
Beatles 118
Beatty, Ralph 176
Beer Bottlers Local #133 161
Bergère, Cliff 55, 60, 63, 65, 67
Bettenhausen, Tony 69, 84, 95, 110–111
Bidamin, Edwin 193
Bigelow, Tom 138
Bignotti, George 140–141
Binford, Tom 108, 138, 140, 142, 145
Blum, Henry 101
Boggs, John 32
Bonneville Flats 147, 155
Bourque, Wilfred 80
Bowman, Charles 172
Boyd, Johnny 86, 109–110
Branson, Don 111, 115, 119
Brawner, Clint 127
Brewery Workers Local #84 161
Bronson, Dave 51–52
Brunson, Arthur 171
Brute, Simon 24
Bryan, Jimmy 84, 102
Bueb, Ivor 88
Builder's Contractor Association 70
Burman, Bob 80
Button, Horace 25

231

Index

Cabo Blanco Fishing Club 74
Cadou, Jep, Jr. 78, 89–90, 92, 100, 111
Cagle, Clarence 16, 70, 98–99, 108, 113, 118, 144–145, 146, 200
Cagle's Mill Lake 187
Calvary Cemetery (Terre Haute) 35–36, 200
Campbell, Colin 122–123
Candler, Asa 162
Capehart, Homer E. 58, 90
Caraccioli, Rudy 55–57
Carter, Duane 93, 104
Cassidy, Dave 12–14, 166
Castellotti, Eugenio 86, 88
Catholic Cemetery Association 35–36
Chapman, Colin 114, 126
Chapman, Oscar L. 72
Cheesbourg, Bill 122
Christie, George 171
Citizens Manufacturing Association 29
Clabber Baking Powder 44
Clabber Girl Baking Powder 5–6, 14, 40, 44–45, 48, 50
Clark, Hezlep 182
Clark, Jimmy 117–118, 120, 122–123, 126
Clemens, Jap 80
Cline, Del 119
Cloutier, Joseph 3–4, 12 -14, 45, 47–48, 84, 85, 91, 141–142, 150, 160–161, 166, 196–197, 200
Coca-Cola Bottling Company of Indianapolis 6, 150, 163, 165–167, 200
Coca-Cola Company 45, 162, 164, 165–168
Cochran, Homer 12–13
Collett, Josephus 180
Collins, Sid 72, 75, 146
Columbian Enameling & Stamping Company 46, 194
Cook, Frederick W. 156–157
Cook, Jim 134
Cook & Reis City Brewery 156–157; *see also* F.W. Cook Brewing Company
Coon, Frank 86
Cooper, Earl 68, 112, 152
Cooper, John 93
Correll, Gus 44
Cortner, Bob 105
Covoert, John 28
Cox, B.C. 29, 32
Cox, Benjamin 29
Cox, Paul 185
Cox, Robert S. 25, 29
Craig, William C. 107
Crockett, Larry 83–84, 129
Cullen, Michael 42
Cummings, Bill 84
Cummins Engine Company 73

Dallenbach, Wally 136, 139, 140
Darby, Reuben 192
Davidson, Donald 93
Davis, Floyd 132
Dawson, Joe 153
Daywalt, Jimmy 107
Dean, Earl R. 164
Debs, Eugene 30
DelRoy, Frankie 132, 140
Demming, Demas 180
Demming Hotel 183; *see also* Hulman Center
DePalma, Ralph 63, 67
DePaolo, Peter 3, 94, 199
DeVore, Billy 59, 65
Dick, David B. 25
Dickey, Frank 108
Donohue, Mark 132
Druing, Adolphus 31
Duesenberg, Fred 154
Duesenberg automobile 151, 154
Duffey, Ike 191
Duman, Ronnie 118
Dunlap tires 118
Dymond, John 24

Early Wheels Museum 154
Ed Sullivan Show 116
Eliasian, Ed 101–102
Elkins, Lee 101, 147–148
Ely, Walter 182
Estes, Bob 92–93
Evansville Brewing Association 158; *see also* Sterling Brewers
Evansville Brewing Company 158; *see also* Evansville Brewing Association

Fairbanks, Crawford 26–27
Fanzio, Juan Manuel 88–89
Farrington, S. Kip, Jr. 74
Faulkner, Walt 68
Federation Internationale Automobile (FIA) 91–92, 117, 135
Fendrich, Mary Josephine 40, 53; *see also* Hulman, Mary
Fengler, Harlan 96, 102, 105–106, 108–109, 116, 120, 123–124, 126–127, 129, 131–132, 138
F.H. McCormack & Company 32
Firestone Tire & Rubber Company 3–4, 11, 58, 67, 71, 115, 119–120, 126, 153
Fisher, Carl 4, 9–10, 13, 51, 53, 79–80, 121–122, 153
Flagler, Henry 188–189, 191–192
Flagler, Mary 189; *see also* Harkness, Mary
Flaherty, Pat 95, 99–101, 106
Florida East Coast #90 188–192
Foltz, Herbert 182
Ford Motor Company 58, 109
Forest Park 185
Fortner, Jack 16–17, 146
Foster, Billy 119, 122
Fox, Bill 64, 92
Fox, Frank 51

Index

Foyt, A. J. 112, 114–115, 118–120, 122, 125, 127, 129, 139–141, 143, 147–149, 200
Frame, Fred 152–153
France, Bill Sr. 92
Frantonne, Frank 62
Frayer, Lee 9
Frisz, Paul 186
F.T. Hulman Wholesale Store 21; *see also* H. Hulman & Company; H. Hulman & Sons; Hulman & Company; Hulman & Cox
Fuji Speedway 125
Fulton Avenue Brewery 157–158; *see also* Evansville Brewing Association
F.W. Cook Brewing 6, 156–161, 186, 200; *see also* Cook & Reis City Brewery

Gable, Clark 65–66
General Motors 10–11, 81, 154
George, Elmer 103, 116
George F. Chester & Son Seed Company 172
Gerhardt, Louis 193
Gifford, Tommy 66
Gill, David 186
Glenn, John 130
Goldsmith, Paul 115, 117
Goodyear Tire & Rubber Company 119–120, 126, 147
Granatelli, Andy 110–111, 116, 122–124, 127, 135–136
Grant, Jerry 132
Gray, Dudley 134
Great Atlantic & Pacific Tea Company 35, 44; *see also* A & P; Atlantic & Pacific Tea Company
Griffith, Al 74
Grimes, Ray 78
Grimm, Kenny 93
Gurney, Dan 120, 122
Guthrie, Janet 144, 146–148

H. Hulman & Company 29–34, 50, 174; *see also* F.T. Hulman Wholesale Store; H. Hulman & Sons; Hulman & Company; Hulman & Cox
H. Hulman & Sons 35; *see also* F.T. Hulman Wholesale Store; H. Hulman & Company; Hulman & Company; Hulman & Cox
Hahn, Ray 198
Halibrand, Ted 115
Hanks, Sam 95, 100, 102, 199
Hannaford, Samuel 29
Hanson, Mel 65
Harkness, Dan 188–189
Harkness, Mary 188; *see also* Flagler, Mary
Harkness, Stephen 188
Harrison, George 119
Harrison, William Henry 20, 190
Harroun, Ray 67, 109, 111–112, 154
Hartman, Carl 172
Hartz, Harry 102, 152

Hartzmetz Brewery 157–158; *see also* Evansville Brewing Association
Hawthorne, Mike 88
H.D. Tousley Company 70
Hedbeck, Phil 114
Henning, H. C. "Cotton" 67
Hepburn, Ralph 56, 62–63, 65, 75, 82
Herb, Marvin 168
Herrington, Arthur 56, 62, 91, 93–94
Hill, Graham 122–123
Hinkle, Tony 144
Hiss, Mike 138
Hobbs, David 131
Holcomb, Harry 80
Holland, Bill 65–66, 72, 114
Holliday, Fred 58
Hoover, Herbert 158
Hopkins, Lindsey 84, 141, 200
Horn, Ted 63, 67, 82
Horne, Byron 66
Horsford, Eben 43
Hoyt, Jerry 84, 89
Hugus, Wright 141–142
Hulman, Anna 32
Hulman, Anton, Sr. 23, 26, 28–29, 32, 34–42, 47, 51, 170, 174, 182–183, 185
Hulman, Antonia 27–28; *see also* Risfinstahl, Antonia
Hulman, Francis 19–23
Hulman, Grace Smith 15, 51, 183; *see also* Fendrich, Mary Josephine
Hulman, Herman 18–20, 22–29, 31–32, 34–36, 44, 47, 49, 174, 177, 180, 182–183
Hulman, Herman, Jr. 23, 26, 28, 32, 34–36, 39, 50–51
Hulman, Mari 93, 152
Hulman, Mary 7, 40, 51, 192; *see also* Fendrich, Mary
Hulman, Theodore 22, 25, 51
Hulman & Company 4–6, 14, 16, 18, 35–39, 41, 44–45, 47–49, 123, 172, 175, 182, 185, 195–196, 200; *see also* F.T. Hulman Wholesale Store; H. Hulman & Company; H. Hulman & Sons; Hulman & Company; Hulman & Cox
Hulman & Cox Wholesale House 25–27, 44; *see also* F.T. Hulman Wholesale Store; H. Hulman & Company; H. Hulman & Sons; Hulman & Company
Hulman Center 183; *see also* Demming Hotel
Hulman Civic University Center 183
Hulman Foundation 47, 150, 168, 175, 182–183
Hulman Links at Lost Creek 186
Hulman Memorial Student Union 183
Hurtubise, Jim 107, 115–116, 118–119

Independent Grocers Association (IGA) 39
Indiana: Flood Control and Water Resources Commission 186; State Conservation Committee 186; State Penal Farm 187
Indiana National Bank 78, 201

234   Index

Indiana State Normal School 179, 180–182; *see also* Indiana State University
Indiana State University 6, 178, 183; *see also* Indiana State Normal School
Indiana Transportation Museum 192
Indiana University 123
Indianapolis 500 9–10, 54–78, 83–88, 92, 95–143, 152–153, 155, 199
Indianapolis Athletic Club 13, 62, 112
Indianapolis Capitols 128
Indianapolis Motor Speedway 2, 4, 6, 9–14, 16, 18, 51, 54, 61–62, 67–68, 75, 79, 81, 86, 89, 91–93, 96–97, 104, 107, 112, 121, 123, 130, 133, 148, 150, 153, 186; Media Center 16
Indianapolis Motor Speedway Museum 143–144, 149, 152
Indianapolis Motor Speedway Network 75–76, 112
Indianapolis Raceway Park 108, 119
Indianapolis Speedway Housing Bureau 57
Ivy Tech 178, 184

J.A. McCarty Seed Company 171
Jackson, Job H. 190–191
Jackson & Sharp Company 190–191
Jacobs, Audry 58
Jake's Manufacturing Company, K. C. Food division 48–49
Jefferson, Thomas 20
Jenner, William E. 90
Johncock, Gordon 119, 122, 130, 137, 143, 145–148
Johns, Bobby 124
Jones, Parnelli 111, 113–116, 118, 124–125, 133–134
Joseph, Alfred W. 175

Keck, Howard 72, 74, 84
Keen, Bruce 81
Keller, Al 86
Kellum, Charles 80
Kenyon, Mel 130, 141
King, Dick 142–143, 200
Kizer, Karl 152–155
Koblinski, Father Hubert 200
Krisiloff, Steve 130
Kroener, Fred 156
Krueger Brewing Company 159

Lamb, John K. 196, 198
Langhorne Speedway 62, 83–84, 129
LaSalle automobile 10
Lawrenceville School 39, 52
Laycock, James 14–15
Laye, Leonard 129
Le Mans race 87–88, 91
Leonard, Joe 126
Levegh, Pierre 88
Light, Leo 195
Ligouri, Ralph 110, 124

Linder, Fred H. 107
Lingen, Germany 18, 53
Lingen Lodge 56, 196
Lockhart, Frank 153
Logan, John A. 183
Loulan, Jim 119–120
L.S. Ayres & Company 67
Ludlow, Louis 58
Lupton, J.T. 163
Lytle, Herb 80

MacDonald, Dave 118–119
Macklin, Lance 88
Malloy, Jim 128, 131
Marcenac, Jean 96
Marchese, Tom 92–93
Markle, Abraham 20
Marmon, Walter 94
Marmon Motor Car Company 80, 94, 151
Marmon Wasp 50, 111, 153–154
Marratta, Robert 168
Marshall, Leonard 12, 14, 177
Marshman, Bobby 118
Marty, Reverend Father Martin 24
Marzotto, Paolo 88
Mayer, Charles B. 19
Mays, Rex 63, 65, 82, 143
McCellom, Marshall 168
McCluskey, Roger 11, 132
McCormick & Sweeney 180
McGee, Jim 127
McGrath, Jack 71, 76, 84–86
McGregor, Alexander 25
McKeen, William Riley 177, 180
McKeen National Bank 177
McMillan, Vernon 186, 194–195, 198
McNutt, Paul 194
Melton, James 59
Merz, Charlie 80
Meyer, Adolph 30, 35
Meyer, Louis 120
Meyer-Drake 77, 117
Michigan International Speedway 134
Miletch, Mel 134
Miller, Chet 71, 75, 82–83
Miller, Eddie 144–145
Miller, Harry 152
Milton, Tommy 68
Montgomery Ward Company 37, 41, 154
Moore, Johnny 67
Moore, Lou 65
Mosley, Mark 124, 131
Moss, Stirling 88
Motorsports Hall of Fame 201
Mundwiler, Reverend Father Fintan 24
Murphy, Jimmy 94
Murphy, Paula 147
Music Corporation of America 118, 130
Muther, Rick 131
Myers, Ted "Pop" 4, 10, 13–14, 16, 64

Index 235

Nalon, Duke 61, 63, 66, 71–72, 75
National Association for Stock Car Auto Racing (NASCAR) 91–92, 117, 129–130, 135
National Association of Wholesale Grocers 46
National Motor Company 80–81, 151
Nazarek, Mike 72, 83–84, 129
Neuberger, Richard L. 89–90
Neubling, John 159
Newby, Arthur 4, 9, 79
Newman, Paul 127
Niday, Cal 87, 138
Nippert, Firmin 180
Nixon, Richard 134
Nunis, Sam 93

Ober, George 92–93
O'Connor, Pat 100, 102, 104
Offenhauser Engineering 60
Ontario Motor Speedway 130, 132–134
Organization of Petroleum Exporting Countries (OPEC) 134
Ortmeyer, Edmund F. 160

Painter, William 163
Palmer, Eldon 130
Parsons, Johnny 68–69, 142
Pemberton, John 162
Penske, Roger 134
Petty, Joe 198
Piccard, Don 121
Piggly Wiggly 37
Pocono Speedway 130, 132
Pollard, Art 125, 135
Porter, Herb 93
Pouelsen, Johnny 116
Prest-O-Lite Company 4, 10–11
Prest-O-Lite Team 10–11, 112
Prest-O-Lite Trophy Race 80
Preston, Rubush & Hunter 165
Princeton Farms 150, 170–173
Pro Golfers Association 107
Professional Drivers Association 129
Pullman Palace Car Company 190
Purdue University 122, 171–172
Purdue University Sanitary Research Board 47
Puterbaugh, Bill 147–148

Quinn, Joe 146

Rainwater, Veasey 164
Rasmussen, Eldon 143
Rathmann, Dick 101–102, 105, 110–111
Rathmann, Jim 105–106, 108, 111, 113, 200
Redenbacher, Orville 171–172
Reece, Jimmy 101–102
Reis, Jacob 156–157
Reis, Louis 156–157
Resta, Dario 120
Revson, Peter 129
Richmond Gas Company 176

Rickenbacker, Eddie 3–4, 9–13, 15–16, 59, 81–82, 111–112, 154
Ricker, Chester 69
Risfinstahl, Antonia 23; *see also* Hulman, Antonia
Roadways, Inc. 113
Robbins, Jim 69, 110
Roberts, Donn 193
Roberts, Floyd 60, 75, 87
Robson, George 59–60
Rockefeller, John 188–189
Rodee, Chuck 121
Roose, Ernest 78
Roosevelt, Franklin D. 46
Root, Chapman J. 164
Root Bottling Company 186, 194; *see also* Root Glass company
Root Glass Company 164; *see also* Root Bottling Company
Rose, Bud 67
Rose, Chauncey 6, 21, 175, 178–180
Rose, Ebb 124
Rose, George 178–179
Rose, Mauri 63, 65–67, 69, 72, 74, 78, 114, 132, 154
Rose-Hulman Institute of Technology 6, 168, 178, 183; *see also* Rose Polytechnic Institute; Terre Haute School of Industrial Science
Rose Polytechnic Institute 6, 35, 180–183; *see also* Rose-Hulman Institute of Technology; Terre Haute School of Industrial Science
Roy Woods Racing Team 141
R.S. Cox & Son 24
Ruby, Lloyd 124
Rumford Baking Powder 48–49
Russo, Eddie 96, 108
Russo, Paul 96–97, 110
Rutherford, Johnny 117, 128, 135, 141, 143, 145, 147, 200
Ruttman, Troy 74, 78, 106
Ryder, Henry 142

Sachs, Eddie 106, 111–112, 114, 116, 118–119
St. Anthony's Hospital 28, 36, 39, 184
St. Benedict's Catholic Church 24, 31–32, 199
St. Benedict's School 24, 26, 39, 52
St. Joseph's Catholic Cemetery 35–36
St. Joseph's Catholic Church 24, 35
Salih, George 104, 123
Savage, Swede 137
Scarborough, Carl 75
Scharoun, Reverend Peter W. 32
Schenkel, Chris 130
Schiller, Jim 81
Schmidt, Peter 86
Schricker, Henry F. 187
Schwab, Charles 159–160
Shaffer, Leo 195
Sharp, Jacob 190–191
Shaw, Boots 152

236 Index

Shaw, Wilbur 3–4, 10–14, 16–17, 55–57, 59–64, 66, 68, 71–73, 75, 77–78, 100, 120, 151–153
Shick, Paul 76
Shorter, Frank 148
Shortridge, William A. 107
Shrouds, Ida Alice 189
Sisters of St. Francis 28, 184
Smith, Ada Grace 33, 170; *see also* Hulman, Grace
Smith, Don 150, 199
Smith, Ezra 25
Smith, Hy 171
Smith, Robert J. 170–171
Sneva, Tom 143, 147–148
Snowberger, Russ 76–77
Snyder, Jimmy 56
Sordoni, Andrew J. 90–91
Souder, George 112
Speedway, Indiana 11, 166
Speedway Motel 119, 166
Speedway Team Company 9–10
Spence, Mike 126
Spoerle, Bill 154
Sports Car Club of America 91, 117, 135
Sportservice 16
Standard Oil Company 188–189
Stanton, Sheldon & Company 24
Stanwyck, Barbara 67
State Board of Tax Commissioners versus Jackson 41
Sterling Brewers 158, 161; *see also* Evansville Brewing Association
Strobel, Don 90
Stutz Motor Car Company 151
Sutton, Len 106, 114
Swango, J. Morton 94
Sweikert, Bob 87, 89, 106, 138, 152
Symmes, (Honorable) Frank A. Jr. 142

Tabbert, Don 141–142
Teamsters Union 38, 47, 73
Teran, Armando 137
Terre Haute, Indiana 3, 6, 19, 20–23, 25, 51, 178, 193–197
Terre Haute Brewing Company 51, 161, 194
Terre Haute Chamber of Commerce 186, 195, 197
Terre Haute Cycling Club 28
Terre Haute Female College 28
Terre Haute First National Bank 177, 201
Terre Haute House 30, 50, 175–176
Terre Haute Phillies 186
Terre Haute School of Industrial Science 180; *see also* Rose-Hulman Institute of Technology; Rose Polytechnic Institute
Terre Haute Star 176
Terre Haute Tribune 176
Thiese, Jim 119
Thomas, Benjamin F. 162–163

Thompson, Charles O. 180
Thompson, Mickey 116
Thomson, Johnny 105, 138
Thorne, Joel 56–57, 61
Thorne Engineering 60
Tousley, Harry 16, 60
Tousley Construction Company 95
Traum, Joe 195
Travers, Jim 84, 86–87
Trevis, Floyd 101
Truman, Harry S. 73, 134
Tucker, Ralph 195–196
Turkey Run State Park 51
Turner, Jack 109
Turner, Roscoe A. 67
Typographical Union 38

United States 10–11: 1875 Revenue Bill 26; Federal Trade Commission 168; Food Administration 36; Food & Drug Administration 44; Guffy Act 194; Lever Act 158; National Industrial Recovery Act 46; Packaging Tax 25; Public Health Service Water Control Advisory Board 187; Robinson-Patman Act 46; Sherman Anti-Trust Act 168; Soft Drink Interbrand Competition Act 168; Taft-Hartley Act 73; Volstead Act 158; War Labor Conference Board 37; War Production Board 159
United States Auto Club (USAC) 93–94, 96, 102–103, 104–106, 109, 112, 116–119, 123–124, 126–127, 130–132, 135, 138–140, 142–143, 147–148
Unser, Al 128, 131, 147
Unser, Bobby 118, 126, 131, 139, 143
Unser, Jerry 104–105

Vance, Edward 168
Vanderbilt, William K., II 79
Vanderbilt Cup 79
Vidan, Pat 118, 148
Villerosi, Luigi 89
Vukovich, Bill 68, 72, 74–75, 77–78, 82–87, 154
Vukovich, Billy 140

Wallard, Lee 72
Walsh, Ed, Jr. 69
Walther, Salt 136, 147–148
Ward, Rodger 72, 76, 86, 105–106, 108, 111, 114, 117, 123
Warner, Fred 81
Warren, Chauncey 179
Watson, A.J. 87, 101, 106
Welch, Lew 65, 97, 110
WFBM-TV 66, 75
Wheeler, Frank 4, 9, 79, 153
Wheeler-Schebler Company 153
Wheeler-Schebler Trophy 80, 153
Whitehead, Joseph B. 162–163

Index

Wholesale Packers and Handlers Union 38
WIBC 72, 75, 76, 146
Wilcox, Howdy 59
Wilcox, Howdy, II 62
Wilke, Robert C. 115
Willan, Dr. L.L. 27
William J. Junclaus Company 165
Williams, Merrill (Doc) 63
Wilson, George 43
Wilson, Woodrow 36–37
Wimmer, Barney 154

Woodlawn Cemetery (Terre Haute) 35–36
Woodward, Joanna 127
Worcester Academy 39, 52
Worchester Polytechnic Institute 28
Wudowici, John B. 19, 21

Yale University 5, 39, 52, 182
Yost, Paul 121
Yuncker, James 162–166
Yuncker Bottling Works 163
Yunick, Henry "Smokey" 116

www.ingramcontent.com/pod-product-compliance
Ingram Content Group UK Ltd.
Pitfield, Milton Keynes, MK11 3LW, UK
UKHW041941140426
5217IPUK00014B/607